# The Donnie Clark

# Myakka Gold

11/22/14

*To Laura & Carl, I hope that you will enjoy my book. Thank you so much, your long time friends. We have had some good times in our teen years, didn't we. Your friend always, Donnie Cl*

by

# Donnie Clark

*Donnie Cl*

the Peppertree Press
Sarasota, Florida

*P.S. Bob, I have a hard time about calling you Carl, like calling Richard Romero (Dick Romero) HA.*

Website: www.thedonnieclark.com

For information regarding permission,
call 941-922-2662 or contact us at our website:
www.peppertreepublishing.com or write to:
the Peppertree Press, LLC.
Attention: Publisher
1269 First Street, Suite 7
Sarasota, Florida 34236

ISBN: 978-1-61493-127-0

Library of Congress Number: 2012918720

Printed in the U.S.A.

Printed October 2012

# Prelude
## The Donnie Clark

I never knew writing a book was going to be so hard! Heck, I thought I'd just write the stories down, my girlfriend Sonya would type them up, and we'd have a book in a few months. Damn if it wasn't the hardest thing I've ever done!

I first started thinking about writing this book when I was in prison. Of course, like a lot of things in life, I put it off. In 2006, I started thinking hard about the book again and everything I had done in my life. So I started writing down notes of things I remembered, visited with old friends, shared memories and photos from family and friends, and this book was started. I had notebooks of stories - seems like in my life I was always making trouble or in trouble or trouble just found me!

Sonya started really typing these stories down in 2008, trying to get me organized, getting me to remember more. She'd spend 10-20 hours a week on this book, giving up a lot of her free time and dancing! And for those of you who know me, I had a lot of stories written down and kept coming up with more as she was typing them into the computer. By the time we finished it was nearly 1000 pages and it took her about two years of typing and trying to figure out my stories. I lived a crazy life, but I'm not sure I'd even read 1000 pages about me!

With a little luck and word of mouth, we found an editor living in Myakka City, Paula Porter. She was able to whittle those stories down and help us come up with the book you now hold. Along the way, we built a website, thanks to my cousin, Mike McLaughlin. Mike also wrote and recorded a song about me called, "The Legend of Donnie Clark".

I don't want to give too much here, but a lot of folks have been wondering just how this book was going to turn out, especially to see if they are mentioned. I didn't write it to tell stories on any folks, I didn't write it to embarrass anyone or make anyone mad. It's just the truth from my point of view. I have to admit, I'm proud of this book and the way I lived my life, mistakes and all.

# Acknowledgements

Sonya Noel, Author, typing and years of toleration
Dr. Paula Porter, Editor
Mike McLaughlin, Songwriter and web designer
Rick Lambert, web designer
Allen Langford, Banker
Nate Bryant, book cover layout
Squire Strahan, book cover layout
Brandon & Kayla Noel, typing
Cande Clark, typing
Amelia Catalano, typing

Special Thanks to:

Former President Bill Clinton
Julie Stewart, FAMM
Sandra Rawls
Cande Clark

And to all of my supporters through the years from writing letters to me or to the Judge or Politicians. If it wasn't for all of you, I would still be in prison.

# CHAPTER 1
# 1940 - 1950

I, Donald Ralph Clark, was born on November 8, 1940, at Bradenton General Hospital in Manatee County to Ralph Spring Clark and Edna Jeanette Clark (Johnson). Dad's family originated from Granby, Connecticut, and Momma's family originated from here.

For those of you who may not know, Manatee County is Florida's 31st county established on January 9, 1855, after separating from Hillsborough County. Bradentown was incorporated as a city in 1903. Bradentown was named after Dr. Joseph Braden who was the first sugar cane grower in the area.

In 1925, the citizens of the town voted to drop the "w" and become Bradenton. Of course, Manatee County was not anything like it is today. In the early '20s, Manatee County experienced a tremendous period of growth with the Florida land boom. Within the first five years of that decade, the population tripled, many new buildings were constructed and tourism increased dramatically.

The Great Depression severely hurt the entire country, but agriculture continued to keep many of Manatee County's residents working. Prosperity returned in the '40s, and by the end of that decade, Manatee County was becoming the thriving area many of you recognize today. The population in 1940 when I was born was documented to be around 26,000 people. But the population steadily grew to 35,000 in 1950 and to 307,000 in 2005.

Most of the roads were dirt roads that had cattle guards to cross over. Highway 70 was a two-lane dirt road from Linger Lodge Road to Country Road 675. All the bridges were wooden except the Green Bridge. Almost all of the land was agricultural land used for cattle, citrus groves and farms. A lot of people lived off the land, from growing their own vegetables to raising their own cows for milk and beef.

Some of the more familiar sites in the area had their beginnings in the county about the same time I did. Sarasota-Bradenton International Airport started in World War II, when it was used as an air base for training bomber pilots and crews. The flights went over Longboat Key, which was used as a bombing target during the war.

Tropicana was started by Anthony Rossi who emigrated from Sicily, Italy to New York City. He moved to West Florida in 1947 and started selling citrus fruit boxes to locals. The demand for citrus from Florida grew larger when Macy's & Gimbel's department stores in New York City started requesting shipments of 1,000 boxes per week.

Dad was working at Tri-City Milk Company when I was born and he had many jobs throughout his life. He traded cows, horses and mules, swapped land, farmed land, built houses, doctored animals, and butchered, as well as being a heavy machine excavator and the owner of several businesses. The most remembered by many folks was his stint as County Commissioner; in fact, he went into office in January 1951 through January of 1959 and then went back into office from 1963 to 1966.

Momma was the homemaker who cooked, cleaned, sewed, canned vegetables, jarred jelly and tried to take care of me, which was her biggest job ever! From making me take a bath in the pond after my encounter with the skunks to threatening to tell Dad about my latest stunt when he came home, she was a busy woman. She knew Dad would tear my ass up if she told him everything that I did, which she hardly ever did.

Momma was deathly afraid of lightning and snakes. She would make Sandra, my sister, and I get into the closet with her when it was lightning. I often remember Momma on cold mornings warming her hands by rubbing them together over the hot stove. Later in her years, she worked for me in the sod company selling retail sod.

Momma and Dad both loved to dance, which is probably where Sandra and I got the dance fever from. Dad and his sister, Bea, won several dance contests, as did Sandra and I. Momma and Dad often went dancing at the Knick-Knack, which was on the corner of 14th Street and Cortez Road. They also went to the Coliseum in St. Pete, which was a big place to go to in the mid '40s with big name bands. They loved to play cards, but the only game that I remember them playing was called "Rook".

My sister, Sandra, was born on February 11, 1944. I always picked on her, but that was my way of making her tough. She's gonna hate me, but you know I got to share some of these memories. She'll get over it, I suppose.

One day I told her that we would get paid by the county if we cleaned the ditches out in front of our house in Samoset. I was around ten and she was around six. So we chopped down the high weeds for about 100 yards; of course, we never got paid by the county and Sandra was so mad at me.

Sandra was bitten on the arm really bad by our horse, Mickie, when she was about five or six years old. She was emptying the bucket of feed into the feed trough and Mickie took a chunk off her arm. Sandra still has the scar on her arm to remember Mickie by to this day.

We moved around quite a bit from living in East Manatee, to Samoset, to the Bayshore Gardens area to Oneco, but I can only re-member back to around 1945. My best recollection was when the war was over and we lived on 9th Street East in Samoset which was a dirt road. I was riding my tricycle when all of a sudden the sirens went off and the women were running out of their houses. Everyone was jumping up and down, hugging and crying because they knew their husbands or sons would be home soon from the war.

My dad did not go to war due to an old injury from being thrown off a bucking horse. The military would not accept him, so he worked for the railroad during that time. All men were required to work for factories, the railroads, etc. if they could not enlist.

One of my daily jobs as a kid was feeding the animals and hanging out with Dad and helping him. I recall riding around with Dad a lot when I was young; I'm sure this was to keep me out of Momma's hair. Speaking of hair, Momma and Grandma Clark never wanted my hair cut, but the longer it got the curlier it was and really blond. Dad was always having people tell him how cute his little girl was until one day he decided to get me a "real man's" haircut. And I'll never forget how mad Momma and Grandma Clark were when we got home.

In my younger years, I stayed a lot at Grandma and Grandpa Clark's house on 12th street in Manatee. I would look over Grandma's picture albums of the family. Grandma was a big believer of taking pic-tures. The other things I always used to look through were the *National*

*Geographic* magazines that she was always getting. Back in those days there wasn't any *Playboy* magazines that I knew of or anything of naked people. So the *National Geographic* was my *Playboy*.

Some of the things that I did when I was real young was helped Dad when he worked on cattle. One of my jobs was holding the bottles of glucose or dextrose up while Dad gave it to the cattle intravenously. Another one of my jobs was digging the gut holes while they butchered the cattle.

In the '40s and '50s we also doctored calves for screw worms. Screw worms were real bad on cattle from 1930 to 1959. Screw worm flies would lay their larva on the cattle and the maggots, when they hatched, would feed on live flesh. If not treated, the maggots would kill the animal within a week after the infestation. The fly would lay eggs around the navel cord on newborn calves or any bloody place on the cow and once the eggs hatched, the maggots started eating the flesh.

The gopher turtles were almost wiped out because they also menstruate and screw worms killed them. It made life rough for the ranchers during the screw worm days because the ranchers had to check their cattle daily. The fly was finally eradicated in 1959, and I didn't see screw worms again until I was in the jungles of Ecuador.

One day Dad and I went out to a pasture to doctor a calf for screw worms. He came back to the truck carrying the bucket that had the feed pellets in it to call the cows up. He handed me the bucket. I dropped the bucket down to my waist to put it in the back of the truck and there was a dead rattlesnake in it. It scared me so bad that I dropped the bucket and ran away squealing.

In the mid '40s, we lived on the corner of 9th Street East and 37th Ave. E. in Samoset. Mr. Thompson lived on the opposite corner from us and he was a truck farmer. A truck farmer grows vegetables to sell locally. I recall Mr. Thompson riding on top of his wagon pulled by a mule in the early mornings going to his field. There would be a couple of black women in the back of the wagon going to work with him in the field. A lot of times I would jump on the wagon and ride a ways with them down the dirt road.

One morning I jumped on the wagon with my harmonica and I played that harmonica with the women just laughing at me because I danced along with my silly music. The women warned me about getting off where I usually get off, but I was having too much fun and stayed on all the way to the field. When we got to the field, Mr. Thompson saw me and was going to take me back home but when we turned around, there was Momma marching up the road with a switch in her hand. Boy, did I get my butt tore up.

Speaking of getting a butt whippin', I remember another time when Dad and I stopped at the Gulf gas station that Andy Romine had on the corner of 15th Street and Hwy 70. While Dad was paying for the gas, I took some candy from a jar on the counter. I was standing in the passenger seat (this was before seat belts were required) next to Dad as we left and he noticed that I was eating candy. He asked me where I got the candy and after I answered him, he pulled the truck over and whipped my butt. He then drove back to the station and made me apologize to Mr. Romine for taking the candy without paying for it. Dad paid for the candy and I believe that was my first and only lesson about taking something that didn't belong to me or not paying for something.

I have to say that my whippin's were memorable especially from Dad. I probably deserved every one of them if not more. When Dad spoke, everybody listened! It didn't matter whose kid you were, if you misbehaved or got out of line, Dad whipped your ass, too! I have a few friends who can vouch for that. When I was younger, I got it with just the hand. Then I graduated to the belt as I got older, and then onto bigger and better things like milking machine hose pipes.

I remember one whipping that I got from Dad with his hand when I was about six or seven years old. We were eating supper and it was a few days before Christmas when Momma piped up and said, "There's a mouse in the house and he's a little strange ole mouse, because he only made small holes in the corners of all of Donnie's presents."

Dad looked at me and asked, "Boy did you make those holes in those presents?"

I nodded my head, yes because I couldn't talk for almost crying. I knew that I was going to get a whipping. He snatched me out of my chair and tore my ass up. After that I don't ever remember sneaking into my presents anymore!

There was a time that I should have gotten my tail tore up when I was with Dad on one of his livestock trading trips. Whether it was mules, cows, bulls or horses, if someone needed to trade, Dad would be there. He traded quite often with a man named Mr. Cress, who had a mule lot where the ComeSee ComeSav feed store is located now.

This one time in particular Dad bought a horse in Venice and later on in the day, while we were in Fort Myers, a man asked Dad what he wanted for the horse. Dad told him that he had $125 invested in him, that's when I piped up and said, "No, you didn't Dad...don't you remember you only paid $75 for the horse?"

I don't remember if that man bought the horse from Dad or not, but I sure do remember the lecture Dad gave me later. He said, "I didn't lie to the man about the horse. My time and expense was worth something and combined with the money spent on the horse it all added to $125."

I learned then to keep my mouth shut when Dad was trading.

Dad had a couple of dairies in the late '40s. One was the dairy that he rented from Mrs. Cobb and the other was the Whiteside Dairy. The Cobb Dairy was on 26th Avenue East, just past Mixon's Fruit Farm heading east on the right.

It was a small dairy, probably about 65 to 70 head to milk. I was too small to do much, so my jobs were washing and cleaning the pot milking machines, washing down the milking barn, mixing feed with a shovel, and driving cows in and out of the barn.

When I was about six or seven years old, Dad had me driving an old '42 or '43 Ford pickup, while he was unloading culled vegetables to the dairy cows. He would stand on the bed of the truck with a pitch fork tossing the culls out, while I slowly drove along. I could barely see through the steering wheel and had to keep the truck going as slow as possible. Because I had to stretch to reach the gas pedal, my feet were not steady and I would make the truck jump. One time I had it jumping so bad that it threw Dad out of the back of the truck. He was so mad, he snatched me out of the truck and tore my ass up and told me to get back in the truck and drive it right.

Another recollection about being around the dairy was when I got my tongue stuck to the milk cooler. The milk cooler was about five foot high with a tank on top which is where the milk was poured into out of ten gallon milk cans. The cooler looked like an old washboard made out of stainless steel pipes. When the milk was poured into the milk tank, it would flow down over the cold pipes into another milk can below and after a period of time, milk ice would form on the bottom outside of the cooler.

Normally I would walk by and scrape the milk ice off with my finger and put it into my mouth, but this particular day I had my hands full carrying milk buckets. So as I walked by, I stuck my tongue out to lick some milk ice off the cooler and my tongue stuck to the cooler. Damn did that stop me dead in my tracks!

I tried hollering for help but couldn't yell loud enough. With all of the machines going it would have been hard to hear anyway. It was awhile before one of the workers, James Meadors, came in and saw me stuck to the cooler. He was laughing at me, but he went over to the sink to get a bucket of water and poured it over my head. Needless to say, that was the first and last time that I licked milk ice off coolers.

The Whiteside Dairy was on 9th Street East and 30th Avenue East. At this time is when the milk prices dropped quite a bit and all of the dairy farmers, which I believe were about 35 in the county back then, started dumping their milk for a few days to try to get the prices back up. Dad would scrape the cream off the milk and bring it home to make butter using Momma's washing machine to do it in. He would give away the butter to people who wanted it, but boy Momma had quite the time cleaning the washer tub out!

Back then, the washing machines were not what they are today. The tubs did the washing, but they had two rollers that sat on the top of the washer so that when the clothes were finished washing and rinsing Momma had to slide the clothes through the rollers to wring out the excess water. The clothes were then hung on the clothesline to dry.

During the late '40s Atwood Groves was located on the south side US 301 in Palmetto, where Canal Road meets 301. There was several hundred acres along the Manatee River and this was the largest grapefruit grove in the Southeast. Mr. Ezell was the local grove caretaker for many groves in the area and Atwood was one of them. This grove had a lot of maiden cane which was hard to maintain if it got out of control. Maiden cane is a thick, tall grass that can get up to four to seven foot tall and cattle love to graze on it.

With it being summer time and the grass pretty much out of control, Mr. Ezell got an idea to fence in the grove and buy some cattle to help keep the grass down. So he bought about 200 head of cattle from North Florida and had them brought in on semi-trucks one rainy night. These cattle were "wild wood cows", which are considered cracker cows raised in the woods. These cows had long sharp horns and weighed about 500 to 700 pounds.

Mr. Ezell had a cattle chute built to unload the cows off the semis, but did not build any cow pens to put them in for a few days before letting them out in the grove. As soon as the gates were opened on the semis, the cows came out running and did not stop for anything, including the fences. All 200 or so cows were scattered from Palmetto to Parrish (east-west) and from the Manatee River to Buckeye Road (north-south).

The next day, Mr. Ezell called Dad to ask him to round up the cattle. Dad had me, Uncle Red Kilcrease, Wayne Terry, John White, Varnell Green, and Dad's helpers from the dairy, James and JC Meadors to help. James and JC mostly drove the cattle truck or the jeep pulling a small stock trailer from place to place to load the cows that we had roped and tied.

I was about eight years old and my job was to stay with the cow dogs. They would trail a cow or cows, get them bayed up in the woods where I would go in on my Welsh pony, which was a cross between a Shetland pony stud and a mare horse. I would start hollering and yelling at the cows and sic'ing the dogs on the cattle so they would run out of the heavy woods where the men would be waiting there to rope them in the open area.

Some mornings Dad and Uncle Red went up in a Piper Club airplane, which Uncle Red piloted, to try and spot some of the cattle. When they returned, they informed us where they had spotted the cattle and we would then go catch them. Rounding up all of these cows took about a total of six weeks off and on, but we caught most of them in the first three weeks.

It was a slow process, but a good lesson learned. Never turn wild cattle out into a new pasture, especially at night, without cow pens because no fence will keep them in. Normally, we kept wild cows penned up until they got familiar with their surroundings and settled down. So with this nightmare experience for Mr. Ezell, he decided to sell all of the cows and mow the maiden cane from then on.

Sometime after our experience with Mr. Ezell and the wild cows, James and J.C. would go over to Palmetto on the opposite (north) corner of Atwood Groves after milking, to mow and pile up maiden cane. The maiden cane was taken back to the dairy where it was chopped into shorter pieces by a machine and molasses was added to it for cow feed.

There were times that I drove the tractor and wagon over to pick up the maiden cane, but either J.C. or James would drive the load back to the dairy. I had to drive down 9th Street to Manatee Avenue, go west towards downtown Bradenton and across the Green Bridge over to Palmetto. From there I would travel north to 10th Street and then east to Canal Road. At this time the Green Bridge was the only bridge crossing the river to Palmetto from Bradenton.

The guys would have all of the maiden cane piled up in small piles so when I arrived they could load the grass onto the wagon with pitch forks. I would drive the tractor along as they loaded the wagon and I would pick oranges at the same time. Once the wagon was loaded, I would make a hole in the grass, like a fort, where I would ride in the wagon on top of the grass with my oranges back to the dairy. One of the guys would drive the truck back to the dairy and the other one would drive the tractor back.

On the way back to the dairy, I would throw the oranges that I picked at the black kids that lived along 9th Street in the Negro quarters (where Tropicana is now). But there was one time they ambushed me. They were waiting for me to come by and they all started climbing on the back of the wagon. I started yelling at whoever was driving the tractor so he stopped and ran them off.

Another day I was heading to Palmetto with the tractor and wagon, and shortly after I crossed over Green Bridge, I was stopped by a Palmetto police officer. He said I was too young to be driving a tractor on the road by myself and he made me park the tractor. He took me to the Palmetto Police station, where I spent the rest of the day.

Dad was a County Commissioner at the time and was in a meeting that morning. I tried to tell the officer that Dad would be mad if I didn't get that tractor to the field, but he insisted that I was breaking the law and held me at the station anyway. Dad came to the station late in the evening to pick me up and he gave the officer hell for keeping me from doing my job. There was not a written law back in those days to state that I was too young to be driving a tractor and Dad made sure the officer knew exactly that when everything was all said and done.

Dad was always helping people with their animals, so I learned a lot at a very young age about caring for animals. My fondest memories of our animals were about our Brahma bull named Sam, and Tarzan, our stud horse. Both were born the same year I was born. Dad trained both Sam and Tarzan so good that they would lie down so I could get on them and ride them.

Sam was 7/8 Brahma and 1/8 Guernsey and was white and grey with brown specks on his hump and neck. Dad put a ring in Sam's nose which allowed him to be tied or led around. Even after the Great Depression and WWII were over, times were still somewhat hard in Manatee County and Dad used Sam to breed a lot of milk cows in the county. To haul Sam was not a problem; he would ride on a flatbed truck or in a trailer, it didn't matter, all we had to say was, "Load up, Sam."

Sam was a true Clark bull. When we loaded him into the trailer or on a truck bed, he knew that he was going to get his "fix". Sam started bellowing real loud as soon as we drove into someone's yard and the cow would bellow back. I would unsnap the chain from the ring in his nose and Sam would jump off the truck. It did not matter about a fence or gate. Sam jumped it just to get to that cow. The owner would come out of the house to greet Dad, but ole Sam was already through with the breeding.

The charge for breeding was $5.00 and most of the time the owners did not have the money. But that didn't matter. Dad took whatever they had. Whether it was chickens, hogs, vegetables, but most of the time he bought their yearlings. Most people did not care to keep their yearlings because they were mostly interested in the milk from the cow.

I remember when we had Sam on a two and a half ton flatbed truck and we were on our way to Palmetto to breed a cow. We had Sam tied to the headboard of the truck and Dad and I were talking forgetting that Sam was on the back. It was raining hard when we made a 90 degree turn onto the Green Bridge. This made Sam's feet slip out from underneath him slamming him down hard on the bed of the truck. Because he weighed about 1800 pounds, this made the truck really shake.

As we made the corner, Sam slid off the truck snapping the chain. Sam slid on his side, dropping about four foot, right into on-coming traffic. But the cars managed to stop in time before hitting him. Dad realized what was happening and stopped the truck.

As Sam was sliding across the pavement, Dad rolled down the window to holler at Sam, "Sam, get your ass back on the truck."

Sam got up and jumped back onto the truck bed and away we went. This all happened in less than a minute. There were about six to seven cars dead stopped with their drivers in shock. As we passed by them, we could see their faces with big eyes and open mouths. They couldn't believe what they had just witnessed.

We only let Sam breed the same cow twice and there were times when Sam was breeding five to six cows a day. Over the 18 years that we had Sam, he must have breed hundreds of cows throughout the county.

Every March, for about six years, I rode Sam in the DeSoto Parade. I really didn't like riding him in the parade because I had a hard time keeping the 30 foot chain between his hump and my crotch. Later on, I started using a short rope for reins, tied onto the noise ring, which worked much better. Sam had a real smooth ride and a really nice lope. I only have one photo of Sam and it's of me riding Sam in the parade. We were always in the back of the parade behind Dad and the others that were on horses. They would shoot their pistols, pop their whips and rope the cops or bystanders.

In the early '50s they came out with artificial breeding, so Sam wasn't needed much anymore. Times were getting better with most people getting rid of their milk cows. But Sam was used to having his fix and there were times that we wouldn't get a call for breeding for two to three weeks.

Sam was never put in a pasture. We kept him chained to a tree, a post or an axel shaft that was driven into the ground. My job was to keep him fed and watered so I would have to move him to another area once he ate the grass around where he was tied.

I can remember a lot of times that someone would drive up in the yard in a pickup but when they got ready to leave, Sam would be in the back of their truck ready to go get his fix. They would knock on the door and tell Momma, "Mrs. Clark, there is a bull in the back of my truck."

Momma would have to go get Sam out of the truck. We tried keeping Sam tied up but when Sam wanted loose, he would break the chain no matter how bad the nose ring hurt.

Sam was about three years old when he got his horns cut off. He got loose and Momma tried to get him back on the chain, but he chased Momma around a guava tree trying to hook her the entire time. Momma told Dad when he got home, so the "Clark remedy" was to get rid of the horns.

While Dad had the Whiteside Dairy, it was only about a mile from our house in Samoset, so when the milk cows came in heat, Dad would call to tell me to bring Sam to the dairy. About half way to the dairy, Sam realized where we were going and he started to run. My hands became sore from pulling on the chain and before long I couldn't hold him back any longer.

After he did his duty, I never had any problems riding him back home; I could actually drop the chain without worry.

I failed second grade at Samoset Elementary School but passed the following year. Dad transferred me to Oneco Elementary for third grade after getting into an argument with the Principal, Mrs. Hager. Because I was out of district, I had to provide my own transportation to school. Most of the time my transportation was horses, Sam the bull, or an 8N Ford tractor. Back then, you could do this kind of thing in Manatee County and I was the only one in our area that I know of that ever rode an animal or drove a tractor to school.

Sam was slower than my horse was but was actually smoother to ride. I put burlap feed sacks on the horses or Sam because I got dirty riding bareback. I normally rode bareback until I got into my teens when I started using a saddle.

Dad tried to sell Sam in 1959 at the Sarasota Livestock Market because he kept getting loose and was becoming a hassle. He was used to the breeding, but the breeding was less and less, so Dad took Sam to the market and showed everyone what Sam could do. He showed them that Sam would lie down so he could get on him. And that he would jump up onto the concrete loading dock while he was still on Sam's back.

When I got home from school that day, I didn't expect to see Sam again, but he was still in the backyard tied to the tree. I asked Dad what happened and he said "I got soft hearted and couldn't sell him."

A few months later, a cattleman named Carl Mann called and told Dad that a college football team was looking for a tame Brahma bull to be used as a team mascot. I think this team was from out west playing Miami in Miami. Knowing that Sam would have a good home, Dad let Mr. Mann take Sam to Miami for the game. They bought Sam and I never saw Sam after that and have often wondered about whatever happened to "Old Sam"!

We had several horses, but they were mostly cow horses. I recall riding my horse, Goldie, to Oneco School quite often. I always ran my horses most of the time wide open wherever I went. I would ride the horse to school and race the school bus in the afternoons on its way back to Samoset, which got me into a lot of trouble. Trouble didn't stop me when it was fun though.

The best time racing the bus was when I flew by the bus along the longest stretch of road on 15th Street between Oneco and Samoset. The bus was going its fastest speed alongside the big canal, which was called the Oneco Drain Canal. The kids on the bus would try throwing things at me but I would be going so fast that they hardly hit me. There was just enough room between the edge of the road and the big deep canal for my horse to pass the bus. As I passed the bus on the right side I would have to lay down on the right side of the horse as far as I could to keep from getting hit. The bus driver, Mrs. Brown, kept telling me not to race the bus.

One day the bus left the school in Oneco and some of the kids that I was talking to said, "There goes the bus."

I didn't get into a hurry because I knew the bus had to stop at the railroad tracks and I would be able to catch the bus there. I started running the horse wide open and as I was getting closer to the tracks, the bus was stopping. There was a large house facing the road alongside the tracks on the north side of State Road 70 which blinded my view of the track until I got right up on the tracks. I went flying by the bus and then all of a sudden, I saw the train.

There was nowhere to go and nothing to do. I threw the reins over the horse's head keeping a hold of them and dove off the horse. With my weight, it jerked the horse around with the train barely missing my horse. The train horn was blaring the entire time. The horse was quite jumpy afterwards and I was scared to death myself. My jeans were torn and dirty, but we were both alive by a miracle.

Mrs. Brown stepped off the bus, white as a ghost and quite shaken. She was yelling at me and told me she was going to tell the Principal,

Mr. Gall. The next day, of course, I had to go to Mr. Gall's office. He gave me a whippin' and said that I had to quit racing the school bus. Boy was that fun while it lasted!

In the mid '40s, the Ringling Brothers & Barnum Bailey Circus train would come through Samoset on their way north. Folks would stand out by the railroad tracks for miles to watch the train go by. The train was about two miles long and every car was painted with circus paintings. We could see the animals in the cages, too. This was quite the event, because they would only come through twice a year, leaving to go north and coming back south for the winter.

My best and most memorable Christmas was in 1947. We got up and went to see what Santa brought us and there laid a Daisy lever-action BB gun with a bunch of packets of BBs. David Thomson, who lived next to us, also got a pump BB gun. David was a year older than me and we played together a lot.

I don't know how many birds we killed with those BB guns, but it was a lot. Richard Strickland, who lived at Granddad's dairy, got a BB gun also so David and I rode my horse over to the dairy and the three of us killed blackbirds most of the day.

Just up the road from our house, in Samoset, is where a bunch of other kids lived. They were the Parrish's, the Meador's and the Cliburn's. There were 16 kids in the Cliburn family and all of us boys played all kinds of games together.

When I was about eight, Dad bought me a key lawnmower. We lived in Samoset at the time and there wasn't that many yards to mow. Luckily Robert Hughes lived in an area with quite a few yards and he also did lawn mowing. So we worked over in his neck of the woods mowing lawns and received $5 per yard for the bigger yards. It only lasted one summer, but it showed me that I could make money myself.

When I wasn't working, I was playing or shooting game. In 1949, Dad bought me my first 22 rifle that was a single shot bolt action. I rode my horse bareback, carrying the rifle and a croker sack, to put the rabbits in that I killed. I believe I hunted rabbits in every citrus grove in Samoset.

Mama was always worrying about me and the rifle, like either shooting someone or myself. When I left the house with the rifle, she would always say, "You be careful carrying that gun on that horse."

We sure ate a lot of rabbits in those days. I only shot cotton tail rabbits though because the brown rabbits or what we called "swamp rabbits" seem to have the wolve in their neck all the time. I'm not sure what it was but it resembled the "bot-fly" that would get on cattle. Sometimes I would shoot a quail or two; most times you only got one shot at them though.

Sometime in the late forties, Dad bought a Shetland pony and buggy along with the harness at a livestock auction. The pony was a cream colored gelding that was well trained. The buggy was very light and had four bicycle wheels, with two flat board seats in the front and back. Also you could disconnect the back from the front and have something like a racing buggy, which was what I used most. We only had it for a month before Dad sold it, but I always used it most everyday going all over Samoset.

I drove it often over to Grandpa and Grandma Johnson's house a lot, which at the time was on 8th Street West. This was about four miles from our house in Samoset on Ninth Street East. Grandpa and Grandma Johnson were poor cracker people who lived in an old wood frame house with an outhouse in the backyard and an icebox refrigerator in the kitchen. They cooked on a wood burning stove, had a garden and a bunch of chickens that were in a large chicken pen. And they always had flowers growing all over the yard.

Sandra and I called Grandma Johnson "Doe Doe". She dipped snuff and Grandpa chewed tobacco and smoked cigars. That is probably where I got my snuff habit from. Doe Doe made lots of shirts and dresses out of flowery colored cotton feed sacks that chicken scratch feed came in. Grandma died in the early fifties and Grandpa lived into his nineties.

My most memorable time going over to their house with the pony and buggy was when I came flying into their front yard. I made a sharp turn into the yard and turned the buggy over which threw me out of the buggy. The pony dragged the over turned buggy through Grandpa's garden, tearing up some collard greens and black-eyed peas before he finally stopped. As I said, we didn't have the horse and buggy long but it sure was fun to ride but, of course, obviously pretty dangerous with me being the driver.

Sometime after I turned nine, I started helping Dad butcher cattle at Ocie Hawkins' slaughter house in Sarasota. We would butcher about 15 cattle every Tuesday morning, starting at two in the morning and working until around seven.

The part that bothered me the most was salting the hides after the butchering was done. The salt would burn the cuts and nicks on my hands that I received from skinning the beef. It would have been much better to bury the guts and do the cleaned up than to work in the hide room. I would take my school clothes with me so I could clean up at the slaughter house and then Dad would drop me off at school on his way home. J.C. and James Meadows, Dad and I were the only ones who worked that early morning shift.

Somewhere in the late '40s, Dad, John White and I were checking one of Dad's small pastures in Manatee on 15th Street, just past Tropicana before 9th Avenue. When we checked the pastures, we were always looking for any signs of screw worms, flies or lice. Dad always used a bucket of pellets to call the cows up, which of course, I acquired the same trait. The cows got so used to this that as soon as Dad would start yelling "Come on Bee bees, come on", they would all come running knowing Dad was throwing the pellets. He threw them in all directions so it was easier to walk among the cows to check them. Sometimes he would spray them with DDT to help get rid of the flies, lice and ticks.

On Christmas day around '48, Dad had 125 acres in Parrish on Chin Road, which he later sold to Steve Chin in the '50s. After we opened our presents, Robert Hughes and I had to go plant watermelons. Neither of us was very happy because mainly we had to work on Christmas day and we were not able to play with the things that we got for Christmas.

Dad soaked the seeds in water while we were planting. There were a few others beside Robert, Dad and I, but Robert and I would take four steps to the other men's two. The seeds were to be planted six feet apart with three seeds to a hill. We knew that we only had to plant half of the field that day.

Dad had the pile of seeds on a tarp. When our quart cans were empty we went back to the tarp to get a refill. Dad said when the pile of seeds were gone we could go home, so Robert started putting about 10 or 12 seeds in each hole. But it didn't take long before Dad caught on and boy did Robert get his ass tore up. And later on I got my ass tore up for planting them too far apart. Welcome to Ralph Clark's world!

With the ass whippin's in mind, I remember Dad had this saying as I was growing up, whenever he would do something wrong and he would get mad at himself, he would say, "I ought to have my ass kicked." After hearing him say this for years, one time at our family gatherings, I told my cousins that when I got big enough if I hear him say that, I was going to kick his ass for him. About 30 years later at a Thanksgiving reunion, my cousin, Anita Kilcrease Henderson asked me if I ever kicked my Dad's ass for him. I laughed and said, "I would have, but I never got big enough!"

I know if Dad was alive today he would be under the jail for whipping these kids' ass for not minding him. That was one thing he did not tolerate and most of us only had to have one ass whipping to know that he meant business.

This is about it for the '40s. If you learned anything from this chapter, I hope you learned that if you haven't taught kids how to behave by the time they are six to seven years old, you never will. And the more you teach your kids about life, the more they learn life's lessons. I can only recollect from about five years forward, but the things that I learned and experienced at such an early age have stuck with me my entire life, especially the ass whippin's.

*Me and Aunt Bea.*

*Me and my mother.*

*Me on a horse.*

*Me when I looked like a girl.*

*A school photo.*

*Me riding our bull Sam*

*The Clark Family in the 50's.*

## CHAPTER 2
# 1950 - 1960

The **Fifties** in the United States and much of Western Europe were considered conservative in contrast to the social revolution of the 1960s. Education grew explosively because of a strong demand for high school and college education. Many modern toys like Hula-hoops and Frisbees were invented in the '50s.

Rock and roll emerged as the teen music of choice in this era with Little Richard, Buddy Holly, and Chuck Berry being the notable ones. But it was really Elvis Presley who was the musical superstar of the period with rock, rockabilly, gospel, and romantic balladeering being his best music.

Also during this time, African-Americans were subject to racial segregation, but the Civil Rights Movement of the 1960s was brewing. Key figures like Martin Luther King, Malcolm X, and Rosa Parks highlighted and challenged those who were against African-American rights and freedom.

Disneyland opened in Anaheim, California in 1955 and market surveys showed 2% of the visitors came from east of the Mississippi River. This prompted Walt Disney, in 1959, to begin looking for land to open a second resort, which happened in 1971 with Disney World.

Manatee County, of course, was steadily growing, too. Most of the roads were still dirt roads and the wooden bridges were still around. Twice in county history, the population almost doubled in a 10-year period, between 1910 and 1920 and again between 1950 and 1960.

The first Sunshine Skyway bridge span opened in 1954 and was 15 miles long crossing from St. Petersburg to Bradenton. The original span was a two lane causeway with a vertical clearance of 150 feet above the water.

As I mentioned before, Dad was a County Commissioner in District IV for several years actually going into office the first time in January of 1951. He ran for County Commissioner for District IV five times and was elected for three terms. He also ran for Sheriff twice and School Superintendent once but was never elected.

Dad loved politics and often tried to get me involved in them as well. I was accustomed to the political ring since I was raised around it. Dad would always tell me not to be getting into trouble, but I seemed to always get into some kind of trouble while he was in office, which did not make my life easy.

Dad did do a lot of good things for the county. He was one of the leaders in promoting and accomplishing the Lake Manatee Reservoir. He was also Treasurer of the State of Florida Water Board in the '60s.

In the early '50s, the county had five Districts with each District having their own budget and expense. Dad's District bought the first dragline and bulldozer that the county owned. Up until that time, the Districts paid an outside company to do this type of work. After his District purchased these two machines, he would rent them out to the other Districts.

Later on, his District built a tile plant on County property, in Samoset, to make concrete culverts for driveways and sold them to other Districts. Dad's District was saving and making money off the other Districts, until the rest of the Commissioners voted to have all of the Districts lumped together. Every two election years, there were rallies where the opponents would give a speech to the public after dinner. The dinners were usually around two to three dollars for mullet, chicken, baked beans, swamp cabbage, grits, and hush puppies.

Roy Baden, who was the Manatee County Sheriff at the time, cooked the meat and hush puppies with Dad cooking the swamp cabbage. My buddies and I were always the lucky ones to help cut and clean the swamp cabbage. So as you can see, in my early years, I was able to see, do, and hear things about politics while being with Dad. That made an impact on me for not wanting anything to do with politics at all!

In the early '50s, he was working with the county crew that was paving the parking lot of the new Manatee Memorial Hospital. His friend, Bob Van Diver, who was visiting from the east coast near Daytona, wanted Dad to check on getting a tag for his house trailer so that Bob could get it moved.

Dad was pretty dirty from working in the parking lot when he and Bob went to the FHP office to check on the tag. At that time, the FHP office was where the Bishop Planetarium is now and Mr. Grayson was in charge. When they arrived at the office, Dad asked the officer behind the counter where Mr. Grayson was.

The officer informed Dad that Mr. Grayson wasn't in, so Dad asked the officer to get him on the radio because he needed to talk to him. But the officer refused to call Mr. Grayson and told Dad to come back later. The officer was not friendly at all and had an attitude to boot.

With Dad being all dirty, he must have assumed Dad was just some regular citizen making a request to speak to the person in charge. Dad, being the persistent person that he normally was, asked the officer again to try to get Mr. Grayson on the radio. By this time the officer was angry and walked around the counter and told Dad to leave the building.

When he approached Dad, Dad grabbed him around the shirt collar and slammed him against the wall hard. As Dad was grabbing the officer, the officer drew his pistol and shot Dad as he slammed him against the wall. Dad then released his hold of the officer and the officer ran out of the room going out a back door.

Dad turned to Bob and said, "That son of a bitch is trying to scare me with those blank bullets."

Bob was scared and completely shaking but said to Dad, "Those were not blank bullets, Ralph, because there's a bullet hole in the wall."

Dad immediately pulled his shirt up and noticed a red spot on his side where the bullet grazed his abdomen. Dad then went out the back door to try to find the officer but couldn't find him. As they got into Dad's car to leave, Clyde Gill, a Manatee County Sheriff Deputy, pulled up to speak with Dad.

Apparently, Clyde had been called to the office due to the officer telling Sheriff Roy Baden that some riff-raff citizen came in and was trying to beat him up. Dad explained to Clyde what happened. So with Clyde knowing Dad, asked him to come to the Sheriff's Office to get everything straightened out, which Dad agreed to do.

As Dad entered Roy's office, Roy asked, "Hey Ralph, what brings you in here?"

Dad answered, "That FHP officer just shot me!"

And Roy said, "You're the one he shot?"

Dad replied, "Yes, I don't know what his problem is, but he sure does have a bad attitude!"

Roy called the officer into his office and asked if this was the man that he shot and the officer replied, "Yes."

Roy asked the officer if he knew who that man was that he just shot and the officer replied, "No."

Roy then proceeded to tell him that this is Ralph Clark, a County Commissioner, and a paid county employee. He then asked the officer, "Are you going to stick to the story that you just told me?"

The officer hung his head and replied, "No."

He then told the officer to leave and to return back to the FHP office. After the officer left, Roy told Dad a few things about the officer as to why he may have had a bad attitude. Roy told Dad that the officer's wife was in the hospital having a baby, and he had to stay at the FHP office because they didn't have anyone else to cover the office.

Obviously, the officer was upset about not being able to be with his wife which Dad understood. Roy asked Dad if he wanted to press charges against the officer but Dad said, "No, sounds like he has enough problems."

Around the early '50s, Dad bought 200 acres near Bayshore Gardens. Back then most of the land was virgin land with pine trees, palmettos, and a lot of rattlesnakes. And after some land clearing, we built about eight or ten houses in that subdivision and moved into one of the houses around 1951. We only lived in it for about a year and a half (remember, I did say we moved around quite a bit).

During this time, we didn't need building permits to build houses, and the subdivisions did not have paved roads. It would take about a year to build a three bedroom house because we did not have plywood and they did not pre-make trusses either. In fact most everything that had to be done to build a house, we had to do ourselves. Like the kitchen cabinets all had to be built from scratch and the door frames for the doors had to be made as well. We actually mixed our own concrete with our own portable cement mixer using oyster shell, sand and cement for the footers and slabs. That's why it took so long to build a house.

I cannot remember all of the people who helped build the houses but the ones that I do remember were Varnell Green, John White, Wayne Terry, Ray Stewart, and James and J.C. Meadors.

Ray Stewart was the junior high football coach at Oneco, but he only worked for us building houses one summer. At the time, Oneco Elementary had first grade through ninth grade. I pulled a lot of jokes on Mr. Stewart and teased him a lot while he helped us that summer, but I got my payback later.

On the first day of school, after that summer, he was my home-room teacher, as well as my History teacher. When I walked into his classroom, he said, "Donnie, get one of those desks and put it right beside my desk because this will be your seat for the rest of the year."

So I had to face the class for the entire year. But the only good thing about my desk being beside his was that I made good grades because he was always on my ass. He even stayed on my ass at football practice but I liked him because he was a good coach. Paybacks can be hell at times…it ain't fun when the rabbit's got the gun!

I remember one day, while building one of the houses, a black man was helping mix mortar when he looked up at Mr. Terry and asked, "How tall is you, Mr. Terry?"

Mr. Terry said, "I'm five foot 18 inches tall."

The black man said, "Nah, you'se taller than that! I's six foot three and you'se a lot taller than I is".

Everyone was laughing while Mr. Terry explained to him what five foot 18 inches really meant.

The midway skating rink was nearby so Sandra and I skated a lot back then. That was the only rink in Bradenton then and this was really our only form of entertainment that was close to home. I actually got so good at skating that I could go down on one skate and strike a kitchen match, holding it in my mouth, and lighting it on the floor.

We also had the Sara-Mana Speed-Bowl (Speedway) that butted up to our property on the north side. On Friday nights we could hear them racing because our house was only ¼ mile away. When we first moved into the house, I built a platform in the top of a pine tree next to the Speed-Bowl so that I could watch the races. I really only used the platform to watch the races a couple of times, because I didn't really like car racing back then and still don't care for it much today.

There were times that Dad went to Wisconsin to bring back Holstein heifers in a semi-truck for Herman Burnett, who owned

Burnett's Dairy. Herman was a County Commissioner when Dad first went into office and was around the same age as Dad. Since there are two Herman Burnetts that I talk about, I'll call this Herman, "Big" Herman. The other Herman is a couple of years younger than I am so I'll call him "Lil" Herman. The two of them are related, I think cousins, but Lil Herman and I rode bulls, butchered, and worked cattle together.

In 1952, Mr. Estrup gave Dad a female bulldog that we named Troy. She was about a year old and was all white with a brown spot around her right ear. When I came home from school one afternoon, I saw the bulldog tied to a stake on a chain. When I approached her, she came to the end of the chain trying to bite me. She was mostly pit bull with mastiff weighing around 80 pounds and was a very mean dog in the beginning. It took a few days for me to get her under control and I did it mostly by using a big stick on her head.

We were soon using her to work cattle, and she ended up being a good cow dog. As a bulldog, she could trail cattle real good and could hold them up in a bunch. And because she was a bulldog, she would catch anything that we would sic her on, I mean anything. Whenever she had a hold of something I could not get her to let go of it. We bred her several times to other big bulldogs and she never had less than ten puppies at a time.

After Dad sold the house in Bayshore, we lived on 9th Street again for a while until he built a new house in Oneco on 33rd Street where he bought 25 acres. We built some dog pens behind the house with a concrete floor and two doghouses in it. I had to feed the animals in the morning before going to school.

When we first moved into the house in Oneco, I had a Guernsey cow to milk twice a day. Momma and I sold the extra milk to the Bennett family who had nine children. Dad ended up having to get another Guernsey cow because the Bennett's were using three gallons of milk a day.

We had one cow that would just take off after she finished eating her feed out of the feed bucket, causing the milk bucket that I was milking her in to spill all over. Boy did that tick me off when she would just run off and spill milk everywhere! So I had to give her extra feed whenever I milked her so that she would finish eating about the same time that I would finish milking her. The other Guernsey cow that Dad bought had a heifer calf. I kept the calf tied up and I would leave some milk in the cow to let the calf finish. I really took a liking to that calf.

One afternoon I went to get the calf to nurse and the calf was lying down. She couldn't get up so I started looking over her and saw the screw worms were eating at a hole in her hip that must have gotten scratched and started to bleed. I ran to the house to get Dad and when he saw how bad it was, he told me to kill and bury her.

So I got my 22 rifle and walked up close to her. As I was looking down the sight of the barrel, she was looking back at me with her big brown eyes with her head turned sideways looking somewhat sad. Tears came to my eyes as I pulled the trigger. I was crying as I buried her and it really affected me all night. It just really hurt me to have to kill that calf that I had grown to love.

From that point on, I never allowed myself to get real attached to anything or any person so that I wouldn't get hurt as I did then. Oh, I've had my feelings hurt a lot, but not like crying like a baby. So now you all know why I am the way I am.

Speaking of animals, all of my life I was around cattle in some form or another. We had pastures scattered that we leased all over the county. The only pasture that Dad actually owned back then was the 125 acres in Parrish which he ended up selling to Steve Chin.

Our biggest pasture was the Connick pasture which was on the north side of Highway 64 and east of the Braden River (where Carlton Arms is now). It was about 600 acres of good Bahia grass that had cross fences with a good set of cow pens complete with cattle scales and a dipping vat. Dad was in a 50/50 partnership with the cows with a man named Coon Lee. Dad also had a horse pasture for horses only and we normally had 20-40 horses in the pasture at one time. When Dad just about lost everything in the late '50s, we only had a few cows left.

Many times, Dad and I took Troy with us to help catch other people's animals whether it was a horse or cow, she could do it. We always had to carry a hot shot with us though, in case she wouldn't let loose of the animal once she caught it. The only way a bull, cow, horse, or hog could get loose from her, aside from using the hot shot, was if the animal's nose tore away from her grip. She always caught the animals in the nose where most dogs would catch animals by the ears.

I remember one Sunday afternoon, Dad, Momma, Sandra and I

were going fishing at Uncle Red's on Caruso Ranch. Mr. Joe Powell of Powell's Nursery in Oneco called Dad for a favor. He had some cows on Lorraine Road and asked Dad if he would come out to catch the Brahma bull that he had in Oneco and take him to the pasture on Lorraine Road. So instead of taking the car, we drove the cattle truck over to Mr. Powell's to get the bull. We took Troy with us to catch the bull, because Mr. Powell said the bull wouldn't go into the cow pens.

When we arrived we let Troy out to catch the bull and he was running away pretty fast when Troy jumped up and caught the bull by the nose. The bull jumped up pretty high trying to sling Troy off his nose but that didn't work. So he continued to run fast at the same time slamming his head into the ground trying to smash Troy. Instead of smashing Troy, his horn caught in the ground and broke his neck. With the bull dead, we had to butcher him. By the time we finished butchering him and took the meat to the cold storage in town, it was too late to go fishing.

Shortly after buying the 25 acres, Dad sold a few lots off the back part of the property and that's where Robert Hughes and Bob Murphy lived. Robert Hughes, Bernard Fagan, and Bob Murphy were my closest friends during this time since they were my closest neighbors, and the Hughes' were friends with my parents as well.

The four of us boys were nearly inseparable from 1954 to 1958. I was called Donnie, Bernard was called Fagan, Robert as Robert, and Bob was referred to as Murphy. We had a lot of fun and did a lot of crazy things over the years.

Robert and Fagan were the more serious ones of the bunch with Murphy and I considered the craziest without a doubt. Poor Fagan was the one who took the blunt of our jokes most of the time and it's a wonder that Fagan lived through it.

That house was the biggest house that we had lived in with three bedrooms and two bathrooms. Dad let me dig a swimming hole and a fishing pond with his dragline from the rock pit. We had an artesian flowing well next to a big ditch behind our house and right next to the well is where I decided to dig the swimming hole between some trees.

I left a large hickory tree that leaned over the pond. This is where I attached a rope from the highest limb. Another oak tree stood behind the hickory tree which had a long limb that ran from the trunk. We made a wooden ladder up the tree. The limb was about 15 feet from the ground and about 20 feet long going straight out from the tree trunk.

When one of us was up on the limb, someone else could throw the rope hanging from the hickory tree. From the oak, we could walk out on the limb about ten feet while holding on to the rope for balance and swing from the tree limb. We would let go when we were out 25 feet or so above the water. The oak/hickory set-up was on the west side of the pond, and on the east side was another large oak with a rope hanging from it. Boy, we had a lot of fun in that swimming hole especially on the east side

We would divide ourselves into two teams and play what we called Gator-Bird. Every time a player swung out over the pond and was able to get back to the bank their team would earn a point. But being able to get back to the bank was not easy.

The opposing team would do whatever they could to knock the swinger from the rope and into the water, hoping to keep them from being able to get back to the bank. Needless to say, there were plenty of scratches and bruises before the day was over.

We laid a thick, wide board across the big ditch next to the well which we used to cross the ditch. This was the path that was used for coming and going between our houses.

Other than getting into a little trouble now and then, we went to the movies a lot. We would go to the State and Palace Theaters in Bradenton, as well as the drive-in theater. We chose the drive-in theater mainly because we could sneak over the high fence in the back of the parking lot. We would hitch-hike to and from the theater. We found ourselves walking more often though because there were that many cars on the road back then.

Fagan and Murphy were born in September of 1940 and both graduated in '58 with both entering the service after graduation. Robert and I were born in November of 1940 and both of us graduated in '59 with Robert joining the service upon graduation as well. Robert and I graduated in '59 because he failed the third grade, and I failed the second grade. We all worked for Dad at the rock pit after school and on weekends.

Dad got into the rock pit business which was located on the East side of 15th Street heading towards Samoset from Oneco. He mined the rock into stone for fireplaces, flower boxes and patio stones and it was very pretty stone that sold really well. He invested into several different types of machinery to try to mine the rock easier, but lost a lot of money doing so. He eventually lost the mine and most everything else, but we were able to keep the house and property in Oneco.

The rock pit is where I learned how to operate the dragline because Dad got frustrated when the dragline operator, Ray Smith, hardly ever showed up for work on Saturdays. So one Friday, Dad came down into the pit where us boys were working breaking up rocks with sledgehammers and told me to get in the car. He took me back to where Ray was working the dragline and told Ray to show me how to operate it.

Ray showed me everything I needed to know except the maintenance part. I was a quick learner when it came to operating machinery, but I have to say, the dragline was the hardest piece of equipment that I ever learned to operate.

Of course, Ray didn't show up the next morning as expected and we had trucks waiting to get loaded. Dad came barreling down into the pit to get me and asked, "Did Ray show you everything about the dragline?"

I said, "Yes, but I don't think I'm ready to load trucks yet."

Apparently he didn't hear me, because he told me to get on the dragline and start loading the waiting trucks. So ready or not, I was going to have to load the trucks.

George Wiley was the first truck to be loaded. He was around 45 years old weighing about 350 pounds at the time. I started the dragline and was waiting for it to warm up when he got out of his truck. He looked up at me and asked, "Son, what do you think you're doing up there?"

I told him, "I'm going to load your truck."

He then asked, "Have you ever loaded trucks before?"

I told him, "No, I just learned yesterday."

He said, "Well, you're not loading my truck!"

So he went to the office to speak with Dad and about ten minutes later, he came back, and backed up to the dragline to be loaded. He said, "Go ahead and load me, your Dad said he would pay for any damages to the truck."

I thought, "Oh boy! That's just great. No pressure here".

It took me about 45 minutes to load him because I was so tense and both legs were shaking. I was a wreck because I was being extra careful keeping my mind on what I was doing. I loaded about ten trucks that day and the last one took about ten minutes. So I got better as the day went on. It wasn't long before I was loading trucks within three minutes.

Dad had a Negro man, McKnight, who worked for him at the rock pit. He often came over on Wednesday or Thursday nights to borrow money until pay day. McKnight would drive into the yard but sit in his car blowing his horn until Dad came outside. McKnight was afraid of Troy and her two half grown pups.

Dad did not like McKnight blowing his horn, so he told him not to worry about the dogs. He said, "If they growl at you, just stomp your foot at them and yell at them to get out of here you son of a bitch!"

After supper one evening while we were watching TV, we heard a car drive up. We heard the car door slam shortly afterwards and the dogs started growling. Then we heard McKnight say, "Get on out of here you son of a bitch!"

Shortly afterwards, we heard McKnight screaming, so I ran outside to get the dogs back. When I got to where McKnight was, he was flat on his back with the pups on each leg jerking and pulling on them while Troy was on his chest. McKnight had both of his hands around Troy's neck as Troy was snapping into the air trying to get to McKnight's arms. I got the pups and Troy off of him and took them to the pens. Needless to say, McKnight never came back to the house to borrow money before pay day anymore.

Fagan and I were leaving the rock pit in the dump-truck loaded with fill-dirt one afternoon. I was hauling the dirt to the Hughes' house along the back roads, because I was only 15 years old and only had my restricted license. We were on 51st Avenue in Oneco, approaching the first railroad track, and I had just shifted into fourth gear.

During this time, there weren't railroad crossing gates or lights at the tracks so you went over tracks at your own risk. As we started to cross the track, an oncoming train's horn blew. I looked to the right, out of the passenger side window, and there it was! I saw nothing but the train's front end. Immediately, Fagan started throwing a crazy fit by throwing his arms in the air screaming bloody murder.

I down shifted the truck to third gear, stomped on the gas, and sped off the tracks just in time for the train to miss the rear end of the truck. By now, Fagan was motionless with his head leaned back and not saying a word. I'm sure he stopped breathing with his heart in his throat.

I only made it about 100 feet from the tracks before I started shaking uncontrollably. I pulled the truck to the side of the road so I could calm down. After a while, my shaking stopped and I was able to drive again.

I do believe that is the most frightened I have ever been. This was not one of my planned jokes and that was the one time I was not laughing! So this is twice now that I've almost been killed by a train.

But there were plenty of planned jokes that poor ole Fagan endured. Like when Fagan, Murphy, and I were going to the Connick Pasture in Momma's Desoto car to check the cattle for screw worms. We entered the pasture off a dirt road north from State Road 64. Because there were also a lot of rabbits along the dirt road, I stopped the car in order for Fagan to ride on the front passenger fender of the car. Fagan wanted to try to shoot some rabbits with my bow and arrow.

I was driving about 25 or 30 miles per hour when I abruptly bumped the brakes. Fagan thought I hit the brakes trying to throw him from the fender, so he jumped away from the car. He hit the ground running, but his legs could not keep up with the momentum of the rest of his body.

After a few seconds, he was somersaulting with the bow still in his hand. I stopped the car and Murphy and I fell out of the car laughing our asses off, but Fagan was hardly laughing.

I was still on the ground laughing when Fagan came walking up to me angry. He was covered in dirt and sandspurs and he started beating me with the bow that never left his hand. I did not stop laughing until the pain took over, which sent Murphy even deeper into laughter.

Once Fagan was through beating the living daylights out of me, we continued on to the pasture. When we got there, we noticed that the neighbor's dogs had caught three cows by the ears. Screw worms were just hatching and starting to eat on their bloody ears.

So we roped the cows and cut their ears off next to their heads and put screw worm medicine on them. We then tied feed sacks around their heads to help keep the medicine intact until their ears healed. When we got home I told Dad what happened. The next morning Dad went back out there and shot and killed four dogs because they were catching another cow when he arrived.

While I'm on the subject of medicine, I'll tell you about the time I was trying to give some medicine to a bull. Smokey Smith had a pasture off 9th Street East in Oneco which began on State Road 70 and ran north along the west side of 9th Street. The pasture was made up of 125 acres which is now a trailer park.

One day, Smokey called the house and I answered the phone. Smokey told me he had just pulled his Angus bull out of a boggy pond and his bull didn't have the strength to get up. He wanted Dad to give the bull some glucose but Dad was in Tallahassee on business for the county so I told Smokey that I could do that for him.

So Fagan and I grabbed Dad's medicine bag, and headed for Smokey's pasture. We laid the bull down broad side, so I could insert the needle into his juggler vein. I had seen Dad do this many times, but as usual, I didn't pay close attention to the details of how he did it but I knew the vein was located close to the bull's windpipe. I must have stabbed that bull's neck ten to fifteen times before I hit the vein. Fagan was having a fit and claiming that I did not know what I was doing.

After I finally found the vein, and gave the bull 500 cc's of glucose intravenously, the bull found the energy to stand with our help by pulling up on its tail and ears. When Dad arrived back home, I asked him how he found the juggler vein all those times. This didn't make Dad happy as he said, "You don't pay attention to anything, do you?"

I told him I was always busy helping him with the fluids and bottles when he was inserting the needle. He then explained how it is done and I never had that problem again from that point on.

After school, one afternoon, Fagan and I were in my bedroom and I was changing clothes. I had just bought a new holster for my 22 revolver pistol and he was looking at himself in the mirror as he strutted around with my holster and pistol on.

I hadn't put a tie down strap on the holster yet which holds the holster in place when fast drawing the pistol, and Fagan was having a hard time practicing his quick-draws. He asked me to hold the holster down while he made his quick-draws. As he stepped back for one of his quick-draws, I snatched the pistol out before he was able to and fired it towards Fagan.

The shot fired surprised and scared us both. Fagan grabbed for his crotch and I threw the pistol on the bed and quickly shut the bedroom door before Sandra could come in. Though she did come to the door asking what had happened but I just told her that one of my firecrackers went off.

After she left, I took Fagan into the bathroom to examine his wound. He dropped his Levi's and the bullet hit the floor. The bullet went through his right front pocket scathing his right upper thigh at the hip area. The bullet made a large gash about a half inch above his penis and entered his left front pocket where it remained until Fagan dropped his pants.

I didn't know what to do besides apply some rubbing alcohol to the wound. As soon as I poured the first drop of alcohol onto the gash, Fagan started hollering. We put some cotton over the wound to help stop the bleeding and I told Fagan to go home, go to bed and that he would be alright by morning. He went home but I called him every half hour for a couple of hours and after a while, the bleeding finally stopped. If Dad had found out what happened, I would have been on the receiving end of another ass-whipping.

Another incident happened after school one day. Fagan went home to change his clothes and was then headed back to my house. With all that time on my hands what could I do beside devise another trick to pull on poor 'ole Fagan?

I started sawing the board that was used to cross the ditch going to Fagan's house using a hand-saw. I only sawed a portion of the board in the middle from the bottom side so Fagan couldn't see that it had been messed with. After I finished, there were only slivers of wood holding the board together.

I laid the board back in its spot and hid behind a big oak tree as I saw Fagan coming and about to cross the ditch. Fagan jumped on the middle of the board and splashed into the water below breaking the board. From that point forward, we crossed the ditch with a little extra care as we never knew when someone else would pull another prank.

The next trick I pulled on Fagan was slightly different. One dark night, I knew Fagan was on his way to my house again so I went out to the ditch and poured gasoline on the board from end to end. I made a gas trail up to and around a cabbage palm tree where I was hiding.

Fagan stopped to check the board to see if it had been sawed. He found it to be sturdy so he began to walk across the board. That's when I struck a match and threw it down on the trail of gasoline. With a "poof" sound, the gasoline ignited, shot down the trail to the board, and the flames blazed through Fagan's legs.

I didn't need to put in so much strenuous effort to get Fagan wet this time because as he let out a hell of a scream, he jumped into the air and went down into the ditch water. He actually looked as though he had been blown off the board instead of jumping off it.

The best trick Murphy, Robert, and I ever pulled on Fagan was when we dug a pit trap. Just before dusk one evening, Robert, Murphy, and I dug out a pit along the grassy trail which led from Fagan's house to Murphy's. Along the path was grass and weeds and we used a wheel barrel to move the dirt that we had dug up to a spot just off the trail so it wouldn't be seen.

It took about four wheel barrel loads of dirt because we dug a hole two feet wide, five feet long, and four feet deep. It took us quite a while to finish the job because we were careful not to disturb the grass and weeds near the hole. When we finally finished digging the hole, we connected water hoses together to fill the hole up with water.

As the hole was filling up with water, we cut limbs from cabbage palms to lie across the hole in order to conceal it from Fagan. We then gathered wire grass to lay atop the cabbage palm limbs. We did a final inspection and the hole looked complete with no signs of a hole at all.

We went to Murphy's house so that I could call Fagan. Acting as if I was out of breath (huffing and puffing really hard), I told Fagan to get to the pond with his shotgun quick because we had a wildcat up in a tree.

We were hiding when we heard Fagan running down the path. We couldn't see him but we could hear him running just a huffing and puffing right towards the hole. Just before he stepped into the pit trap, we were only able to see him fall into the hole and his upper body smacking into the other side of the hole. The collision with the muddy wall caused the shotgun to fly from his hands.

We ran to Fagan laughing our asses off but the first thing I did was make sure I got to the shotgun before Fagan did. I knew if he could get to that gun one of us would have been dead but actually Fagan was too busy moaning in pain to get up and do anything to us. Poor 'ole Fagan!

For some reason Fagan kept hanging around us even after all of the shit he went through. You know if it wasn't Fagan it would have been someone else; he just happened to be the lucky one I guess. There's more about Fagan to come so hold on.

The four of us used most of our money that we made at the rock pit to buy food and supplies to go camping on the weekends and in the summer. We camped mostly along the Braden River on Caruso Ranch but we did have another campsite on the north side of Highway 70 which was a part of Caruso Ranch as well.

Speaking of camping supplies, I remember one day sitting down to make my camping list for food when I came to mayonnaise. When I realized I couldn't spell 'mayonnaise', I drew a picture of a jar and wrote 'Blue Plate' on the jar's label.

Later that afternoon, we all went to Barney's Market in Oneco to get the list of supplies. Barney's Market was located where Walgreen's is now. I thought Robert, Fagan, and Murphy would never stop laughing after they saw my list and my drawing. This prompted one of them to ask why I didn't just write "mayo" instead of drawing out an entire picture. Of course, that would have been too easy for me to think of.

We camped on Caruso Ranch because Uncle Red ran the ranch which was a little over 5,000 acres at the time. It ran along the north side of Highway 70 from Caruso Road east, almost to Lakewood Ranch Blvd., and then on the south side of Highway 70 from Linger Lodge Road along the river, again almost to Lakewood Ranch Blvd. There was a lot more land on the north side than on the south side, and Uncle Red always knew when we were there camping.

There were times that we rode our horses and went into other pastures that we didn't have permission to be in while camping along the Braden River. As we entered another pasture we would pull out enough staples so that all four strands of barbed wire would be on the ground. One of us would stand on the wires so that the horses could cross over to the other side. Once across, we would replace the staples with nails so that when we were ready to leave all we had to do was lift the wires off the nails, drop the wire back down and lead the horses across again.

We always marked the post so that when we wanted to reenter at a later time we knew where to go in. This made it easy access to go into other pastures and we called it the "Cracker Gate".

We called our camp "Fish Ford Frontier" or FFF when we camped at our campsite along the Braden River, east of Linger Lodge. We built a large wood burning stove to cook on and used lighter wood for the fire. I have many great memories of us camping out; including times we would swim and run through the woods naked which we did most of the time except in the winter months.

We would pack up, normally, on a Friday evening and stay until Sunday evening. In the earlier years, we rode the horses to camp but there were times that Dad would have someone haul us, with all of our supplies, to the campsite in one of the rock pit trucks. But on weekends when they didn't need the truck at the rock pit, I drove it camping.

There was one time we went camping on the north side of State Road 70 where the Rosedale Country Club is now located. We took the truck this weekend and I was driving. Robert and Murphy were in the front with me and Fagan was in the back with all of the camping supplies.

We were going through the woods and came up on some bee hives that someone had set up to get honey. With our windows rolled up, I told Robert and Murphy to watch as I bumped the bee hives as we passed. We were almost passed the hives as I stopped the truck and by this time Fagan saw what I had done. Fagan jumped off the truck and ran as fast as he could toward the woods. Instead of chasing poor 'ole Fagan, the bees swarmed around the truck and nearly covered every inch of it.

We could hardly see out of the windows. Some even started buzzing up through the floorboard where the two dump levers were. We quickly took our shirts off to fill up the holes on the floorboard. It was obvious that my bee prank backfired on us!

Another incident like this was in 1955 when the four of us took Troy camping along the Braden River. There were times when the river was quite low that you could walk on the sandy bottom to Linger Lodge. When it was low like that, the only water was in big potholes that had fish trapped within them and that's when we would use our bow and arrows to shoot the fish, which were mostly garfish. This particular trip was one of the times that the river was real low with the pot holes along ever so often. We could actually ride the horses down in the river bed in most places.

While Fagan stayed at camp, Murphy and I were atop of the bank, about ten feet above Robert who was down in the river bed shooting fish with his bow and arrow. We were trying to sneak down to where Robert was to scare him. We didn't see the cow that was not far from Robert that was pawing and snorting at him for some reason.

As we were walking along a cow trail through vines and palmettos, we stepped into a yellow-jacket hole. They immediately came swarming out after us and we started running towards the river screaming. As we reached the river, we almost ran into the cow. Now we had the cow and the yellow-jackets after us.

When Robert saw us coming with the cow and the yellow-jackets following, he dropped his bow and arrow to dive into the pot hole. We dove in shortly after Robert and when we all came up for air Troy was latched onto the cow's nose and they were in the water as well.

Once I got Troy to let go of the cow's nose the cow ran away so we went back up the steep embankment to see where the yellow-jacket nest was. We found it and saw the yellow-jackets coming and going out of the hole. I told Troy to catch them as she started snipping and snapping at them. It didn't take long before a bunch of them were after us again. I yelled for Troy to come as we were running to the river to get away again.

Later that evening, after Troy was bitten all over by the yellow jackets, she was lying by the campfire with her head all swollen and her eyes nearly swollen shut. She was just another victim of another prank of mine.

I have to mention a memorable camping trip with Steve Marshall. Steve, Robert and I went through school together and also played junior high football. There were times that he would go camping with the four of us.

There's one particular camping trip that comes to mind more frequently than all of the others. When he had camped with us before, he had a real bad habit of leaving can goods on the stove while heating or cooking them and they would explode.

After this happened a few times, I told Steve that we were going to tie him to a tree if that happened again. Well, apparently he didn't hear me tell him that because he put a can of baked beans on the stove and forgot about them. Of course they exploded and went everywhere on everything, including me.

I jumped up and Steve took off running. He ran towards a high patch of palmettos and I saw Murphy and Robert coming towards us, so I hollered at them to catch him which they did.

We were all naked as jaybirds so we brought Steve back to camp and tied his hands behind him around a pine tree. I got a staple and drove a staple into the small rope between his wrists attaching the rope to the tree so he couldn't get loose. I told Steve he wasn't going anywhere until he promised NOT to put any more can goods on the stove without watching them real close.

Several minutes went by but Steve still wouldn't promise so I took my knife and cut a palmetto fan cutting the fan part off leaving only the stem. As most of you know, they have sharp teeth on each side of the stem that will cut you if you're not careful.

I walked over to Steve and asked him again to promise not to put any more can goods on the stove but he still wouldn't promise. So I started hitting his "peter" with the palmetto stem and Steve went to hollering. Finally I stopped and Steve promised he wouldn't put any more can goods on the stove. I guess the "Clark remedy" worked because he never put any more can goods on the stove.

Bill Elmore called Dad to ask him to bring Troy over to catch his horse one time. The horse was located in a big pasture with a set of cow pens at one end of the pasture. Dad told Mr. Elmore to stay in the cow pens with the bridle in his hands.

The horse ran off with his tail in the air and with head shaking high as well. When the horse started running to the other end of the pasture, Dad hollered for Troy to catch him. So Troy ran after the horse and jumped up to catch him in the nose but the horse reared up and knocked Troy loose with his front feet.

By the horse knocking Troy off his nose, it tore a big gash in the horse's nose. The horse immediately ran into the cow pens right up to Mr. Elmore as if he was begging for him to put the bridle on him. He obviously didn't want any more of Troy and that was the first time that I had ever seen a horse do that.

Another horse incident like this was when I had Troy catch one of my horses. The horse reared up like the other one did and knocked Troy off tearing his nose as well but Troy ended up hurting her back hip pretty bad. This injury slowed Troy down quite a bit but she still caught the animals just as good, it just took her a little longer to get to them.

Somewhere in the mid '50s is when Floyd and Roy Smith came into my life. Floyd is one of the many "boys" that has lived through many of my antics over the years. He came from the mountains of Tennessee with his Mom, Dad, his brother Roy and sisters Grace and Brenda. I don't know anyone who does not like Floyd; he is truly one of a kind and what a jokester he is.

Floyd and his family moved to Oneco in the early '50s and they lived about a mile and half south of us growing up. The first time I can remember seeing Floyd and Roy were at the swimming hole, sometime around 1956.

I remember them flying through our front yard on their bikes, with Troy and pups chasing and trying to bite them. With their feet up on the handle bars, they would just coast right into the pond. After laughing, of course, I would holler at the dogs and they would finally return to their normal place, lying on the front porch.

Most of the time, there would be ten or fifteen boys in the pond at one time. The group was usually split into two groups, with the older boys who included me and my friends being one group and the other group being the younger boys like Floyd, Roy, Ricky Hughes and Eddie Boyette.

There was about five or six years age differences between the two groups, so the younger boys, more or less, stayed away from the older boys. When the groups did mix, we all played pretty rough and as you can imagine, the younger boys usually got the brunt of it.

Around 1958, C.R. Montgomery and I were butchering at his place one day, which was on Whitfield Avenue. C.R. was a big Dutchman who stood close to six foot five and weighed about 350 pounds. In his early years, he worked for Ringling Brothers & Barnum Bailey Circus taking care of all the animals needs and even bought and sold animals for the circus. When the circus moved from Sarasota to Venice in the late '50s, C.R. went his own way. The only thing he had to do with the circus from that point on was mostly butchering meat for the circus animals as well as for the local zoos.

Floyd and Roy rode up on a girl's bicycle while C.R. and I were butchering. Besides it being a girl's bike, the first thing I noticed was a big gopher turtle in the basket attached to the handlebars. Floyd asked C.R. if he was into buying gophers, and C.R. answered yes. Floyd asked how much he usually paid for a big gopher. C.R. replied, "For real big ones, I'd pay $500."

Floyd's eyes got real big, and he asked, "How big is 'real big'"?

C.R. pointed to a big bunch of bamboo and said, "There's a pig pen over there behind those bamboos, with a 'real big' gopher in it".

Floyd and Roy were anxious to see how big C.R. was talking about so they took off running toward the bamboo patch. Before long, they were running back with even bigger eyes. Floyd asked C.R., "Where did you catch that big gopher at"?

C.R. and I were laughing by this time from the looks on their faces. C.R. told them he caught the gopher at Rattlesnake Slough. Floyd and Roy wanted directions to Rattlesnake Slough, so C.R. explained the three mile trek as he pointed east.

They headed back behind the bamboo and were gone for quite some time. When C.R. and I finished butchering, I walked around the bamboo patch and found Floyd and Roy riding on the turtle's back. They both had a stick in their hand, acting like they were riding a horse, hitting the back of the turtle shell to make it go. The turtle was about 400 pounds and actually came from South America. C.R. ended up paying Floyd and Roy two dollars for their gopher.

After Fagan, Robert, and Murphy went into the service, I started taking Floyd and Roy with me to do different things. There were others that would sometimes join us like Marvin Cameron, David Young, David DeSear, Herman Burnett, and Billy Miller.

Speaking of David DeSear, I knew David and his family all my life. We worked together and had fun together like going dancing and rodeoing. He was another one of the many who took the blunt of most of my jokes and tricks that I pulled on people.

David was pretty good at most things that he had done in his life except that he had a big problem with drinking. I tried all I could to get him to stop drinking so much. David would tell me that he couldn't because he loved it too much. He died from it in early 1990 at the age of 42.

He and the other boys were with me most of the time and the things that we did included things such as working cows, patching fences and cow pens, butchering, breaking horses, picking okra and black-eyed peas, cutting swamp cabbage, catching rattlesnakes and skunks, playing games at night on horseback, riding the bucking barrel, tractor work, clearing pine trees from vacant lots, catching alligators, fishing, and going to rodeos. Just about everything under the sun!

At one time, I had a one-ton Dodge pick-up truck that I used to go to rodeos and for hauling meat after butchering. Sometime later, I built a wooden cattle rack to haul cattle in and I also nailed a thick board across the top of the cattle rack about a foot or so from the front. This way the younger boys could ride on top of the cattle rack.

They would sit on the board overlooking the cab with their feet resting on the boards below. Normally, two or three of us bigger boys would ride inside the cab of the truck, and three or four smaller boys would ride on top.

One time, we were on Saunders Road or 63rd Avenue which was paved then but narrow and bumpy. As I approached the railroad tracks, which were three feet higher than the road, I normally would slowed down to go over the tracks. The railroad tracks were located where "new" Highway 301 is now.

I was going a little faster than I should have been because I wanted to give the boys on top a little scare. As we hit the top of the tracks and started going down the other side, I hit the brakes.

With the abrupt stop, the boys came down head first onto the hood and cab of the truck. Because they were holding onto the board, they brought the board down with them. A couple of them bounced off the cab, onto the hood, and down onto the road.

Us boys in the cab could not help but laugh our asses off even though the boys were skinned up and sore. Luckily there were no bones broken or any other serious injuries. Looking back, it's a wonder one of them wasn't killed. Floyd and Roy can definitely vouch for that.

I remember another time that Floyd and Roy were riding with me when I was pulling a small trailer. I was hauling a dead cow to butcher for cat meat that we picked up in Palmetto. As we came off the Green Bridge I turned left onto 8th Avenue or Manatee Avenue going east.

During this time there was a railroad track in east Manatee just before you got to 9th Street East.

As we crossed the tracks, I looked in the rear view mirror to see the trailer had come unhitched and the runaway trailer was coming around to pass me. Floyd and Roy were totally unaware that the trailer came unhitched. So as the trailer passed my door, in order to get it stopped and to keep it from slamming into the car lot on the northeast corner, I jerked the steering wheel hard to the left which caused the trailer to run into the front left tire.

That sudden swerve, combined with the trailer's impact, scared the living daylights out of Floyd and Roy. They had no idea what the hell was happening and they just started screaming. The impact also caused the dead cow to be flung out of the trailer into the middle of the road.

I looked around to see if anyone had seen what happened, but only found two men in the nearby used car lot checking out vehicles. We jumped out of the truck and hooked the trailer back up and then backed up to the dead cow to winch her back into the trailer.

Within a few minutes, we were driving away from the scene with the two men's jaws dropped and heads shaking. I'm not sure but Floyd and Roy probably had to change their britches when we got home. But that was definitely quite a scary incident.

Floyd sure can think fast when he has to. One time, we were driving down the road and came up on a girl riding a horse. She looked good from the back with a nice looking body wearing a halter top and had long hair. As we approached her, Floyd leaned out the window and whistled at her. And she turned her head towards him and gave Floyd a big smile. Damn what a shock we had; damn was she ugly! This surprised Floyd and he quickly said, "Boy that sure is a good-looking horse that you're riding!"

We laughed and laughed! And of course, I still kid him about that.

In the summer between tenth and eleventh grade, I worked for the county operating different equipment, because I normally covered for someone else who was on vacation. I mainly ran a dragline cleaning the canal on the west side of Val Massey's dairy which was called the Oneco drainage canal.

This is when I first met Cande Wilgus, who was 12 at the time and she often helped Val at the dairy. I remember I was trying to finish this one canal so that we could move the dragline the next day onto another job when a thunderstorm came up. It was raining really hard with bolts of lightning striking everywhere and I normally would stop the machine when it got like that but I was trying to hurry to get finished.

I had the bucket full of black muck and was picking it up from the bottom of the canal when all of a sudden I felt the machine start tilting into the canal. I instantly dropped the bucket back into the canal but when I did, the machine dropped back down and made an enormous loud boom sound. I was shaking really bad and scared half to death knowing that the machine and I were that close to toppling into the canal.

So with the rain and thunder so bad, I thought the hell with this, I'll just go to the feed barn and wait this out. I got into the county truck and drove towards the barn but got stuck about 100 yards from the barn because of all of the rain. I wasn't about to try to get the truck out so I jumped out and ran towards the barn.

I came upon a one wire electric fence so I dropped down on my hands and knees to go under it and saw something move real quick. Much to my surprise, there laid a coiled ground rattler right by my hand which made me immediately jump up, and of course, get shocked by the fence. I ran into the feed barn and collapsed onto the feed sacks shaking like hell. I must have laid there for about five minutes when Mr. Massey came in. I told him what happened and all he could do was laugh at me. Maybe this was a payback on me for some of the pranks that I had been pulling on so many people.

I once had a pet coon for one night but I can't remember who gave it to me. They asked me if I would like a pet coon and said it was real gentle and playful but they didn't want it anymore because it made too much of a mess and was always getting into things. I ended up taking it but I was already dressed to go out, so I just put the coon in a rabbit cage out back.

I came home around midnight but no one else was home and I was real tired so I went to bed. It wasn't long before I felt something crawling up the foot of the bed. At first I thought I was dreaming so I shook my head a little, but it kept coming closer to my head. (Keep in mind – I totally forgot about the coon at this point) I was scared not having a clue what was on my bed so I froze, not knowing what to do.

It got right up to my head and put its cold nose on my cheek. I dove out of bed and ran out of the room clicking on the light on my way out.

Low and behold, there stood that coon in the middle of my bed looking at me like I was stupid. After my heart finally came down out of my throat, I picked up the coon to take him back outside. On my way out the back door, I noticed Momma's kitchen was a disaster. Momma kept a can of used grease on the counter top and next to it was leftover cornbread from supper. That coon had grease and cornbread crumbs all over the counter everywhere. Then I saw where the coon had pried open the window screen to get inside. Needless to say, I gave my one and only pet coon to Bob Murphy the next morning. Momma would have been so mad if she came home to find her kitchen like that!

Speaking of leftovers, breakfast in the Clark household was eggs and leftovers. Whatever was leftover from supper the night before was put in a frying pan and heated up, then Dad would beat several eggs together and throw them in the pan and mix with the leftovers. So that was breakfast, scrambled eggs and leftovers.

Dad always expected me up when he got up and I remember a time that I didn't get up when he got up. I normally heard Dad's alarm clock go off and got up when he got up. This particular morning, I had gone to bed late and I didn't hear the alarm go off. Dad always got up around six 'o clock to cook breakfast and he knew I wasn't up when he went into the kitchen.

This particular morning I was awakened by him jerking me out of bed by my arm, kicking me in the ass as I went a ways up off the floor and then slapping me in the back of the head with the other hand. I went head first out through the bedroom door crashing into the washing machine. I always thought of this incident as a "wax job"; he was cleaning the wax out of my ears. But from that point on, no matter what, I always heard the alarm and my ass was out of bed and dressed before he got into the kitchen.

Shortly after my pet coon incident, I started catching skunks. Bill Boyette wanted live cottontail rabbits that he was going to use to train his greyhound race dogs with. He told me he would give me three dollars for each live cottontail that I caught.

One of my classmates, Bob Withers, told me there were a lot of cottontails in the orange grove behind his house. So one night I went to his house with a cast net planning on catching some rabbits. Unfortunately, the moon was too bright and we were unable to get close enough to throw the net over the rabbits. After an hour of trying, the only thing we came close to catching was a skunk.

Rather than getting 'skunked' and leaving there empty handed, I threw the net over the skunk. Turns out we got 'skunked' in a totally different way. The skunk sprayed as soon as the net fell on it.

We kept our distance and watched the skunk work its way out from underneath the net. While the skunk was shimmying out, I got the bright idea that I wanted to start catching skunks. My idea was that I would de-musk them and sell them as pets.

The very next day while I was studying in the library at school, I looked up a book on skunks. I read that a skunk's tail would be straight up when spraying its musk and it would kick up its back legs in order to spray upwards. The book didn't provide any information about removing the skunk's musk though.

After my little bit of research, I thought that all I had to do was throw the net over the skunks and after releasing the net, I could jump on the skunk and hold its tail down so that I wouldn't get sprayed. Of course I wore heavy gloves so that I wouldn't get bitten.

I got home from school and James Davis, my neighbor, wanted me to ride some green, broke horses for him. While I was riding his horses, I told him of my idea with the skunks. He told me that he knew how to cut the musk glands from the skunks and that he would show me how to do it.

After I finished riding his horses for him, I returned home and called Bob Withers, Richard Strickland, Murphy, Fagan and Robert. We all planned to meet at my Granddad's dairy to try to catch some skunks because Richard said that the dairy was a reliable place to find them.

As soon as we drove into the pasture later that evening, we spotted a skunk. I was the only one without a head light because I was going to be the one throwing the net over the skunks. The job for the others was to shine their lights on the skunk for me to see. They jumped out of the car surrounding the skunk to keep it from running off or escaping into a hole. When I got out I immediately threw the net over the skunk.

The skunk started spraying immediately as the net fell on it just as the other one had done. All of the guys ran back about 30 feet from the skunk with their headlights still shining down on the trapped skunk. I put my gloves on and jumped on the skunk with both hands. My left hand went around the skunk's neck as my right hand held its tail down. That is when all hell broke loose.

Even with its tail held down, I managed to find myself covered in a cloud of skunk spray. I felt like I was in a fog with all of those lights shining on me with a frantic skunk to boot. I started gagging and nearly puked as I remained on top of the skunk. I held him for some time before realizing the book was not completely accurate or at least misleading.

By now, the other boys were about 100 feet back from the skunk as the smell was overwhelming. I was getting madder and madder by the second because I didn't know what to do. I threw the lead lines of the cast net from over the skunk with my right hand while keeping my left hand around its neck. When I finally got him out of the net, my eyes were burning and I was gagging desperately for fresh air. I couldn't think clearly enough about what to do, but I did know I had enough of that skunk.

Surprisingly, some of the skunk's teeth made their way through my gloves and into my skin. When I finally let the skunk out of my grasp, throwing it down away from me, the skunk hit the ground running. Being that I had already been sprayed, I didn't want the skunk to get away so I ran for the car to grab my own light and took off after it.

I caught up to the skunk and snatched it up by its tail as I got up beside it. I still didn't know what to do so I swung the skunk around by its tail with me spinning around and around with my light flashing on it. I was happy to notice it wasn't spraying anymore. I stopped swinging it around and just held my arm straight out with the skunk dangling by its tail in my hand. With its feet moving frantically, the skunk was trying to do everything it could to climb up to its tail. Its head could only get as far as his upper belly and no further.

Curious to see what it would do, I held it for a little longer in that position. Even though he couldn't do anymore spraying, the skunks back legs were constantly pedaling away. With my light in one hand, I grabbed one of its back legs with a couple of my fingers and I was sprayed again just as soon as I grabbed the skunk's leg. I let go of its leg and the skunk stopped spraying. I grabbed the legs again and I was sprayed yet again.

We didn't bring anything to put the skunk in because I was under the impression all I had to do was hold its tail down to keep it from spraying. But I wanted to take the skunk to James' house so he could show me how to de-musk it.

The other boys would not let me in the car, with or without the skunk. They were all cussing and raising hell due to the smell which I had gotten used to by now. So I sat on the car's fender and rode the four miles or so to James' house while holding the skunk in my outstretched arm.

When we arrived, James started showing me how to de-musk the skunk. He started by making a loop out of hay string so that he could lasso it around the skunk's neck while I remained holding it with my outstretched arm. It felt as though both my arm was going to fall off from holding the skunk straight out in front of me like that for so long. Once the string was around the skunk's neck, I stood on the string with one foot to keep it from squirming around so much. Both its back feet were still moving as if it were running in place.

James was careful to keep his hands away from the skunk's moving feet while he prepared to make the incision with his razor. With tweezers, he grabbed the skin near the skunk's asshole and started cutting around the asshole. He couldn't find the skunk's musk gland and ended up cutting the skunk's asshole completely out. That's when it became clear to me that he knew less about skunks than I did, however that skunk was unable to spray any more after that point.

Once again I didn't know what to do with the skunk so I put it in a box, but I picked up its asshole to examine it. I found two small, green glands that were about the size of a jelly bean on each side of its asshole. I also saw many yellow pores around the asshole which were apparently where the musk was shot through. When I got home, I went out back to the cow pens and put the skunk into a rabbit cage.

Momma could smell the odor nearly as soon as I got home and was having a fit. She threw me some soap and towels and told me not to bring my clothes into the house. She said I needed to jump in the swimming hole and scrub hard. I used the entire bar of soap and still had the smell of skunk all over me.

I grew quite use to the smell so it didn't bother me, but everyone else could smell it on me. That first morning when I was walking down the hall going from class to class, no one would walk behind me and those walking towards me would gag and run the other direction.

In my classrooms my teachers made me move my desk, from its usual position, to the very back of the classroom, next to the open windows. Back then, classrooms didn't have air conditioning so the open windows helped quite a bit. This is how it was for the next two months until I got out of the skunk business.

I became better and better after that first night of catching skunks. The other boys stuck with me too. They even held the skunks by their tails with the hay string around its neck while I cut out the musk glands.

The way that I demusked them was by making a V-cut with a razor. The point of the V started at the beginning of the tail and two incision lines would each be cut down on each sides of the skunk's asshole. I would then use the tweezers to pull the V-shaped skin flap back exposing the two green musk glands on each side of its asshole.

We caught over 20 skunks that I put in a large cage out back behind our house. We built the skunk cage that was eight feet wide, 14 feet long with a six foot high roof that had heavy rabbit wire making up the sides. The wire was buried about a foot deep into the ground to help keep the skunks from digging out.

But as it turned out, we didn't bury the wire deep enough into the ground because the skunks were always digging holes along the base of the cage. Every time I went to feed and water them, I had to throw sticks or rocks into the holes along the base of the cage to cover the holes they made.

The last skunk that I caught I put into a toolbox which was on the back of a jeep truck. I was pulling some pine trees down and burning them in order to clear a lot for a contractor in west Bradenton. Every time I would lift the lid on the toolbox, I would have to work around the skunk to keep from getting sprayed.

After about four times in and out of the toolbox, I decided to snatch the skunk from the toolbox and let it go. About ten minutes later, I heard a woman yelling at her barking dogs. As I turned around I saw her dogs chasing the skunk into someone else's garage.

I ran to the garage that I saw the skunk run into and found it hiding behind the hot water heater. The woman finally came over to get her dogs and I made the owner of the house very happy as I recaptured the skunk from the garage. She was so happy that she gave me five dollars. It turned out that was the only money I ever got out of the two months being in the skunk business!

Another one of our adventures was when we were all around 16 years old, Murphy, Fagan, Robert and I started making moonshine. We were still working at the rock pit at the time as was Milt Kennedy. Milt was around 55 years old and had served three different sentences in state prison for making moonshine. Every chance we got we would ask Milt about how to make moonshine. After we thought we had all of the answers, we started getting together all of the things to make a small batch.

First we had to get a five gallon crock, and then buy some sugar at one store and some yeast at another store. We always had horse feed so we didn't have to buy any corn. We mixed all of the ingredients in the crock at the swamp on the west side of 33rd across from our house (where Wong Kai Imports is now).

This is where we hid the mixture until it was ready to brew. We checked on it daily and when it stopped bubbling meant it was ready to brew. There were times that we would have dead rats floating in it but we would just throw them out. After a while we put croker sacks over the crock to keep the rodents out.

We then bought a small single burner Coleman stove, a two gallon pressure cooker and about 20 foot of 3/8 inch copper tubing with a male adapter to attach to the pressure cooker. After we removed the pressure valve on the cooker, we inserted the male adapter inside the hole, and then coiled the copper tubing around inside a 55 gallon oil drum. We did the drum preparation by our calf pens behind the house.

We cut a hole at the bottom side of the drum to put the copper tubing through for the moonshine to flow out of and then clay puttied the hole around the tubing so that the water wouldn't leak out. We then filled the drum with water from the ditch, which came from the flowing well beside our swimming hole. This is what took the longest time because we carried the water from the ditch to the drum in buckets.

We laid a board across the calf stalls to place the stove on top of in order to heat the pressure cooker. Once the brew was ready to go, we then went to the swamp to get the crock. We had to put the drum up on blocks and then light the stove. After straining the brew from the mash, we poured the brew into the pressure cooker three quarters full.

When the brew was boiling, the steam would rise, go into the tubing and down into the drum of cold water which would then condense into alcohol. This entire process took about 30 minutes time and we used a quart jar to catch the moonshine in.

I remember the first batch we made, we filled the pressure cooker up too high and it boiled out of the copper tubing. We learned from that to make sure that we only had it three quarters full. The first true batch of moonshine we made I was waiting for it to come out of the tube. I could hear it coming so I put my nose down there and could smell it. When it came out I caught it in a mayonnaise jar lid and swigged it down.

As soon as it went down, I couldn't shut my mouth. I was gasping and gasping for air. I took off running to the closest orange tree and climbed it for an orange. I bit into it, peeling and all, and started sucking the juice to cool my mouth and throat. The guys were laughing their asses off at me.

Once we got the moonshine to perfection, we prepared a batch every Friday afternoon. We would have moonshine for the Friday night dance at the teen club. We would only have about a quart jar full but we never made it back home with any.

Around this same time is when Robert, Fagan, Murphy and I started breaking horses for Dad. Dad had a pasture in Parrish which had about 40 horses in it and we would bring home two or three of them, at a time, to break them. Once we got them to the house, we would tie them to trees for a few days so they would get used to being tied.

We would then take them near the swimming hole and tie the rope around the lower part of their necks near their shoulders. The rest of the rope was fed between their hind legs going around one of their back hooves. Then the rope was brought back up through the loop around their neck. By pulling on the rope through the loop, their one hind leg would come up near their shoulder making the horse have to stand on three legs. The horse would naturally jump around and fall down and go crazy as this was very uncomfortable. This process normally only took a day because it wore the horse down pretty good.

Usually the next day, we would jump on their backs to get them familiar with something being on top of them. We did everything to take the spook out of them, such as waving and throwing a croker sack at them, to stomping our feet down hard as we come up to them real fast. We would also put saddles and bridles on and off them.

There were four of us working the horses this way, and we kept it up until they wouldn't spook, fight the rope, buck, or fall down any more. By this time they were all lathered up, give out and were breathing hard and not moving or fighting the rope anymore. We would then leave them alone and go swim for a while.

We would repeat this process for hours until the horses would no longer flinch from any type of contact. Finally, it was time to keep a bridle on them, untie their foot and ride off on them for the big test. Usually it was late in the afternoon when we first rode them. But the next day would be the true test because the horse would be ridden all day.

This was the best way to break a horse if you ask me. They never bucked, spooked, bit or kicked when I worked with them in this fashion.

Robert, Fagan, Murphy and I were in the same Future Farmer's of America (FFA) class together and Raymond Lee was our agricultural teacher. Towards the end of the school year, the FFA went to several other schools to compete in the state championships for several categories. The categories included soil/cattle/hog judging, horseshoes, softball, parliamentary speaking, etc.

Late one evening, we were on a very crowded bus on our way home after a competition in Lakeland. Jim Simmons, another classmate, had to take a leak badly. He decided to take a leak in an empty soda pop bottle but before throwing the bottle out of the bus window, he slung some on me and a few others. Although he probably already knew, I told him I'd get him back for that. Little did he know I had to take a leak as well!

So I took my handkerchief from my pocket and pissed in it, soaking it very well. I then threw it at Jim, but he ducked causing it to hit Fagan in the face. This surprised Fagan and he madly jumped on me and rubbed the piss soaked handkerchief in my face. While Fagan was smearing my piss in my face, Murphy followed by pissing in his handkerchief.

There was about eight of us in a piss fight amongst a bus that was already crowded. There were three people in each seat before the fight started but most of the ones not in the fight crammed towards the front of the bus. There were a few empty seats in the back where we had our piss fight. It's a good thing Mr. Lee was on the other bus or else we would have been in a heap of trouble.

By the time we got back to the school and got into Robert's car to head home, the four of us were stinking of piss and our skin was real sticky. We decided to go to my house and jump in the swimming hole fully clothed to get rid of the stench.

Monday morning's FFA class rolled around following the piss fight from the previous Friday and we were to take the bus to the agriculture plot where our vegetables were growing. This bus happened to be the same bus that we had the piss fight on and the windows had been up all weekend long. Needless to say, inside the bus reeked of piss with a lot of heat mixed in. We had to put every window down due to the awful smell.

Mr. Lee was the last one to board the bus and made a horrendous face as he stepped into the aisle. Not one person spoke up to explain the smell. And it was the next class who had to wash out the bus.

Not too long after this incident, the four of us decided to catch a few small 'gators in order to release them in the Manatee High School gold fish pond. James Davis had a trot line set out near the Braden River dam and told us he knew there was a bunch of little 'gators there. So we followed James and brought an aluminum 'John boat' to try to catch some of the 'gators while James worked his trot line. We tried catching them but the noise from the boat would cause them to go under water before we could grab them.

We decided to go close to shore so I could get out of the boat with a headlight battery in one hand and a free hand to catch the 'gators. I waded along in waist deep water snatching the 'gators from the surface one by one. They'd make their grunting sound as I picked them out of the water and I threw them over into the boat which was a good ten feet away in much deeper water.

After I caught about seven or eight, James hollered for me to get in the boat before I lost my ass to the momma 'gator. I looked around for her but continued hunting since I didn't see her. I picked one or two more up and heard the boys in the boat hollering at me to get back into the boat quick. I looked over at them to see where their headlights were fixed and saw the momma 'gator coming at me fast.

With the headlight reflection on her two red eyes, they must have been a foot apart which meant that she was one huge alligator. The gator was 75 to 100 feet from me when I saw her quickly approaching. My adrenaline immediately started pumping with my friends yelling for me to hurry and get in the boat.

I dropped the little 'gator as well as my headlight battery which caused my headlight to drop from my head. Without hesitation, I swam as fast as I could for the boat. The last I saw of the big gator before heading for the boat was her ducking under the water with me in her sights.

I was in the boat as soon as my hands touched the bow. The other boys had their lights shining on the area from where I just escaped. I must have just made it, because the water was swirling around like something big just went under the boat. It scared the hell out of all of us, especially me! I didn't think I could make it to the boat before the momma got me. Needless to say, our 'gator hunting was done for that night.

But we wanted more little gator's having only caught ten so the very next night, we went to a different place but with a gig so we could gig bigger 'gators to eat; but our main purpose was to still catch more little ones.

Uncle Donald had a pasture leased in Elwood Park for his cattle and the pasture had a small man-made lake with quite a few 'gators in it. He also had a canoe there which we were able to use without making any noise. After arriving we unloaded the aluminum boat which would be used to gig the bigger gators. We shined the lights out over the pond only to see red eyes everywhere.

Robert and Fagan were in our boat to do the gigging while Murphy and I took the canoe to catch the little ones. Robert had a four-prong, heavy gig with a one inch thick metal pipe handle that was about ten foot long. The two boats were side by side and easing up on a four foot gator for Robert to gig. He gigged the 'gator in the middle of its back but had a hard time lifting the thrashing 'gator out of the water. In a frenzy, the 'gator bit himself and the gig handle a number of times.

The four of us had our headlights on the gator as Robert suddenly brought the gigged 'gator out of the water and over Murphy and my heads. He swung the gator around in order to drop it in the back of the boat. Murphy and I ducked so the 'gator could make it over us but as we both ducked, we ducked to the same side of the boat, causing the canoe to overturn and soaking us to the bone.

Surprisingly, the canoe sank and so did our headlights. We quickly swam to shore as there was not enough room in the other boat for the four of us and a gigged 'gator. Another unexpected incident meant another abrupt end to yet another 'gator hunt. But we did get one gator to eat.

Early the next morning, we headed off to school with the ten little 'gators we had caught. We put three in the gold fish pond and the other seven were put in the first seven lockers that we could find unlocked. What a nice bunch of guys we were, huh?!

The Fish and Game Officers had to come in order to take the gators away. I actually tried to talk them into giving me the gators but they would have no part in that.

Speaking of nice guys, the four of us were going home in Robert's car from the Manatee County Fair one night. I was riding shotgun and Murphy and Fagan were in the back seat. At the fair, Murphy won a small walking cane with an American flag attached to the handle.

As we were approaching the Green Bridge, Murphy told Robert to slow down and pull over closer to the curb. Murphy said he was going to poke one of the fishermen in the ass with his cane.

As we came up on this fisherman who was leaning over the bridge railing with a rod and reel in his hands, Murphy leaned out of the rear window behind me and poked the fisherman square in ass. Just as he poked the fisherman, I slapped the side of the car door and let out one of my patented, ear-piercing screams.

Anyway, the combination of the cane to his ass, my piercing scream and the loud slap to the side of the car, caused the fisherman to spin around wildly with his hands up in the air. Before he realized what happened, his hands were empty, with his pole splashing into the water below. All he could do was shake his fists in a rage of anger as we drove off laughing hysterically.

For as long as I can remember in the '50s, Dad bought a new

Pontiac every year. Why every year you might ask? Because they only lasted a year due of the abuse Dad put them through. He would go through the woods or ditches chasing cattle with his car. At times, I would sit on the front passenger side of the hood as he chased cattle or yearlings. Once he got them tired, he would pull up beside them and I'd jump for their neck and head to wrestle them to the ground.

It was in 1957 when I caught my first rattlesnake while mowing some commercial lots north of the Sarasota Airport. I noticed the big rattlesnake crawling out of the grass so I stopped the tractor and got the hoe to kill it. When I got to the snake, he didn't go into a coil; he just kept crawling real slowly so I pushed the hoe down on its head in order to reach down and pick it up around the neck. Once I started picking it up I had to use my other hand to grab the middle part of it because it was over six foot long and real fat and heavy.

Here I had this snake not knowing what to do with it and didn't have anything to put it in. There were some men in a nearby warehouse that saw me with the snake and yelled at me so I walked over with the snake. I asked if they had anything I could use to put it in but they only had a cardboard box that was 4' x 4" x 4" which made a very long but narrow box.

I put the snake in the box except for its head which I had to count to three before I could let go of it but once I got it in the box I put the box in my truck. I started mowing again and later on caught the mate which was about the same size.

My plan was to take them to C.R. Montgomery's so he could sell them for me but both snakes died two days later. C.R. told me the reason they died was because you cannot pick up that big of a snake by its neck. The weight of the snake will break their necks so that's why they died.

I caught several more snakes that I sold to C.R. but none of them died. I always kept croker sacks in my truck just for snakes that I caught. Most people would poke at the feed sacks to see if there was a rattlesnake in them before they would get into my truck.

In 1958, I had two tractors with mowers to mow pastures, vacant lots and orange groves for people. I kept had a hoe and croker sack on the tractors with me to put live rattlesnakes in. We used to have a hell of a population of rattlesnakes around the county back then and I would sell them to C.R.

One particular day, I went over to West Bradenton to mow a couple of lots for someone which was quite a ways for me to drive to only mow a few lots. There were a few houses built in this subdivision but quite a few overgrown lots that still needed mowing.

When I started mowing the first lot I already had a rattlesnake in a croker sack on the back of the mower. As I started mowing the second lot, it was closer to some houses and I noticed some men working in their yards. I mowed a few passes around the lot and got off the tractor like I was checking something on the mower. I checked to make sure the men were not paying any attention to anything I was doing, and that's when I turned the rattlesnake loose.

I jumped back on the tractor to start mowing again and when I got back around to where the snake was, he was stretch out and crawling around where I had just mowed. I jumped off the tractor, started hollering and throwing my arms up and running around the snake which made the snake coil up. I noticed the men's attention was on me now so I ran to the mower and grabbed the hoe and sack. I went over to where the snake was and poked at him some to make him strike at me with me jumping back out of his way.

Now that I had the neighbors full attention, I put the flat part of the hoe on its head and reached down picking the snake up and slid him back in the sack. I jumped back on the tractor like it was all in a day's work.

Shortly afterwards, both men came over, after talking to some more of their neighbors, asking me to mow more of the lots. I don't remember how many lots I ended up mowing because of that snake!

Another snake incident was when Freddy Alcathie was helping me mow some vacant lots. I was on my way to check on him when a seven foot black indigo snake crossed the road in front of me. I stopped to catch it, but this time I didn't have a croker sack in my truck so I dumped my tools out of the toolbox in order to put him in there for the time being. I had a hard time getting that big long snake into such a small toolbox but I finally did.

I then headed on to where Freddy was mowing. Once I got there, I walked over to where he was mowing and started staring at the mower as if something was wrong. Freddy stopped the mower and I told him to get a crescent wrench from my toolbox. As told, Freddy went to the truck, jumped up on the flatbed and opened the toolbox.

Because the toolbox was so small and the snake was so long, the snake flopped out at his feet. Freddy fell off the truck landing flat on his back. I stood there laughing like hell but of course, he didn't think it was very funny.

Speaking of Freddy…his brother, Ned, liked my tricks or jokes no more than Freddy did. The ones they hated worse happened when I would stop to pick them up for work. Their parents had a hard time getting them out of bed in the mornings but then again they didn't have a hot shot like I did.

I'd go into their bedrooms with them still sound asleep and poke one with the "hot shot" then run to the other before the first one realized what had hit him. They would leap out of bed screaming like in convulsions and run by their parents who were standing in the door way laughing at them. Before long, all their parents would have to say was, "Here Donnie comes pulling up in that truck of his!"

They were out of bed real fast, so a little prodding goes a long way with some people!

Thinking about prodding people reminds me of the time that a few of us boys took prodding to a higher level than we should have but it sure was fun. It was around the end of June in 1958, Fagan, Murphy and I were swimming in the pond, on a Saturday afternoon. We got tired of swimming and swinging from the rope so we went back to the house. It was around dark and we were looking for something fun to do. We went into the garage and saw two bushels of ripe tomatoes that Momma was going to jar. One of us came up with an idea of going to the hard road, which was SR70, to throw them at the cars as they went by. But in those days it could be five or ten minutes before a car came by.

So we decided to take Momma's DeSota car and go to town where the blacks lived and throw them at the Negroes. I drove with Murphy riding shotgun and Fagan in the back with the bushel of tomatoes. We headed to the Bradenton and drove towards downtown past Main Street which was 9th Ave. back then.

They started throwing the tomatoes at the Negroes and I slowed down as we got to the Negro movie theatre where there was a hell of a line of them waiting to get in. They were all dressed up and you could see the tomato stains on their clothes. It was bad…it was real bad.

Some of them started running towards us but I took off down the street. Fagan and Murphy continued to throw tomatoes at the ones walking along the sidewalk. Thanks to the car for not breaking down because we would have been dead if we would have been caught by the swarm of them.

We soon ran out of tomatoes and we were heading back to get the other bushel but I knew Momma would be really mad if she found both bushels gone. As we were leaving downtown, I remembered that the Gulf Coast Experimental Farm had tomatoes. The Experimental Farm was where Bradenton Middle School was or where PAL is now.

As we were driving back to the Experimental Farm we came across Freddy Tolar, so we flagged him down and told him what we were doing. After talking to Freddy, we talked him into taking his car. We knew the Negroes would be looking for Momma's car and they wouldn't look at his as the "trouble maker" car.

We stopped at the Experimental Farm to pick some more tomatoes but since it was dark, we couldn't see real well. We picked mainly green tomatoes but we decided green tomatoes were better than no tomatoes. We only got to throw a few tomatoes on the back streets because once we turned one corner all of a sudden we were surrounded by cops.

They jumped out of their cars and blinded us with their flashlights. They asked if we were having fun, then told us to get out of the car with our hands on top of the car. Freddy was the only one that had clothes on because the rest of us still had our swimming trunks on. The cops started patting us down, and then Murphy started giggling at the cop that was searching him. That pissed the cop off and he called Murphy a smartass.

They put all of us in squad cars and took us to the Bradenton Police Station. They made us wait for Matt Britt, who was Chief of Police in Bradenton at that time. The entire time we were waiting, the blacks were all outside looking in the windows, cussing and hollering at us.

We were there about 30 minutes when Mr. Britt came in to question us one at a time. We all told him that the tomatoes came from my house so we only got charged with disturbing the peace which was a

$25.00 fine for each of us. He released us and allowed us to come back the next morning to pay the fine.

Now, Dad was County Commissioner at the time and I knew I was going to be in big trouble. I dreaded telling him but knew that I had to; I just wasn't real sure how I was going to do it or when.

The next morning, Dad and I took Troy to get Mr. Patterson's bull back into his pasture which was where Evers Reservoir is now. After we got the bull back into the pasture and was headed home, I finally got the nerve up to tell him. For some reason he didn't whip my ass but he was really mad.

Monday afternoon is when he got really mad. He went to a Commissioners meeting that morning and sometime that afternoon he got into his car and smelled something rotten. When he opened the trunk there was Troy. Both of us had forgotten about her when we got back from Mr. Patterson's the day before. We often carried Troy with us in the trunk and because I had to tell Dad about what had happened, and knowing he was as mad as he was, neither of us was thinking about Troy.

I was really upset about this...Troy died because of me. I loved that dog and I was sick over it. And it didn't help matters any to read in the Bradenton Herald the next morning "County Commissioner's son arrested for throwing tomatoes at Negroes."

Most of you have probably heard about "shotgun weddings", well I had one of them myself. My first marriage was to Betty Lou DeSear when I was 18 years old and a senior in high school. Betty Lou was 16 years old and a sophomore; both of us were attending Manatee High and she was the daughter of Everett and Mildred DeSear.

I made a mistake and she came up pregnant and I'll never forget the day that I found out. Dad and I were going to doctor a cow and I was getting the intravenous set ready with the needle and glucose. He was driving down the road and all of a sudden he said, "The DeSear girl was over at the house today and told your Momma that she was pregnant".

I jabbed that needle right into my hand...I was numb. I couldn't believe it but Dad and Mr. DeSear thought that this was the greatest news. And it wasn't long before they loaded us up in the car and drove us to Georgia on Dad's birthday, March 19, 1959, for us to be married.

We lived together at my parent's house for one week because that's what I agreed to. Our fathers said that we would get used to one another but I just couldn't live the rest of my life with someone that I didn't love. I did not feel that would be fair to Betty Lou or the baby.

On September 20, 1959, Betty Lou gave birth to our daughter, Sherie Clark and there is no denying that Sherie is my daughter. We stayed married for about two years divorcing sometime in 1961. She married Bill Sexton shortly afterwards and he adopted and raised Sherie like his own. He was definitely the father to her that I never allowed myself to be.

I still feel bad about the entire situation but I know Sherie was better off without me and Bill did a wonderful job being her father. Sherie is a very bright, intelligent, beautiful woman and I am grateful that she had the life that she had.

She later married Joe Vickers and they had three wonderful, also very bright, intelligent and beautiful girls. Their oldest daughter is Sorrell Dawn who was born on March 8, 1983 with their second daughter being Joanna Michelle who was born on October 18, 1984 and their youngest daughter is Jamie Lynn who was born on November 24, 1985. Jamie has three of my great grandchildren, Kaylin, Landon and Kason and Joanna has one, Micheal.

At the end of March of '59, shortly after I was married, there was a Rodeo Cowboys Association (RCA) rodeo at the High School at Hawkins Stadium. There was a FFA bull-ri ding event in the rodeo, and since I was a member of the FFA some of my classmates talked me into entering the bull-riding event.

This was the beginning of my bull-riding career if you want to call it that. I had never ridden a bucking bull before, just bucking calves, cows or horses. Because I was chasing girls during this time, I wasn't wearing boots and jeans like I had been most of my life. I was going out dating and dancing a lot so I normally wore dress pants with loafers or dress shoes, which is what I was wearing on the first night of the rodeo.

They had what was called back then, a two header which was one bull to ride the first night and another bull to ride the second night. I had no reason to believe I couldn't ride a bucking bull. Though I never really gave it much thought.

When I got on my first bull, some of the other boys had to explain to me what I needed to do to ride the bull. Mainly like how to sit on him or how to pull and set the bull rope while keeping my free arm up without touching the bull.

When I was ready I nodded my head and out the chute we came and right off his back I went. He bucked me off like a fly on his back. The bulls were Brangus bulls that weighed between nine to twelve hundred pounds and they were green bulls, meaning that they had never been bucked before.

I was so mad at myself and was telling Dad about it when I got home. Of course, he started giving me some advice because he rode bulls back in his day in the Arcadia Rodeos before he and Momma got married. Back then the bulls were not as stout because they were simply grass fed bulls which didn't make them as strong or big. He said that you could ride with your hand; no need for spurs. I thought if Dad could do it that way so could I.

So the next night, I rode my bull and won first place on him but I thought I would die before that whistle blew. I still wore my dress pants with loafers and boy did he tear me up. When I got off that bull, I picked my loafers up off the ground and started running. I left the arena as fast as I could, running to the nearest empty horse trailer and fell on my knees inside of it holding my crouch with tears running down my face.

All I could do was moan because the pain was so bad. I just laid there rolling back and forth trying to ease the pain. Some of the guys and girls followed me back to the trailer to check on me. They all busted out laughing because I was rolling around in the back of that trailer in horse shit. But I didn't care at that point; all I knew was the pain. As they say...no pain, no gain!

From this point on, I was hooked on bull-riding until I remarried later and had to make sure I was healthy to work. What an experience it was to be on top of such a large ferocious animal and attempt to stay on for eight seconds. The adrenaline pumping experience is unbelievable!

I graduated in June of '59 but definitely not at the top of the class. After graduation, I worked various jobs and continued to rodeo with the money I made. I also continued to help Dad with his various adventures as well.

Speaking of adventures, this reminds me of one of Floyd's lasting impressions at a rodeo one time. He often went with me to the rodeos that were close to home, especially the ones that had calf-riding for the younger boys. I'd enter him in the calf-riding competitions and he would win his event almost every time!

We were at the Fourth of July Arcadia rodeo in '59 and Floyd was riding our Shetland pony in the grand entry parade. One of Pat Hansel's bucking bulls, named Pa, broke out of the bucking chutes and started running through the riders and their horses that were in the parade.

Of all of the horses for the bull to get, he ran right to Floyd and the pony. The bull hooked the pony under its belly throwing the pony and Floyd into the air with Floyd landing close to the fence.

Dad ran to Floyd as he was climbing the fence and Floyd was crying when Dad got to him. Dad asked Floyd if he was hurt and he said, "No".

That's when Dad said, "Then shut up that crying and go catch the pony".

Of course this was Dad's way of making you tough or maybe I should say another one of the many "Clark remedies" that we all learned through the years.

Dad entered him and me in the same rodeo in the "All Round" category, which meant that we would participate in all five events. The events were bull riding, bareback riding, saddle-bronc riding, bull-dogging and calf roping. This was to be the first time a father and son had ever entered an "All Round" event like this so Dad and I were both pretty excited.

At this point, the only thing that I had even tried was bull riding and bareback riding. So Dad bought some steers and calves for us to practice with. Steve Chin had a roping arena in Parrish where we could practice at.

One afternoon we went to Steve's for our first practice. But before we ever got started, a steer jumped out of the pens and went running down the dirt road. Dad jumped on his horse and took off after him. He got up next to the steer, lunged for his head but the steer was going really fast and Dad had all of his weight on the steers head when all of a sudden the steers head went into the ground. All you could see was Dad and the steer doing a somersault. Dad ended up breaking his arm which didn't allow us to practice together or participate in the Arcadia rodeo.

Wendell Cooper ended up replacing Dad at the rodeo. I first met Wendell, I believe, in April or May of '59 at a horse show in Venice. My sister and I were entered in some of the events. Soon afterwards he and I became good friends and started going to rodeos together. Wendell started dating Sandra shortly afterwards and became my brother-in-law for nine or ten years a few years later.

He was a real good auctioneer who worked for Pete Clemons at the Okeechobee Livestock Market for close to 40 years. He also auctioneered at the Manatee County fair steer sale and private sales from time to time as well as a Rodeo announcer.

He's one of the few guys that I've known that lived, breathed, and acted like a true cowboy. Being a cowboy was his life and he died as a true cowboy with his brand along with other ranchers brands branded on his pine coffin. He was very poetic and wrote some very good poems throughout his life mostly about cowboys and horses. He was very head strong on many subjects especially about women. He liked his liquor and acted like a drunken Indian when he was drunk.

Never in my life have I been in so many fights as I was when I was with Wendell. I've met a lot of "wanna be" cowboys, who wore the boots, hats and jeans that talked like a cowboy but couldn't back up their cowboy talk. But Wendell could and did do just that.

He was an only child and as a child was given most everything he wanted. Wendell was a very superstitious person about certain things like giving me hell for eating popcorn or peanuts before riding bulls. He believed it was bad luck if you ate either of these two things prior to riding bulls.

There were not many things that we saw eye to eye on. It wouldn't take an hour with the two of us together before we would be arguing about something. I think the best times that I can remember, without us arguing was the several months before he died.

Wendell and I had fun at the Arcadia rodeo even though I didn't do that well. It was a two-header, which meant that you had to do everything twice. The bull-riding was the first event and I drew a small brangus bull that weighed about 800 pounds and was a good bucking bull but was a bad chute fighter. We got out of the chute, and he bucked good but fell broad side with me. When he came up he started bucking again but my bull rope was loose and I bucked off.

I ran over to the judges to ask for a re-ride because he fell on me which they gave me but no one could understand why I requested a re-ride. Everyone knew that I made the whistle before the bull fell and actually had the bull riding won. But I had to take the re-ride because the judges gave it to me not knowing I rode out my eight seconds. On my re-ride, the same bull bucked me off before the whistle blew so I blew my chance of winning that round.

As the calf roping event was starting, I was behind the chutes adjusting the stirrups on the saddle for the saddle-bronc event when the announcer called for "Clark". There was another rider by the name of Clark, Tommy Clark, and Pat Hansel got the two of us mixed up a lot of times. This was one of those times because Pat came to me saying that if I didn't get over to the roping box they would be turning the calf out.

I immediately noticed Wendell's roping horse, Chief, tied behind the calf pens with the rope and pigging string on the saddle so I jumped on him. I put the pig string in my mouth and backed Chief into the roping box. This was my first time roping a calf in a rodeo so I was a bit nervous.

When the calf came out, I was right behind him ready to throw the rope but the calf made a sharp turn to the left. Not knowing that the girt was loose before I jumped into the saddle, Chief went to the left after the calf with the saddle and I going off to the right.

I threw my hands out in front of me to the break my fall because I was falling head first into the ground and I cracked my right wrist as soon as I hit the ground. With my wrist cracked, I still had bull dogging to do. Between Dad and me, it just didn't seem like this rodeo was meant for either of us to be there.

For the bull-dogging event, I came out of the box and got right beside the steer. And like my Dad did, jumped on the steers head with all of my weight. I had my right arm under his right horn around the front of his head and as we went down his head slammed into the ground with my right hand between his head and the ground.

All I could hear was something breaking and I immediately thought it was my wrist that was already cracked. When his head hit the ground the rest of his body came over my head and shoulders standing me on my head underneath him. With both of our legs in the air everyone thought that we both broke our necks.

Some men ran out to get us untangled and once we were separated the pain was really bad so I was moaning really loud telling them that my wrist was broken because I heard it break. My wrist was swollen and I was in a lot of pain, but it wasn't my wrist that broke. It was actually the steer's horns breaking because after he started running off I saw both of his horns hanging down.

That was the first and last time that I entered all five events in a rodeo. I rode bareback and bulls for a while but eventually gave up on bareback riding because I never really got good at it. Besides I couldn't stand the pain on my tailbone.

I did get to be a fairly good bull rider though and for about two and a half years bull riding was my only event. I went to most all rodeos in Florida with a few in South Georgia. Riding bulls was one of the most thrilling things that I have ever done in my life and I rode bulls every chance that I could get.

Wendell never did adapt to the "Clarks" way of living. He used to make fun of me for having croker feed sacks as saddle blankets and girths. The girth was made by folding a sack long ways until you got to the width you wanted it. About six inches or so from each end of the folded sack, a small slit would be made so that an O-ring would slip through it. We always had plenty of saddle blankets and girths even if they were homemade. But he never had anything "homemade" like that because he had to have the best.

Thinking of homemade things reminds me of the bucking barrel that we made. After the first few months of bull riding, I made a bucking barrel to practice on in our backyard, next to the swimming hole. There were four trees, almost 20 feet apart, in a square that I tied a 55 gallon drum to. With the drum laying down I cut four holes into the drum, two at each end, about two feet apart. Instead of using rope through each hole, I used a quarter inch chain feeding the chain into the holes because the rope would be easily cut by the barrel otherwise. I then tied a one inch rope about eight feet long to each of the four chains. I then tied four large tractor inner tubes to the other end of the ropes. At the opposite end of the tubes I tied another one inch rope that was then tied about 12 feet up each tree.

Once this was completed, the barrel ended up being about six feet off the ground. A bull rope was put around the drum so the rider could have that to hold on to. With a person at each of the four ropes pulling down or pushing up on them, the rider was about three to four feet from the ground at any given time.

That barrel was hard to ride but the ground seemed harder sometimes. Harold Burnett, Wendell, Buddy Yochim and James Pipkins were the toughest barrel buckers. If they didn't want you on the barrel, you were going off! No one could stay on if they were the buckers.

On the first day that we tried it out, there were about 20 boys there to try to ride the bucking barrel. After everyone had their turn, there was blood all over the barrel mostly from skinned knuckles, and busted mouth's or heads. The worst time would be when a tube would break. We sure did use a lot of tractor tubes but we soon learned to check the tubes for small tears.

Once someone felt that they could ride the barrel good enough they went on to trying to ride a bull. Though this was quite different from an actual bull, this did offer all of us a lot of practice and mainly a good time. Which, if you haven't figured out by now, that's what I'm all about!

In the fall and winter of 1959 a bunch of us boys built a small bucking arena beside an abandoned house that was owned by Woody Townsend. Woody was just starting his subdivision called Peacock Manor, south of Oneco. We rounded up anything that would buck or even try to buck to have a little rodeo.

We used this particularly bad steer with long, sharp horns which belonged to Varnell Green that he kept in our Sarasota pasture for our rodeos. The steer would run in the swamps which made him hard to catch and he would try to hook everyone except me. For some reason, he would see me and go the other way.

I was in the swamp trying to catch him when he left the swamp for the open field. As I was just getting out of the swamp, I heard someone screaming my name, so I began running towards whoever was yelling. That's when I saw Harry Romine up a little pine tree. He was near the top but the tree was so skinny that it was bent over towards the ground.

The steer was trying to hook him in the ass or back, but couldn't quite reach Harry with his horns. All the other boys were up in trees as well or at least hiding behind them. The steer saw me coming with a rope and took off.

We were all laughing at Harry as he dropped from the tree. Harry, Gilbert, and Dickey left shortly after that as they wanted nothing more to do with the steer. We did eventually catch the steer but boy what a job!

I had a bunch of boys help me gather the livestock like, Floyd and Roy, Herman Burnett, David DeSear, Gilbert Albritton, Harry Romine, and Dickey Betts. Some of you may not recall who Dickey Betts is but he first started playing music at our little rodeo dances along with E.J. Stewart and a few others that were putting a band together.

Later on he played with the Allman Brothers as well as wrote and sang one of the bands famous songs 'Ramblin' Man'. We used the abandoned house as our dance hall and we had a lot of fun square dancing and jitter bugging after the rodeo.

Back then I didn't think Dickey would amount to much because he wasn't into working just playing music. This reminds me of the time I had a job to do for Steve Chin planting pangola grass on his 400 acres that he bought on the south side of SR64 just pass Bear Bay Road.

I had my truck loaded with sprigs and took several boys with me. I only remember three of them being Gilbert Albritton, Dickey Betts and my cousin, Jim Kilcrease. When we got to the field we found the field was covered with water from the night before when it rained.

Steve had a bulldozer there to pull my truck through the field as we spread the grass with our hands from behind the truck. Both Gilbert and Dickey said that they were not going to work in the muddy water and they wanted me to take them back home. I told them they could hitchhike or walk back, but I was going to plant the grass, which the rest of us did.

A few days later as I was going by Dickey's house, Dickey was sitting under the cedar tree playing his banjo. I pulled over and shut the engine off. I said, "Dickey, "If you don't get off your ass and get to work you are going to amount to nothing".

Boy, how wrong was I because it wasn't long before he was playing for the Allman Brothers. After playing at our rodeo dances and the redneck places on old U.S. 301, I didn't see Dickey from then on until

I was dancing at the new Water Hole in Oneco in the early eighties.

A long haired hippy looking man came up to me and said, "Donnie Clark, you're not going to speak to me?"

I looked closely at his face and saw that it was Dickey. He changed from a redneck to a hippy so I didn't recognize him at first. So I guess all of the sitting around playing music paid off for him.

We didn't have the arena long but we sure had a good time. It was free because Woody paid for the material that we used so it was fairly cheap except for gas to haul the livestock from the pasture to the arena and then back again.

While I was still married to Betty Lou, Wendell and I went to a dance at Robarts Arena in Sarasota. Around this same time, my feelings for Cande were becoming stronger but with me being married prevented us from being together. We did see each other from time to time at teen club dances and rodeos and as time went on we became more involved with each other. Cande was at this dance but her parents did not like her being with me so whenever we met somewhere like this we would dance as much as we could.

Wendell and I hadn't been friends too long and he kept dancing with Cande even cutting in on our dances. When the band took a break, I reminded Wendell of my situation with Cande and told him to dance with someone else. As usual, Wendell had too many drinks and he didn't appreciate me telling him what to do.

At the time, my shoulders and back were sunburned real bad and he pinched me on the shoulders asking me what I was going to do about it which made me cringe in pain. Now I had in the back of my mind what Dad said to me before I left that night. He was running for office again and told me before I left the house not to get into any trouble. So when Wendell asked me what I was going to do about it, I told him that we could settle it tomorrow morning. Well that just made it worse because he wanted it settled now.

We argued for a while and decided that we would fight right then with the understanding that we go outside alone, just the two of us. I wanted someone out there with us though watching out for the law, and if the law showed up that I would run from the fight. So we got Harold Burnett to be the lookout guy as we went out under a light to fight.

We squared off with Wendell throwing the first punch and missing. But I followed through with a punch to his mouth knocking him to the ground. I helped him up, which I had never helped anyone up before during a fight, and gave him my handkerchief to wipe the blood from his mouth.

I didn't really want to hurt Wendell but I did want to show him that I wasn't going to take his crap anymore. After Wendell wiped his mouth he said that I just got a lucky punch and he wanted to try again. So we went at it again but after the second time of me helping him up off the ground he decided he had had enough.

The next morning Wendell came by the house, upset about the night before, saying that I beat him up while he was drunk. I told him that I knew he was drunk and that was the only reason that I helped him up both times. But I also said that if he wanted a real ass whipping that we could go out to the cow pens behind the house right now. I explained to him that I only fought him because I was tired of him bullying me around and that I wasn't going to take his crap anymore.

We never fought again after that but the next time I saw his mother she gave me hell for busting Wendell's mouth. She said that I could have really messed up his teeth. I don't remember him bullying me around after the fight though.

Thinking about taking someone's shit reminds me of the time Buck Godwin took a lot of people's shit. In the late '50s is when I first met Buck. We became good friends and are still very good friends today. Buck likes to dance as much as I do and we could be found at a lot of country dances throughout our younger years. Buck would call the square dances and dance in them at the same time. He is a soft-hearted man for having been brought up in the country and one of the hardest working men that I know. We sure had some good times together.

I'll never forget about the time that he fell into a septic tank. Now Buck may have a different point of view on how this particular situation happened but my version is this...

One Friday night, when I was about 20, Buddy Yochim, Buck and I went out 'jukin' (now simply referred to as dancing). We drove Buck's car to the Bamboo Lounge in Palmetto because we heard a good band was playing. Buddy had a fake ID showing that I was 23 years old. The funny thing is, at 20 I looked to be 17 years old, but they let me in anyway.

We arrived fairly early and found there to be only a few girls, so we left and headed to Anna Maria Island. We knew the bars on the island closed at midnight and the Bamboo Lounge stayed open until two in the morning, so we could come back later. We were having a good time at the Anchor Inn Lounge with Bill Floyd's band playing.

Whenever the band took a 15 minute break, Buck would go out to his car to take a few swigs from the whiskey bottle he kept in his car and be back before the band started again. Well, the eleven o'clock break arrived and of course Buck did his usual thing with the few swigs of whiskey. The band was just about to start back up, so Buddy and I stepped out to find out what happened to Buck. We looked everywhere but only found his car.

It was then that I thought about the girls we had been dancing with earlier in the evening and remembered they told us they were going to the Bamboo Lounge later on. Buck was getting pretty drunk and with the girls already gone we thought he probably left with the girls and forgot to tell us.

So we hopped in Buck's car and drove back to the Bamboo Lounge. When we arrived, there was no Buck to be found. Not really knowing where he was, we thought he would show up there eventually so we decided to stay and dance until two o'clock. Well, closing time came and went. We waited around until about half past two and then decided to go on home.

The next morning, we drove Buck's car over to his house hoping he would be there. He was there alright and boy was he mad as hell at us for leaving him at the beach. You see, it turned out that Buck had to take a leak after he got his swig of whiskey, so he walked around the building to do so.

None of us knew it, but the lounge must have had sewer problems because the lid was off the septic tank. Buck, not even knowing the septic tank was there much less that the lid was off, didn't see it until he fell into it.

What took so long for him to get back into the lounge was the fact he was busy trying to wash himself off. Then after finding us as well as his car gone, he was mad as hell because he knew it was up to him to find his own way back home. Maybe it was that he stunk so badly because the only ride he could find was with a milkman in the milk truck going back to Bradenton. From there, Buck had to walk the rest of the way back to his house. Boy was he one pissed off person at Buddy and me!

From camping to working to playing to pulling tricks on everyone, I think I might have to get serious one day. But then again, I don't think I can ever stop pulling tricks on people. That's just way too much fun!

I hope you have enjoyed my teenage years. I remember more things about them than I did in my earlier years. I enjoyed life, I played jokes on people but I'm not real sure how everyone stayed alive or at least did not get badly hurt. If you learned anything from this chapter, I hope you learned how to have fun, enjoy life and always be happy!

*Sandra, Dad, Momma and I.*

*Dragline & bulldozer with Dad as County Commissioner.*

*My graduation photo.*

*At a rodeo, L to R, Bill Miller, Herman Burnett & Donnie Clark.*

*Rodeo Clowns, Donnie Clark& Bill Miller with Sam.*

## CHAPTER 3
# 1960 – 1970

The *Sixties*, was also labeled the "Swinging Sixties" because of the different attitudes that emerged. The term "hippies" evolved from the social/cultural youth during this time. Rampant drug use became prevalent as well, which included drugs like LSD and marijuana.

Some of the most memorable assassinations occurred in the 1960s like President John F. Kennedy, Malcolm X, Martin Luther King, Jr. and Robert F. Kennedy.

Blacks began to challenge segregation in the south through boycotts, sit-ins and freedom rides. And in 1969, the birth of the gay rights movement came to light.

The Soviet Union and the United States were involved in a space race, especially after the Soviets had cosmonaut Yuri Gagarin orbited the earth. The space race really became heated up when America put the first men on the moon who were Neil Armstrong and Buzz Aldrin in July of 1969. The immortal words by Neil after placing one foot on the moon was, "That's one small step for man, one giant leap for mankind."

Some popular American automobiles from the '60s were the Pontiac GTO, the Plymouth Barracuda, and the Ford Mustang. The Chevrolet Corvette was reinvented in the '60s. With every available option, the GTO cost was around $4500 in 1964 with the Barracuda costing $2500 and the basic Mustang costing around $2400.

American forces officially arrived in Vietnam in 1961 and the war escalated in 1963. After 1966 with the draft in place, more than 500,000 troops were sent to Vietnam. There were a lot of uprisings and protests with this war. And the voter age-limits were challenged by the phrase, "If you're old enough to die for your country, you're old enough to vote."

A recession hit the economy in the early '60's with building construction being hard hit. It didn't help Florida that Hurricane Donna came through the upper Keys and came ashore near Fort Myers on September 10, 1960, packing 135 MPH winds. It left devastation as it moved north-northeastward through the interior of the state where it exited near Daytona Beach the following day.

Manatee County was growing but was still a safe place to live. Kids were able to walk to the local stores by themselves without fear of getting kidnapped. Parents were able to leave doors unlocked and keys in cars without them being stolen.

More of the main streets were being paved, but most side streets were still dirt roads. Most of the wooden bridges were now concrete except for the few in the eastern part of the county.

In the late '50s to early '60s, Tropicana had to accommodate for the growing demand for its juice, so they built a complete citrus processing plant in Port Canaveral. This allowed them to load 1.5 million gallons of chilled juice onto the SS Tropicana and ship to the northeast part of the United States. Tropicana became the first company to sell bottled orange juice overseas in the mid '60's.

Dad studied the water aquifers and often told me that we would be out of water in Manatee County if we didn't build a dam. Everyone at the time thought because we had lots of water why pay for it now. But Dad kept pushing it until finally it was in the process.

I believe Manatee County Reservoir was started in the early '60s because I remember times that we had the Clark Cattle Company, which was about this same time, and we would stop at the dam site as it was being built. Dad would always count the number of times the pilings were driven after hitting the hard bottom. "If the piling doesn't move anymore with six more hits, it's good," he would say.

He wanted it built right and he was on site whenever he had the time to be there. He also had influence in getting the Port of Manatee started. I guess he was pretty much involved in a lot to do with the county growth back then because he was County Commissioner for so many years. And being County Commissioner he always knew what was going on, where and when.

Dad lost his County Commissioner seat in 1959 and lost most everything else too due to the rock pit business. So he decided to plant three acres of okra to help pay for our living expenses. Dad used his stud horse, Tarzan, to plow, cultivate and hill up the rows as well as plant the okra. He planted it on some muck ground near our house.

The first day of picking, the okra was about two foot tall. There was only Momma, Dad, Sandra and I picking in the beginning. We started at daylight wearing long sleeve shirts and rubber gloves in order to try to help from getting so itchy from the hairs on leaves. After picking we would rub vinegar all over our arms or anywhere else that we were itching. The vinegar was the only thing that would stop the itching.

Sandra had to leave the field at seven o'clock to get ready for school and be on time to catch the bus. She was a sophomore in high school at the time. But Momma, Dad and I would stay and finish picking around noon.

On the first day of picking, my back was so sore from bending over so long and carrying a bucket I got to thinking of an easier way to pick okra. So when Sandra came home that afternoon from school, I told her of my idea making picking bags.

I already had two clover seed bags and some copper wire that I removed from some poles near the cow pens. The bags were small which were just right for picking okra. All Sandra had to do was sew the copper wire around the opened end of the bags in order to keep the bag open. Then sew a strap to the bag which could then hang around your neck.

The next morning Sandra and I came out with our picking bags hanging on our shoulders. Dad asked, "What are you doing with those?"

I said, "We are using them to pick with."

Dad said, "They won't work; you might as well get your buckets."

When the four of us started down the rows, it wasn't long before Sandra and I left them behind us. We were picking two rows to their one because we were able to pick with both hands while they had to pick with one using the other one to carry their bucket. The funny thing was when Sandra got home from school that day, Dad told her to make more picking bags.

I got mad at Dad when he told me that he sold the okra for $12 a bushel when the going rate was $18. He told the buyers that they could pay that price until the season was over, in other words, not any higher or any lower. Dad ended up being right again because about three weeks later the price dropped to $8. So with the agreement from our buyers, we were still getting the $12 for about another month or so.

The third week of picking our okra, Dad ended up buying a Negro man's okra field named Walker Stewart and it was located where the Red Barn Flea Market is now. Dad bought the field because Mr. Stewart couldn't get any help picking it.

We would pick our field one day and the other field the next day. We did have more help picking though. Some of the ones that I remember helping were Floyd and Roy, Billy and his sister Terri, Herman and David DeSear.

At this time, I was still working cattle, as well as helping Dad. It was around 1960 when Dad and I made a few trips to Mississippi to buy some dairy heifers to resell to the local dairymen. We had a GMC straight-job truck with a 16 foot cattle rack on the back which meant we could only haul about 11 or 12 cows per load. We bought some of the heifers in the country, but most were bought at the dairy sales in Pontotoc and Tupelo.

On our first load that we picked up from the Pontotoc market, Dad told me to take the truck into town and get someone to build a wooden dividing gate which would separate the load of heifers. As I headed to town, I was going down a steep hill with an intersection at the bottom. I started to slow the truck as I approached a red light and pushed on the brake pedal but it went all the way to the floor board.

Realizing the brakes were gone, I started down-shifting and blowing the horn like crazy. The oncoming vehicles realized what was wrong and stopped so I could go through the intersection without killing myself or someone else.

As I made it through the red light, I was going uphill again and noticed a GMC dealership on the right so I whipped into the parking lot going about 25 miles an hour. Two men had to jump out of the way as I headed for a steep incline which finally made the truck come to a halt. I just sat behind the steering wheel shaking. Soon the service manager was at the truck door asking if I wanted my brakes fixed.

Another time as Dad and I were heading home with a load of cattle, we approached a red light on a four lane road in a small town. While we were stopped at the light, all of a sudden, we heard some yelling and screaming which made me look back to see where it was coming from. I saw a convertible with the top down, filled with a total of six girls and boys wearing nothing but their swim suits stopped next to us.

They were jumping out of the car just a hollering and carrying on. That's when I saw what was happening...cow shit was spewing into their car through the cracks of the cattle rack on the back of the truck. There was shit all over them and throughout most of the car. By the time they were all out of the car, the light turned green and Dad and I took off laughing our asses off. Don't you know that was one hell of a sight!

On a different trip, Dad had been driving for nearly ten hours and decided it was time to wake me up so I could drive for a while. It was about four in the morning and raining. I really wasn't one that could ever drive and stay awake at night but I had to make the switch with Dad.

I had only been driving for about 30 minutes when I was pulled over by a highway patrolman. I remember him approaching the driver's side window and asking for my driver's license. He then shined his flashlight in my face and must have noticed that I looked sleepy.

Dad was awake by now but not real happy. The cop said he saw me weaving back and forth all over the road and told Dad to drive from there as I appeared too sleepy to handle the wheel. I had been asleep the entire time that Dad drove close to ten hours straight, and yet I couldn't seem to keep my eyes open. Dad climbed behind the wheel once again and gave me hell for not being able to stay awake. We more than doubled our money on the heifers we bought during these trips.

For several years I worked Bartow King's pure breed Brahma cattle for him. Mr. King called me one night from the hospital to tell me that his son, Bobby, would be able to help work the cows that Saturday. He also mentioned that he had seven bulls, about a year old, that needed to be castrated.

On Friday evening I checked the almanac for the zodiac signs and saw the Scorpio sign for that day and the next day which meant that neither day was good for castrating. If you castrate an animal under that sign, the animal would bleed to death but only on animals that have reached their sexual maturity. Most people do not believe in the zodiac signs but my Dad surely did and I, through time, surely do as well.

I called Bobby King to ask if we could work the cattle the following Saturday and he asked, "Why not this Saturday?"

So I told him about the signs and the probability that the animals would bleed to death if castrated under the Scorpio sign. Apparently he did not believe in the signs like Dad and I and said that it would be okay to go ahead with it. Now don't forget, Bobby was just out of college and was going to be an eye doctor.

After we got finished working the cattle, worming, spraying, branding, etc. , only the bulls were left to castrate. Being that they were fairly big, weighing about 700 to 800 pounds, me and a couple of my buddies, David DeSear and Billy Miller had to rope them and throw them on the ground. Bobby had a stainless steel tray with doctor tools inside of it and after he cut out the first bulls nuts, the animal immediately started bleeding very badly. Bobby said it would be okay that the blood would soon coagulate, but I knew better than that.

Once the third bull was castrated, the first bull was already lying down because of so much blood loss. Once Bobby realized what I said might be true, he decided not to finish castrating the other bulls that day. By the time I got home that evening, Bobby was calling to say that the first bull was dead and the other two didn't look good.

After supper, Billy and I went back to the King's to pick up the first bull to butcher and the other two were dead by then. We ended up butchering all three bulls for cat meat because they had been wormed that day. Bobby was there when we started loading them and I asked him as I was laughing, "So you're going to be an eye doctor?"

He answered saying, "Yes."

Then I said as I was still laughing, "I sure hope that I don't have to have you work on me!"

Robert King is now retired but was one of the best eye doctors in Manatee County but I'm sure he remembers his bad experience castrating bulls. There is a time to be patient and I am sure Bobby King would say patience does pay off sometimes. I often wonder if he ever paid attention to the almanac after this.

We all know that paying attention to little things sometimes does pay off. I didn't pay close attention to much growing up but I remember the time that I definitely paid attention when Fred House tried to renege on a job he asked me to do.

I would pick up odd jobs from time to time so moving cattle for Fred House was just another odd job. In the early '60s, he asked me to move his cows from a pasture in New Pierce, which is located between Whitfield Avenue and Tallevast Road east of new Highway 301, to his ranch not too far away on Prospect Road. There was about 125 head of cattle that I was to pen and haul to his ranch for $250 and I knew it would take me most of the day to do it.

That night, at supper, I told Dad what I had to do the next day but Dad also needed me to help him do something. So he decided we should get up early in the morning, drive the cattle over to the ranch with the horses and dogs and be finished before 8 o'clock in the morning. I thought this should work well and then I could help Dad the rest of the day.

So Dad, Billy and I were on horses with Sandra, Floyd, and Roy Smith in the car. At day light, we were in the pasture with the dogs working the cattle into a bunched up group. Moving cattle around in a group helps settle the wilder ones down and gets them more into the habit of staying in a group.

Once we were sure we had them under control, Sandra opened the gate so we could drive them out of the pasture and start down the dirt road. She went ahead of us with Floyd and Roy standing in drive ways along the way to keep the cattle out of other people's yards. Dad was ahead of the cattle so they wouldn't try to run away and the dogs kept circling the cattle to keep them in a tight group with Billy and I pushing up the rear.

We didn't have any trouble with the cattle and in less than an hour, we had the cattle in the cow pens at Mr. House's ranch. Dad and the rest of the crew went home while I stayed at the cow pens waiting for Mr. House. After waiting quite a while, I decided to go back to the house knowing Dad would be waiting for me to help him.

As I was leaving, I met Mr. House on the road and he said, "I thought by now you would be penning the cattle."

I told him that the cattle were already in his pens and he looked at me very surprised and asked how I did it so fast. After I told him how we moved the cattle, he said he wouldn't pay me but $100 because I didn't haul them in my truck. I told him we agreed on $250 and that he wasn't going to pay me just a $100.

After his reply stating that $250 was too much money for so little work, I simply told him that was quite alright with me and that I would be on my way to return with a horse and dog to drive the cattle back to the pasture from which they came from. After looking at me rather stunned and realizing that I meant what I said, he decided he better pay me what we had originally agreed on.

Thinking of people agreeing on things, it was very seldom that Wendell and I agreed on anything but he was easy to pull tricks on which I did at every opportunity. Of the many tricks that I pulled on him reminds me of when I stopped by his house which was on Lockwood Ridge Road one afternoon. I asked his Momma if he was home and she said he was in the back pasture patching some fence. Looking from their barn in the far back corner of the pasture under some oak trees, I could see Wendell.

That's when a brainstorm hit me...I was going to try to sneak up and scare Wendell. Keeping my eyes on him, I got down on my hands and knees to start crawling toward him. As I got closer, when he turned in my direction, I would lay flat on the ground. He was almost to the corner post, stapling the barbed wire with a hatchet and I was about 50 foot behind him when I rose up to start running hard towards him.

When I knew he could hear the sounds of my feet and as he was starting to turn around I let out one of my blood curdling screams. As Wendell was turning around he brought the hatchet up high like he was going to hit something or somebody. He was also trying to run backwards at the same time saying, "Oh…Oh…Oh!"

I fell on the ground rolling around laughing. I was still on the ground when Wendell walked up cussing me saying that he could have killed me with that hatchet. After I finished laughing I told him that he was too scared to kill anything or anyone. He told me the reason he was so jumpy was because there were times when some of the animals, mostly the monkeys, from the Ringling Bros Circus would get loose in the woods behind Wendell's pasture.

Another time that I snuck up on someone was when a buddy of mine, Freddy Alcathie and I snuck up on Cande and her girlfriends while they were camping. In early 1960, they were camping on Johnnie Lou Glisson's property, which was also one of Dad's pastures, off 63rd

Street East, which is now the retirement community, Hawaiian Village. Cande, my sister Sandra, Johnnie Lou, Velma DeSear, and a few others were there.

Later that evening Freddie and I wanted to sneak up on them while they were standing around the camp fire. We hid behind a big clump of palmettos and started throwing dried cow manure at them. They all started screaming and jumped into their sleeping bags. We could hear them talking and Velma said, "I bet its Donnie doing that".

Then Cande said, "If it is Donnie I know he wouldn't hit me".

So Cande stood up from her sleeping bag, put both hands on her hips and yelled "Donnie is that you?"

That's when I threw another cow chip at her and she screamed jumping back into her sleeping bag. That got me laughing as Freddie and I walked up to their camp sight.

Another prank was on Buddy Yochim's brother, Sidney. Most school days after getting off the bus, he would go by our swimming pond, set his books down and jump for the rope that was hanging about three foot from the bank. He would then swing out over the pond several times before going home.

So I got a bright idea…I climbed up the hickory tree and cut the rope so that there was just a few threads holding it together. The next day, I saw Sidney getting off the bus so I went into my bedroom in order to watch him from my window. He did his usual thing…put his books down, jumped for the rope and swung out several times but the rope didn't break. Not sure why it didn't break but I intended to go out there after he left to fix it but got distracted with something else and forgot about it.

The next afternoon, Buddy, Elmer Tharp and Sandra were all at the pond. Sandra swung out over the pond, back and forth several times. Then Buddy climbed up to do the same thing, but as he went out over the pond, the rope broke. It was a real cold day and Buddy had boots on as well as a heavy western jacket. Sandra said that Buddy's facial expression was priceless when the rope broke and it was quite the sight to see him trying to swim back to the bank with the heavy jacket and boots on. He actually just about drowned and boy was he ticked off when I told him that the sneaky trick was actually meant to be for Sidney.

After Dad got rid of "Old Sam", I was able to get a young pure breed Brahma that I also named Sam. I was working cows for Harry Booth and mentioned to him that if he ever had a pure bred bull calf that didn't have a mother that I would like to buy it. Within a few months he called to say he had a bull calf that the mother's tits were ballooned and was quite mean to handle.

Since he was only a day old, I went to Granddad's dairy to get a couple of gallons of colostrum milk for him. We had about four nurse cows that was nursing several calves so after the colostrum milk was gone I was able to put him on one of the nurse cows.

From the very first day that I got young Sam, I started working with him. I first started to teach him to lay down by squeezing his hump and pushing him down to the ground at the same time I would say, "Down Sam...down".

I worked with him for at least an hour every day and by the time he was two months old I had him laying down, kneeling and praying. I had him to pray by kneeling on the left front leg with the right leg stretched out in front of him with his head bowed between his front legs.

I never did put a ring in his nose but I did have a halter on him. I let Floyd ride him since he only weighed about 75-80 pounds and I would let him play like a bull fighter with Sam. I could sick Sam on Floyd like a dog and when Floyd thought he was getting good at bull fighting I would let go of Sam's lead rope hollering, "Catch him Sam."

Floyd would holler, "No Donnie, No!"

It would be too late, because Sam would already be head-butting Floyd in the ass throwing him into the air.

Sam was another good ole bull that I had a lot of fun with. By the time Sam was a year and a half old, I started using him in the clown acts at some of the rodeos that Billy Miller and I performed at.

For the clown acts at the rodeos, Billy and I would put Sam in the bucking chute with Billy on his back. Sam would come out bucking and Billy would make believe that Sam bucked him off. I would then act like I was the bull fighting clown and fight Sam off. Billy would get up as Sam would butt Billy into the air with his head. Of course, Billy wouldn't be butted very high because Sam wasn't that big yet.

After that act, I would make believe that I was hurt by lying on the ground calling Sam to me. Sam would come and lay down beside me and I would crawl across his back as if I was injured. Sam would then get up and carry me out of the arena.

Young Sam sure liked to be scratched behind the ears, under his chin and dew lap, but he liked his balls to be scratched the best. After going through his one hour workout training, I would make him lie down and start scratching his balls.

First, he would lay his head back on the ground all stretched out on one side and as soon as I would start scratching his balls, his back hind leg would raise up and his eyes would roll back in his head with only the whites of his eyes showing. He would lay there like this until I stopped. So if you ever want to tame a wild mean bull, if you can get to scratch his balls, you would probably get him to be gentler or definitely like you more.

Young Sam was a good bull but since he was a pure bred he was lazy. He definitely was not as rambunctious as old Sam was except for the one episode of him clearing the midway at the fair.

I took him to the fair to perform with Billy and I during our clown act in the horse arena somewhere in the early '60's. After the show was over, I was leading Sam down the midway back towards the live-stock barns. Sam was a little rambunctious after the show, which was strange, but it was because I had him up tied real close, meaning he could only stand up or lay down, most of the day.

The midway was overly crowded and we were approaching a big-ass Negro woman who had several kids with her. Sam was still a little jumpy and she was walking fairly slow which left me with a hard decision on how I was going to get Sam around her without causing a big scene.

Before I could make a decision, Sam took it upon himself and head-butted her hard in the ass. Of course this stunned the woman, because she turned around with a mad look on her face with a hand ready to slap one of her kids. She hadn't turned all the way around but caught a glimpse of the bull only inches from her ass and she nearly went berserk. She started screaming, grabbing a hold of kids, and took off running through the entire crowd of people in her way.

I didn't get to see how many people she knocked down as I had my hands full with Sam, but when I finally took a look down the midway

I saw enough room that a truck could have been driven through. Now that was funny even if it did scare the shit out of her!

Young Sam only lived to be 18 months old. Dad had 12 Holstein heifers in a pasture across the canal from our house and told me to put Sam in with them to breed them. The very next day, the Core of Engineers (COE) came into the pasture to spray the canal with herbicide to kill the weeds. There was also a weed called crotalaria which is highly toxic once it goes into a wilt and then gets eaten.

With the COE spraying the weeds, this made the crotalarias go into a wilt and the heifers and Sam ate them. All 12 of the heifers died and Sam only lived for about a week. I tried doctoring him the entire week, but he was too far gone.

I often think about both old Sam and young Sam and would like to raise another Sam again. Both of them were a lot of fun and I sure enjoyed being able to have my clown acts with young Sam. The funniest one, that wasn't really an act, was when he bullied his way through the midway and head-butted that lady in the ass.

In my younger years, butchering wasn't that much fun because I mostly had to dig the holes for the guts and salt the hides, but as I got older I enjoyed it a lot more and got damn good at it. I often helped C.R. butcher horses and cattle for cat meat and I also used his place to butcher crippled cattle and horses. I paid five or ten dollars for the dead animal, butchered it there, and cut the meat in three pound chunks for the cats and he would buy the meat from me.

One day, while C.R. and I were butchering, a man pulled up in a pickup, with his German shepherd in the back of the truck. At the time, C.R. had a large spider monkey, that he called Blue, who roamed free around his property most of the time.

No sooner than the truck stopped, the dog jumped out after Blue, chasing him up an oak tree not too far from where we were butchering. The man immediately yelled at the dog and made it get back into the truck. C.R. told him not worry about the monkey as the dog couldn't hurt him. The man finally came over to where we were butchering and began talking to C.R. about selling him some canker-eyed cows to butcher for cat meat.

It wasn't long before Blue came down from the tree and made his way over to where some other monkeys were in cages. The dog jumped out of the truck once again and lunged for the monkey. But the dog wasn't as fast as ole Blue. When Blue jumped into the air, he landed on the dogs back with his head facing toward the dog's tail.

I couldn't believe what I was seeing when Blue grabbed the dog's tail with one hand and started biting down hard on it. With his legs wrapped around the dog's torso and one hand clenching the dog's tail, Blue then began poking the dog in the ass with his free hand. The dog was howling in pain the entire time while spinning in circles trying its best to bite Blue in order to free him from the grips Blue had on him.

The dog finally fell to the ground, rolling over and over until Blue let go. The dog got up and ran through the orange grove to the road howling in pain. The man ran and jumped in his truck to go catch his dog. When he returned with the dog, he was all curled up lying in the back of the truck. We could see his tail was definitely broken because it was on a 90 degree angle and bloodied. The monkeys little fingers poke small holes in and around the asshole as well.

I must say that is one of the funniest things I have ever seen between two animals! Too bad they didn't have "Funniest Home Videos" back then because that would have been a good one to send in.

David DeSear, who helped me butcher at times, did not like butchering at night at C.R.'s place because of all of the animals and the noises they made. But mainly because of some of the animals may have been out of their cages.

One night, David and I were butchering and we were each carrying a quarter of a beef into the cooler. David entered the cooler carrying a front quarter just ahead of me and he was trying to hook his quarter onto the meat hook when I yelled at him, "David, don't step on that snake!"

David looked down and saw the huge snake at his feet and immediately dropped the front quarter almost knocking me down getting out the door. After dropping my quarter of beef and almost pissing my pants from laughing so hard, I finally told David to come back because the snake was dead.

A few weeks earlier, C.R. lost his entire reptile show trailer because the heater went out and it froze overnight killing all of the reptiles. C.R. had an 18 foot Boa Constrictor which he planned on preserving but he ran out of embalming fluid so he put it in the cooler until he was able to get more.

C.R. told me about it and told me to make sure not to step on it while being in and out of the cooler. C.R. had the snake lying in a large flat pan wrapped in a big circle and had it covered with a canvas so that the beef blood wouldn't drip on it. I actually forgot about the snake being inside the cooler when we first started going into it. David must have pulled the canvas off a little that was covering the snake while trying to hook the beef quarter up on the meat hook.

I remember getting pretty damn scared myself while I was there late one night butchering a cow. C.R. had all kinds of circus animals in cages like lions, tigers, monkeys, elephants, hippos, etc. The animals that were at his place were not all his. He let some of the circus people keep their caged animals at his place and they would come during the day to feed them and work with them.

I was butchering by myself and it was very dark except for the overhead light. I heard sounds coming from the dark from all the animals that were in cages all around me. There were as many animals there as were in some zoos and it was kind of spooky at night because you didn't know if any of them were out of their cages.

I was bent over on one side of the cow skinning it when a 55 gallon metal drum went flying by me. I jumped as I straightened up looking directly at this huge elephant a few feet from me. It startled me so much that I was going backwards fast with the skinning knife in my hand waving it back and forth as if to fight off the animal.

Of course, the elephant wasn't coming after me; he was just getting a drink of water out of the drum. And I guess once he finished drinking the water he must have hit the drum with his trunk which sent it flying by me. But it sure as hell scared the shit out of me.

I started yelling for the elephant's caretaker to come get the elephant. The caretaker was asleep inside the trailer and simply forgot to chain the elephant's foot back up for the night.

I started doing a lot of custom butchering for people who raised their own beef in my late teens and into my twenties. I would pick up the animals on a Saturday morning which ranged from five to eight head and load them in the cattle truck. Billy Miller would bring the one ton Dodge truck with the butchering equipment along with four or five ten gallon milk cans filled with water. We used the water to wash our hands with and rinse some blood off the beef.

We went to the woods at Rattlesnake Slough, which is where Lake Evers Reservoir is now. We had a block and tackle that we attached to a big tree limb to lift the beef up with and we used the cattle truck to hold the beef up to allow us to remove the guts and saw down the back bone. Sawing down the back bone was the hardest job and took the longest time when butchering.

We cut cabbage palm frowns to lay the beef on in the back of the Dodge truck once it was cut into quarters. Each quarter was then tagged with the person's name that we were butchering for so as to not mix up several people's beef. Most people wanted the heart and liver and we were able to keep the tail, tongue, brain, cheek meat, butcher steak and the tripe.

After we finished butchering, we would then take the beef to the different store coolers in town wherever the customer wanted the meat cut and wrapped for them. We got paid five dollars for the butchering and five dollars for the delivery of the beef to the coolers, plus we were able to keep the hide which normally brought eleven cents per pound.

Billy and I had two different spots where we butchered with each spot having a big tree that we used for hoisting the beef up. We would leave the guts and trimmings at the one spot for the buzzards to eat on for a while and go to the other spot the next week. This way each spot would be cleaned by the buzzards in a two week time span.

Buzzards are not picky about what they eat and I guess some would classify me in the same category as buzzards because I'm not that picky about what I eat. I ate my first earthworm somewhere in the early '60s.

David Young, Floyd, Roy Smith and I were digging earthworms behind my house to take with us fishing. David said he would give me five dollars if I'd eat one of them. So I picked one up, took it over to the well to wash it off. With it wiggling in my fingers, I leaned my head back and dropped it into my mouth. I stuck my tongue out with the worm wiggling on it so David could see that the slimy worm was definitely in my mouth and I swallowed it down with one, big gulp. I opened my mouth and moved my tongue around proving that I had completed David's dare.

One didn't seem good enough as David felt he was tricked. So I picked up another one and did it again. But before I could swallow the second one, the first one was starting to crawl back up my throat. That's when I began guzzling down lots water, which made the worm go on down my throat.

Damn, it surprised me how long it would take for the first worm to get down into my stomach for good. I ate four worms before David believed me and finally gave up the five dollars. Wendell used to say that I was responsible for starving the buzzards in Manatee County because I ate all that they would eat.

Wendell got grossed out one night when he came by to pick up Sandra for a date. I had just come home late and was in the kitchen eating supper. As Wendell entered the kitchen we started talking and suddenly he started wrinkling his nose. I asked if he had ever eaten chitlins before and he said, "Sure, I have."

So we kept talking about upcoming rodeos and Wendell asked me what I was eating. I told him cornbread, collard greens, rice and chitlins. Wendell looked at the chitlins and said, "I haven't ever eaten chitlins that look like that!"

Apparently Wendell thought fried pig skins were chitlins. With Wendell leaning against the counter I said to him, "Look in the pot on the stove and you'll see the chitlins better."

Wendell lifted the lid, his nose really wrinkling up, and he turned his head from side to side at the same time slamming the lid back down on the pot saying, "OH MY GOD!!"

He ran out the back door and I immediately starting laughing. I was still laughing when he came back inside and said, "I thought that smell was coming from an open septic tank!"

Then he asked, "Where the hell do chitlins come from?"

I said, "They are hog intestines with the shit cooked out of them!"

You should have seen the look on his face and Sandra told me the next morning that Wendell wouldn't kiss her that night because he knew that she had eaten chitlins for supper.

When I wasn't making people mad from a joke being pulled on them I was working or riding in rodeos. I went to rodeos off and on during the late '50s and early '60s with Billy and Herman. There were times that Floyd went with me to the rodeos that were farther away.

This is when I would take the camper, which was a slide-on wooden style camper that I put in the back of the one-ton Dodge truck. The camper had single bunk beds on each side and a double bed that went over the cab of the truck with an aisle down the center.

Around this same time I started what I called the "Oneco Jump". This was one of the craziest things that I've done in bull riding and pretty dangerous as well. Normally, most bull riders would ease down on their bulls back and start to pull and tie their rope. But I would jump down on the bulls back with both legs going between his shoulder blades and stomach. There is usually a small opening between the bull and the chute which allowed my legs to go through in order to keep them tight if the bull starts bucking in the chute. I couldn't do the "jump" on the bigger bulls because there wasn't enough room for my legs to go down on their sides.

All the other bull riders thought I was crazy for doing this because I could really get hurt. The first time that I did this, a bunch of the other riders asked me why was I jumping down on my bull like that, and I said as I was laughing, "I want my bull to be awake when he comes out of this chute!"

Riding bulls was the most exciting but most dangerous thing I've ever done. But boy did I love it. I rode bulls every chance I could get. At rodeos, when a rider wouldn't show up, I would ride exhibition on that bull. So at times I would ride two to three bulls aside from my own.

Bull riding back then wasn't like it is today. Today bulls are from cows and are of good bucking stock. They are a lot better taken care of and are trained at a young age to be good bucking bulls. The riders are much better than in my time. They start at a young age by riding calves, sheep, and little steers and workout in gyms as well as some doing gymnastics. They also have bucking machines to practice on where we only had the bucking barrel.

In my days of bull riding we didn't use the techniques that the bull riders use today. I never knew to use my free arm as a counter balance I just knew to keep it up and away from touching the bull. Also they lean over the bull with their chest out and their chin up letting their lower body move with the bull while keeping their upper body in the center.

We didn't have protective vests or helmets like they do either. And the bull ropes are made much better. They have a doctor or medical team available for any injuries, where we may have had an ambulance available for us. Bull riders today have insurance and sponsors but I had my own doctor bills to pay and my own expenses. I don't remember ever hearing about sponsors back then.

I worked all week to go bull riding all weekend. But I never took bull riding seriously. Not serious enough to make the money these guys are making now. The entry fees were $10 and first place usually paid around $100 and normally only three places were paid.

Not long after I started bull riding, I bought an 8mm camera and projector so that we could see what we did wrong while riding. Uncle Red took the film and cut the good part out and spliced them on a big reel which ended up being about three years of film on one big reel.

I let Buddy Yochim borrow the film one time to show someone and supposedly the film got burnt up in a house fire. So needless to say I only have about four pictures of me riding bulls.

But I just loved getting on the back of a huge, ferocious bull. The thrill and adrenaline was something else. There are three things about bull riding that will never change. First is that you will get hurt, second is when and third is how bad. I believe within the next 20 to 30 years the Professional Bull Riders (PBR) will be worldwide and the most popular sport.

There were five of us from Manatee County that were entered in the Melbourne rodeo. David DeSear entered in the bareback event while Herman Burnett, Billy Miller, Bill Richardson, and I entered in the bull riding event. The stock contractor was Pete Clemons from Okeechobee and he had a good string of bulls.

Bill drew a bull named Spider which was a cross between a Holstein cow and Brahma bull. He was a real good bucking bull that would catch most of his riders and Bill was no exception. The bull threw Bill off and mauled him real bad causing his chest and stomach to be bruised and skinned real bad.

When David rode his bareback, he got bucked off and the horse kicked him in the back. He was actually kicked before he even hit the ground. Both Bill and David were in bad shape by the time the day was over.

THE DONNIE CLARK

We went to the hotel that evening to get cleaned up for supper and both Bill and David were still in quite a bit of pain. Bill was lying in his bed and said he didn't really want to go with us for supper. David could hardly walk and was limping pretty bad. But the four of us ended up going to supper and I was the last one out of our rooms which were on the second floor.

Herman and Billy were heading down the stairs and David was limping along behind them. David had just started going down the stairs when I came up behind him and gave him a hard shove on his back. He went head over heels down that stairs making a lot of noise which startled all the people sitting in the lobby. He laid at the bottom of the stairs moaning in pain while Herman, Billy, and I stood over him laughing hysterically.

You wouldn't believe what happened after we helped David off the floor. He stood up straight and his back wasn't hurting anymore. He didn't have a limp anymore either.

When Wendell and I rodeoed together he normally drove his own truck. I started working at the cattle market in Wauchula, day worked with cattle, or butchered. On weekends that we didn't have rodeos to go to, we would all practice riding the bucking barrel.

In 1961 and into 1962, I worked at the Arcadia Livestock Market for a while, but then went to work at the Wauchula Livestock Market on Thursday afternoons. I would work in the sales ring where the cattle were auctioned off. Before I started working in the ring, it would take them until four o'clock in the morning to sell 1200 head of cattle, but after I started working the ring we would normally finish by two in the morning.

Ornery bulls or real mean Brahma cows with horns liked to hold things up, causing problems for the other guys working in the back pens. I didn't care how big or bad they were because I was there to get 'em in and out wherever the holdup was. I would run there to get the cattle moving so that there wasn't ever a long wait for the auctioneer to start the bidding again.

They would enter the ring, the auctioneer would start the bidding and before the final bid came in, I was trying to get the animal on out the exit gate. I used croker sacks to pop the animals with instead of a whip. I could pop them as hard as anyone using a small

98

whip could. I mostly used the sack to get the animal on out of the ring by waving the sack at them which would anger them and make them hook or charge at it, like a matador. Most all of the livestock were wild and mad before entering the ring, mostly because they were probably hit with a hotshot five or six times before getting into the ring.

The ring was shaped like a half-moon measuring 20 feet long and 12 feet wide with a solid wood gate at each end. Inside the ring, there were solid boards about three feet high with benches built in for the buyer's to sit during other sales like horse sales or dairy cattle. This allowed the buyer's to be inside the ring in order to look over the livestock before their purchase. But during the time of the beef sales, these benches were never used because the animals were too wild and crazy, so the buyer's sat in the seats up in the stands. So I used the bench boards to run along with the cattle in hot pursuit.

I would open the gate from the inside of the ring for the cattle to enter. By the time I'd get the gate shut, the animal would be at the other end and ready to charge back towards me. That's when I'd wave the sack trying to distract the animal and often times having to jump up on and run along the wooden bench.

With some of the bad ones that didn't want to exit the ring, I would get close to its head and run out of the ring ahead of them with the animal just a few feet behind me. Just before they would hit me with their head or horns, I'd jump up and grab for the top board of the lane with both hands. The charging cattle would then hit my legs throwing both of them in the air causing my legs to reach the top board. The animal would continue on down the alley way to its assigned pen.

I had various job offers from the buyer's and cattlemen who wanted me to work for them full time while I worked the ring. Most of the time, I would haul a load to and from the market and I bought and sold some cattle as well. Several times, I won cowboy hats and boots at the market raffle as I had three chances to win considering I sold, hauled and bought cattle. You received a number if you sold, another number if you bought, and another number if you hauled.

So my chances were better than everyone else so I won more than anyone else.

I hauled and bought cattle long before I worked the market though and I actually worked the Arcadia livestock market for three months before working at the Wauchula market. I enjoyed doing that for some reason; maybe it was the thrill of it, kind of like bull riding.

One Labor Day weekend in Immokalee, I remember the time that I drew Pat Hansel's best bull, "Pa". Pat's dad had raised Pa since he was a calf and he was a Charbray bull, which is 5/8 Charolais and 3/8 Brahma, that weighed about 2000 pounds.

His first jump out of the chute was the worst that I had felt. When he jumped out, his back feet hit the top board inside the chute which ultimately snatched me hard to the right and I instantly hit the chute gate. When I hit the ground, I hit hard on my back knocking the breath out of me.

Once I was able to get up, someone suggested that I ask for a re-ride because the gate knocked me off, so I did and the judges obliged. After I got back into the chute with that bull, I asked myself, "What the hell is wrong with you, this bull has just about killed you once?"

But I tried again and again he bucked me off, slamming me to the ground hard, and knocking the breath out of me once again. The judges were laughing at me as they asked, "Do you want another re-ride?"

I said, "HELL NO!"

That was quite a bucking bull that I never did draw again but he sure was a good bucking bull. That was probably the "Bodacious" of our lifetime because he was so big and strong.

As I said before, Wendell and I were complete opposites when it came to quite a few things. It wasn't just what we ate or getting into fights it was about snakes. He did not like snakes at all so when I had a rattlesnake underneath the seat of the truck one day he went berserk.

There was a woman who wanted a gentle horse for her daughter and they lived on Prospect Road. We had a pasture with horses in it on Gocio Road. I stopped by Wendell's house to see if he wanted to ride with me to deliver the horse.

He was in pain, walking slow and bent over because he just had his appendix removed two days before. Actually, he still had stitches in his abdomen, but I thought he would like to get out of the house, which he did.

We headed south on Lockwood Ridge Road which was paved but real bumpy especially in my old Dodge truck. I was going pretty fast and Wendell was bent over towards the dashboard holding his stomach while bouncing in the seat.

A lot of time I had croker sacks under the seat with rattlesnakes in them along with other cattle equipment in the floorboard. As Wendell leaned forward on the seat his heels came down on one of the feed sacks. The rattlesnake moved and immediately started buzzing his rattlers real loud.

Wendell forgot all about his stomach pain because he almost jumped out of the truck and probably would have if he could have gotten the door open. The truck was old and the door had to be opened from the outside. So he sat back in the seat with his feet up on the dashboard.

I was trying to explain to him not to worry because the snake was in the sack, but I couldn't help laughing at him the entire time. He calmed down a little but was still cussing me for having snakes in my truck.

As we got to the pasture I backed up to the loading chutes taking a bucket of feed and a rope with me in order to call the horses into the cow pens. The horse that I was going to get was gentle and a very good horse for kids but hard as hell to catch.

After throwing several times at the horse, Wendell said, "Give me that rope!"

I did and Wendell caught it on the first throw as the horse came running by. As he roped it he quickly handed me the rope which I grabbed real tight but the rope ran right through my hands. Damn did I have a hell of a rope burn!

It seemed like forever before I let go of the rope and then I started holding my hands under my armpits. Wendell was holding his stomach to keep from breaking any of his stitches open because he was laughing like hell at me.

Once we got the horse roped, she was as gentle as a kitten. We headed over to deliver the horse with Wendell's feet on the dashboard still cussing me about the rattlesnake. Wendell stayed in the truck while I unloaded the horse at the lady's house. I was saddling and bridling the horse for the little girl to ride when I suddenly heard something sounding like gun shots.

I walked around to the front of the house to see what the noise was and there stood Wendell with my whip in his hand. He was popping the feed sack over and over trying to kill the snake. I yelled, "Hey, I could get $5.00 for that snake!"

He yelled back, "I'll give you the $5.00 but that snake and I are NOT riding together in this truck anymore!"

Betty Lou and I were divorced in 1961 which was the best for both of us. It wasn't fair for her to be married to a man who didn't love her. She met Bill Sexton and married him sometime later. I think she has had a pretty good life with Bill and I'm happy for that.

Cande and I became more serious after my divorce. We found out she was pregnant in early 1962 and we took off to Sylvester, GA, to get married in April. Her family did not like it at all that she got wrapped up with me and wasn't at all happy about us running off to Georgia to get married either. She lived with her parents until she graduated from high school in May, then we lived with my parents for about six months until we bought a house.

We had the worst flood in September of 1962 that I've ever seen in Manatee County. It rained 18 inches in 18 hours. When I arrived at the Market in Wauchula that Thursday at noon it was raining hard and Friday morning around 2 AM when the sale was over it was still raining just as hard.

I bought five or six yearlings at the market, got them loaded in my one ton pickup and started home around three in the morning. I was just about to Ona on SR64 and hadn't met a vehicle on the road since I left the market. Those of you that know that area know that it is pretty sparse as far as population and it was even a lot less populated then.

It was a dark, dreary, wet night to be traveling, when all of a sudden I came to an area on the road that was covered in water. I hit the water before I could get the truck stopped and the motor drowned out. I was able to pull over to the side of the road where I tried to dry off the spark plugs and distributor cap and waited about ten minutes. The truck started with a skipping sound at first but soon was running smooth.

I started down the road again and it wasn't long before I saw headlights coming towards me. The lights started flashing high to low beams at me, so I stopped alongside of the other vehicle. The driver asked, "Sir, where are you going?"

I answered, "Bradenton."

He then said, "If I were you I'd turn back because the water up ahead is over the Solomon Bridge".

I thanked him, but told him that I was going on as far as I could go. I actually drowned the truck out twice before I got to the Solomon Bridge. The water at the bridge was only about a foot and a half feet over the bridge so I went on across real slow. With only one car and being real dark with hard driving rain, the entire trip was very spooky. I got the feeling that I was the only one left.

As I passed Lorraine Road on SR64, I had to slow down again as I approached the right curve because there was water running over the road all the way to the next curve to the left. There were cars and trucks all along the roadway that were drowned out and some cars had water up to their windows. Even though my truck was higher off the ground, I still couldn't tell where the road was, I just kept between the cars and trucks that were along the roadway off to each side.

As I started into the left curve just before Rye Road, I could see that the water was getting deeper. I also noticed up ahead that there were some road flares burning and two cars with their parking lights on. I went another 150 feet or so when the water reached my fan and drowned out the truck again.

I didn't have any tools to take off the fan belt in order to go through the water, so I got out of the truck to start wading towards the two cars parked up ahead. When I got to them I realized they were Manatee County Road Department cars. I knew the workers and they were giving me hell for being out in that type of weather. But they did have tools to help me with the fan belt so they went back to the truck with me to get the belt off.

When we got back to the truck the water was even deeper and had already risen up to the engine. So we decided to wade back to their vehicles to wait it out. Once we reached Rye Road, we noticed boat lights coming up Rye Road toward us. When they got to us I realized that it was Clyde Gill with two other deputy sheriffs. They were out making sure no one was stranded in houses along the river near Rye Bridge and they had their jeep and boat trailer parked up the road on SR64.

I told Clyde that I was stranded and he said that he could pull me out with the jeep because the motor was waterproof. By the time we got my truck to higher ground his jeep was starting to sputter. Clyde shut the jeep off and we pulled the oil stick out only to see that the oil was milky looking like there was water in it.

With my pickup having the cattle rack on it, the yearlings were standing in about two foot of water so I opened the tailgate to let the water out. Because of the depth of water and the length of time my truck sat in the water we still were unable to get it started. So the county men took me to Dad's house because it was going to be daylight soon.

The rain began letting up shortly after daylight which allowed Cande and I to tow the truck to Barfield's Service Station in East Manatee. The mechanic and I had to drain the oil from the engine, transmission and rear end fluids because of all of the water.

We then took the yearlings to a pasture and gave them shots for colds. Dad and I were raising cross-bred dairy heifers on milk bottles and a few calves on what nurse cows we had left. We were starting to build our herd back up.

It rained so hard for so long that they were standing in water that was up to two feet deep at Dad's. Because of all of the water and due to them being so young, we decided to move them to Everett DeSear's hay barn about a mile or so away.

We had to make several trips moving them and had to treat them for colds as well. With all of the trouble of getting the calves moved and giving them medications, the calves all died within five days.

I have never seen Manatee County with so much water in such little time. I know, in some areas of our county today, if we were to have this kind of a rain again we would have some of these same types of major flooding problems.

Several weeks after the flood, Cande and I went to a dance at the Coliseum in St. Petersburg with several other couples. This particular day I took Cande on a motorcycle ride which bounced her around quite a bit. Her due date was a couple of weeks away so we didn't think anything of it, until we were at the dance that evening and her water broke.

She did not have a clue as to what was wrong with her. She went into the bathroom with a trail of the Clark women in tow and she soon found out that she was going into labor. We rode with Wendell and Sandra, who were still dating, so when she came back to the table and Wendell found out what was going on, he said, "You better call a taxi because you ain't having that baby in my car".

I don't remember what vehicle we drove back in but we went by the house to pick up her things and then went to the hospital. Her labor pains were still a few minutes apart but her grip on my hand was quite painful. I tried telling jokes to get her to laugh but nothing worked. After about 45 minutes of her trying to break my hand, I left and told her to call me after the baby was born.

Tammy Renee was born on October 29, 1962, and weighed a little over six pounds. Now I had to really get serious with a house, a wife and a kid to provide for which meant most of my playing days were over. Not my jokes and pranks, needless to say, but my rodeo days and stuff like that came to a halt.

Cande and I lived with my parents until we bought a house and five acres from Uncle Donald and Aunt Mary in Elwood Park. There was a lot of work to do on the house before we could move in and we went over in the evenings after work to get it fixed up.

Shortly after moving in, we built a small slaughter house on the property for butchering the cattle. The butchering barn was a lot better because I had electricity and running water. With an electric saw to saw the back bone and an electric hoist to lift the animals up made the work a lot easier. Floyd and Roy helped also but their job was the toughest because they had to dig the gut holes. Oh, how I remember those days.

We also got more money for the hides because we could salt the hides and sell them when we wanted to. Most of the hides were sold in Tampa at the Baker Hide Company. I would take them with me and drop them off as I was taking a load of cattle to the livestock market.

I made several walking canes out of the bull dicks also. I had fun with them because people were always trying to figure out what type of wood it was. Some people would try smelling it while others would bite into them. You should have seen the faces of the ones that tried biting into them when I told them it was a bull dick.

Other than butchering beef for people, there were times that people would call me because they had a dead animal due to lightning strike, cow dying during birth, hit by an automobile, etc. There were also times that I would be called on a dairy cow with acute mastitis. I would cut off the infected tit(s) and inject the cow with penicillin in each of her quarters. If the cow died, I would butcher her for cat meat but if the cow lived I would use her to raise other calves on her remaining tits.

Around this same time, I went to work for Jim Guthrie taking care of his cattle, which he was just starting in the cattle business. He had a pasture in Palmetto with about 125 head of beef cows. It was a good job for me because I could still work the Wauchula market on Thursdays and he would let me off other days if someone had a dead cow or horse for me to butcher.

Even though he hired me to take care of his cows, I mostly worked at his fish house located in Palmetto on 10th Street. Mr. Guthrie bought saltwater fish from the local fishermen and sold them to wholesale fish companies, but also sold retail fish at the fish house as well.

We would go to the docks and load the fish into trucks in order take them to the fish house to get them into the large vats that had ice and water in them in order to get the heat out of them. After they were chilled, we would put them into wooden fish crates. We put three to four inches of ice in the crates first, and then 100 pounds of fish, followed by another three to four inches of ice on the very top and they were kept in a cooler while they were waiting to be shipped.

The hardest work was lifting the heavy boxes of fish and ice which weighed 125 pounds. Mr. Guthrie's biggest sales were mullet, red snapper, and grouper but he also bought and sold trout, sheep head, sand perch, flounder, pompano, drum, and red fish.

His pasture was about two and half miles north of the fish house. Once or twice a week, after checking the pasture, I stopped and bought some bar-b-q from a Negro who ran a small bar-b-q business at noon time. Then at other times I would go with Butch Scizzo, who was Mr. Guthrie's adopted son that worked at the fish house as well, to eat at a local restaurant.

Butch would have nothing to do with me on Fridays though because I made my own plans for lunch. There was a Negro restaurant beside the fish house and they served chittlins and rice on Fridays, with turnips or collard greens and cornbread. This was before integration, but I loved my chittlins.

So about noon every Friday, I would go into the restaurant and eat my chittlins with all of those Negroes. Butch would always raise hell with me for doing this because he didn't want to eat with them which meant he had to eat alone somewhere else. Maybe I started the integration in Manatee County because I was the only white person in that restaurant.

Sometimes Butch would clean some fish and send them over with one of the little black boys who worked with us. They would fry them for us and we would get a loaf of bread and have fish sandwiches for lunch. It was okay with Butch to use them to fry the fish but he wasn't going to eat with them inside of the restaurant.

One day Mr. Guthrie told me to take a fish truck and one of the fish house workers to the train depot in Bradenton to get a load of crossties. At the time, the depot was located along Manatee Avenue at the railroad crossing where the Eye Depot is today.

The fish house worker was a Negro boy named Booney, who was big, stout, and very strong. We had about half of a load of crossties already loaded when a man came walking beside the tracks towards us asking what we were doing. I said, "We're loading these old crossties".

The man asked "Who told you to get these crossties?"

I answered, "Jim Guthrie".

He said, "You just unload those ties because no one has permission to take them".

When we got back to the fish market I told Mr. Guthrie that he better not ever do that to me again. I said, "I don't steal and I sure don't steal for anyone else".

I was real mad because I had no idea he didn't have permission to get them.

One Friday, at noon, Booney and I had to go unload a boat load of mullet and bring them back to the fish house to be processed. With all of this to do, we weren't going to be going home until about 7:30 that evening and Booney wasn't happy that he had to work so late.

Being mad he was dragging ass and it didn't take long for me to get on to him about getting to work. Booney was much bigger than me and he bowed up at me ready to fight after I started bossing him around.

Now this scenario looked good to Butch, so he took out a five dollar bill and put it on a scale with a weight on it and said to Booney and me, "The one who doesn't get thrown into the fish vat gets the five dollar bill."

I said to Booney, "Your ass is going in the fish vat!"

We locked up and were all over that fish dock and I got a real good hold on him. I picked him up and threw him into the fish vat with the ice water and mullet. Just before Booney went into the vat, he let go of my neck and tried to catch himself before going in.

Booney came out of the vat as I grabbed the five dollars off the scale and put it in my pocket. He was completely soaked and was holding his hand and told us a fish fin had poked him but we couldn't see anything so he went home to change clothes.

When he got back Mr. Guthrie dug a fish fin from Booney's hand about one and a half inches long. It's no wonder that he didn't get any more than that, but Booney never bowed up at me again.

One black boy named Joe, who was around 11 years old, would hang around the fish market and run errands for Mr. Guthrie. I took a liking to the boy and would often take him with me on trips to the pasture. Several times he even came home with me to spend the night.

One day, Cande came by the fish market to see me and while she was there someone stole $80 from her purse that was inside the car. The car was parked behind the fish house and there was no way to know who took the money. Then I realized that Joe wasn't around.

About two hours later, I saw Joe and his friends walking down the sidewalk drinking sodas and eating candy. I saw him again, several other times during the day, enjoying even more sodas and candy. I knew then that Joe took the money seeing how he never had any money besides what little money Mr. Guthrie gave him. But that particular day, I knew Mr. Guthrie had not given him any money, because he said he hadn't when I asked him.

Just before closing time, I was in the back of the fish house when I saw Joe standing next to Mr. Guthrie who was rocking in his chair by the big front door. The chair allowed Mr. Guthrie a good view of the stores and across the street as well as through the fish house as to what was going on around him.

Seeing Joe standing there, I walked up to him, grabbed him by the arm, and started leading him to the back of the fish house. As we got to the back of the fish house, I asked him where he got the money to buy all of the candy and soda. And of course, he told me Mr. Guthrie had given it to him but I told him that I knew he was lying because Mr. Guthrie had already told me that he didn't. I then asked him where the rest of the money was and he finally admitted that he spent it all.

By this time, we were on the back dock of the fish house and near the three foot piece of water hose that I had cut just before going to grab him. I grabbed the hose with my left hand while holding Joe's arm with my right hand and started whipping Joe's ass and legs with the hose. By the time I finished whipping him, a bunch of Negroes had gathered at the back of the fish house to see what was happening because you could hear Joe screaming and yelling from a long way's off.

When I let go of his arm, he slipped on some water causing him to skid into some fish boxes. I snatched him up by the arm and kicked him in the ass and off the dock onto the ground. Joe was up and running for home still screaming and crying.

I never had anything to do with Joe again. It's a wonder the other Negroes didn't jump me considering what they just witnessed but I was so mad at that time it wouldn't have mattered if they did!

Wendell and Sandra got married in October. They lived in a trailer park off 15th Street and then they moved to Belle Glade not long after they got married. He was going to work at the market for Pete Clemons.

Dad started talking to me about going in the cattle business with him. There was a lot of land that was available to be used for agriculture or as pastures back then and the county had the green belt law in effect. With the amount of pastures available, Dad was very persistent in talking me into going into business with him but it sure did take some time.

I was making damn good money during this time. I was making $125.00 a week working for Mr. Guthrie, $50.00 for working at the Livestock Market on Thursdays, and on Saturdays I would make anywhere from $50.00 to $75.00 doing custom butchering for people. But my biggest income came from butchering the cat meat which was

$100.00 to $200.00 a week. At times I also worked other people's cattle for them on Sundays.

So it was pretty damn hard to give up this kind of money to go into the cattle business because he was only able to pay me $65.00 a week. Going into the cattle business meant that I would have to quit working with Mr. Guthrie, as well as the market. But I finally decided, after giving Cande a near heart attack that he and I would go into the business on a 50/50 deal. I continued to custom butcher as well as butcher for cat meat.

We named the business Clark Cattle Company and our brand was 3-C. We used this brand when we branded the cattle on their right hip and three "V" notches on their right ear.

The county bought 20 feet of right of way along SR70 from Linger Lodge Road to SR675 on both the north and south side of the road. They had new fence put up 20 feet behind the old fence and allowed Dad to get the old fence posts and barbed wire. Take a guess on who got the job of getting the fence posts and wire down. Of course, it was Floyd, Roy, Tom Harrell, David DeSear, Billy Miller, and I.

Our first pasture to fence and cross fence was 125 acres at Gateway, which ran along the south side of SR70 from the Braden River west to the Division of Forestry fire tower. The other boys worked part time but Roy and I worked from sun up to sun down tearing down the old and building new fence as well as building a huge set of cow pens. I still don't know how just the two of us did all of that hard work to this day. I guess it was just being so young at the time.

SR70 was a two-lane washboard dirt road from Linger Lodge Road all the way east to SR675 back then even though the Florida map listed it as a paved road. While we were removing the fence posts and wire along the right of way we had several tourists stop to ask where SR70 was and when we told them they were on, it they were mad as hell. Most of them were traveling pulling Air-Stream travel trailers and having to go very slow because of the washboard road. We also fenced a pasture of 80 acres on Cortez Road that we called the Cortez pasture which was located where Home Depot is now.

The cattle market was cheap in 1964 so Dad borrowed money from the bank to buy some cows. But he bought more cows than we had pastures for, so we had to buy a John Deere tractor and a John

Deere silage harvester, as well as a feed wagon from a dealership in Fort Myers.

So we then bought an 8,000 gallon used fuel tank, making a bulk holding tank for black molasses. I built two farm wagons with plywood sides leaving about a two foot opening all the way around the wagons which allowed the cows to stick their heads in to eat the grass. I blew the grass inside the wagons with the silage harvester and parked them by the molasses tank and water. This seemed to work because the cows ate all of the grass.

Along with buying these cows, Dad also bought some big poor steers. We put them in the pasture that we called the Prospect pasture which was on the corner of Prospect Road and the old Saunders Road, which is now 63$^{rd}$ Ave. E. This was a good pasture because it was on muck ground. I fed the steers every morning with citrus pulp that we bought from Tropicana. Boy did they get fat on this feed!

We sold them to people who wanted a fat steer to put in their freezer. We let them pick out which steer they wanted and I would shoot and butcher the steer for them, as well as take the quarters to the store for cutting and wrapping.

Most all of our pastures had catch pens which helped us load and unload the cattle. The exception was the Gateway pasture that had cow pens for working the cattle as well as a head catch chute. This pasture was where we brought the cattle to after buying them at the market in order to brand them and dehorn them.

Dad was a big believer in cows without horns. A dehorned cow wasn't able to hook another cow and would be able to go through the chute without getting hung up. And a dehorned cow made her look younger as well.

All of our new cattle were dehorned, branded, ears notched and cobalted as well as sprayed for flies or lice. Dad's favorite saying was, "We're making these cows look more like heifers than the cows that they are."

There were times that we brought a load of cattle to a pasture that they were going to be in instead of to the Gateway pasture and we wouldn't have a place to dehorn or brand them. So Dad would pull up to a lighter stump, which is a dead pine stump that is highly flammable, and get a hot fire going on the stump. Once the fire was good and hot,

David DeSear, Dad and I would get inside the cattle truck with the cows while Floyd and Roy would get the branding irons on the fire to get them real hot.

I would catch the cow by the head as David grabbed the tail and we would shove them to the side of the cattle truck. We both had to put our bodies against the cattle to hold them in place. Once we had the cow in place, Dad would holler for the branding iron or the dehorner or the dust or whatever was next.

Now this was one wild way of working new cattle especially the cross Brahmas. None of us were too worried about the cattle hurting us because we were always watching what Dad was doing. We were more afraid that he would brand one of us because he was always so careless with the branding iron in his hand.

I would go by the pastures most every day to check on the cattle. I normally had my truck loaded with hundred pound bags of citrus pulp when I got to the pastures. I would go to the cow pens and call the cattle as I poured the citrus pulp into small piles inside the pens. It didn't take long for the cattle to come running into the pens.

While they were eating, I would look them over for flies and if I saw any I would dust them with marlate. Very seldom did we have to use horses or dogs to pen our cattle, because the citrus pulp feed worked so well. It also worked well whenever we needed to move cattle from one pasture to another. When we had a real wild one that wouldn't go into the pens, we would just get rid of that one.

The Gateway property had a lot of rattlesnakes on it and I was catching rattlesnakes to sell around the end of February or early March of '63. C.R. told me that someone wanted fifty live rattlesnakes and I knew it was that time of year that cattlemen would be burning off their rough woods pastures. So I went to talk to Philip McLeod, who was in charge of the Forestry Service at the time, to ask him to keep an eye out for rattlesnakes for me.

Within a few days, Philip called to tell me that I should be able to find some in an area of woods that was going to be burnt within a couple of days. A few days went by and the woods were burnt off so he and I rode over the burnt woods looking for gopher turtle holes with shiny white sand at the entrance of the hole.

On warm days with the sun shining, the rattlesnakes would crawl out of the gopher holes to lay in the sunshine and by doing so they would rub away any ashes that were left from the fire which made the sand shiny and white. Every time that we found a hole that looked this way we got a rattlesnake or two out of that hole. We were also able to get gopher turtles, rats and rabbits out of some of them as well.

Uncle Red went with me several times when he would burn the woods off at the Caruso Ranch. He would get down on his hands and knees at the entrance of the gopher hole to line me up with the curve inside of the hole. Most all gopher holes had curves in them, either turning right or left. I would be about four to six feet back from the entrance of the hole, as Uncle Red was lining me up with the curve in the tunnel.

I would dig down with post hole diggers until I hit the tunnel at the curve then I could shove a cane fishing pole or a garden hose down into the hole to make the snake start crawling out of the hole. As the snake passed by the hole that I just dug into the tunnel, I would pull it out with a snake hook and put it into a box or burlap feed sack.

I remember the last time Uncle Red went with me was when we went to the Caruso Ranch property which was along Linger Lodge Road near where Jigg's fish camp was. We got out of the jeep, walked over to a white shiny hole and he got down on his hands and knees to line me up as usual. I started digging when all of a sudden I heard Uncle Red yell. When I looked up I saw him jumping up out of the way and noticed a rattlesnake crawling real fast back down into the hole.

I dropped the post-hole diggers and was just able to grab the snake by the tail before it got back down into the hole. As I jerked on its tail trying to throw it out of the hole I saw the snakes head coming back to bite me on the arm. I immediately turned it loose and the snake went back down into the hole. I began digging on the hole again finally getting the snake out and into a snake box.

Uncle Red had heart trouble back then and when I looked to see where he was, he was leaning on the jeep taking some heart pills. Laughing, I said, "Uncle Red, I see some more gopher holes over there."

He told me that he was done catching snakes and that he was going home. Apparently, what happen was, the snake was out in some burnt ashes away from the hole and we didn't see it when we walked up. But it crawled right beside Uncle Red's arm as he was on his hands and knees into the mouth of the hole.

I caught twelve more snakes in a small area in front of Jigg's Landing and it only took me two weeks to catch the 50 rattlesnakes for C.R. I'm not sure why but I never did get paid for catching them.

The first time I remember meeting Lee Sly was sometime in 1964 when Cande and I were cutting through the woods on a tractor. Back then you could cut through the woods off Highway 64 at the end of Lena Road and come out on Caruso Road.

As we were cutting through the woods, we saw a young boy driving a red jeep and when he saw us he started coming towards us. He pulled alongside of the tractor and got up onto the tractor asking me if I had seen any rattlesnakes. I told him, "No, but then again I'm not really looking for rattlesnakes."

He introduced himself and we introduced ourselves and after talking a few minutes, I wished him luck on finding his rattlesnakes and we parted ways. Once I got to know Lee, I knew Lee was the type person to give the shirt off his back if he liked you, but if Lee didn't like you he really didn't have much to do with you.

People really had to do something pretty bad or be a bad person for Lee not to like them, though. Which is why I'm not sure why he liked me, though I never did anything real bad to him, but I sure did pull a lot of jokes and tricks on him. I was also pretty critical of most of the things that he has done through the years.

Lee's the type of person who likes to do things that no one else has tried to do. His favorite saying is "Can't never did do nothing!"

Somewhere in the '80s, Lee found the Lord and the Lord has ruled Lee's life ever since. Lee doesn't do anything until God tells him to. I can make Lee so mad that the devil comes out in him though. But it takes people like Lee to make the world go around.

He and I are alike in some ways and much different in others. We both have done well with some of our wild ideas but then some of the others were definitely failures but we sure had fun doing them all. Each of the failed ones was always at our own expense too which made it seem worse.

Neither of us saves money...if we got it we spend it and if we don't have it, we make do. Lee cares about what people think about him but I don't. I enjoy life and have fun no matter what the cost. Sonya calls it "Gator hua hua" or that I let my alligator mouth overload my Chihuahua ass.

I have quite a few memories of some of my incidences with Lee, whether they were tricks I pulled on Lee or jokes that got pulled on Lee. I asked Lee for his input but he said that this was my book and that I needed to tell my story the way that I remember it.

Dad and I bought some hay equipment in Brooksville. We mainly baled hay for our cows but we sold some of it as well. We baled most of the hay at Pursley's sod farms in Palmetto and Ellenton and actually baled more hay than our barns could hold.

There was a bunch of us baling hay at Pursley's one day when I had Lee cussing me like the devil. After we finished baling the hay, the boys threw the bales into Woody Townsend's cattle truck and Lee was stacking it. The top layer of hay was about 12 foot from the ground after it was loaded on the truck.

It was late and we were all tired. We were getting ready to leave, so I told Lee to just stay up there on the top of the bales to ride back to the barn, which he did. As we left, I turned onto Ellenton-Gillett road, heading south.

When we got to the barn, Lee jumped down from the top of the hay bales just a cussing and raising hell with me. He told me as we were going towards the overpass in Palmetto, on Hwy 301 where Highway 41 crosses, it seemed as though the top bales were too high and that they were going to slam right into the overpass.

Lee didn't know what to do but he said he was yelling at me to stop, but I didn't hear him. He said that he had to lay as flat as he possibly could on the bales and hold on to his hat at the same time. He also said that his hat actually hit the overpass as we went under it. I was laughing my ass off at him once again and he was getting madder by the minute.

Cande became pregnant with our second child shortly after having Tammy with only eleven months between the two. Our second child, Duane Bret was born September 19, 1963 and weighed eight pounds and six ounces.

In 1964, Dad leased 2700 acres in West Bradenton along the Sarasota Bay on 34th Street West and 53rd Avenue West, west of Manatee

Community College. The lease was for 15 years, but the first three years of it we were only able to use 250 acres because Manatee Fruit Company was using most of it to farm gladiolas.

The acreage was actually farmed ten years earlier and the owners wanted someone to use the land, in order to get the green belt tax write off. When Dad and I looked over the property, not only did we notice that the front part was grown up with myrtles and weeds it was also being used as a dump.

The first thing that we did was put fence up all along 34th Street going down into the Sarasota bay surrounding the 250 acres. A "wino" and I worked for several weeks with a tractor pulling the myrtles up and hauling the trash off. He and I only cleared 25 acres and Dad got someone to bulldoze the rest of the land pushing everything into piles in order to burn. The front part that we finally got cleared was poor, sandy soil. We planted part of the property in Bahia grass and later put some of our cattle on it.

It was about this same time that Dad and I were guests of Leroy Pearson on a hunting trip to Gulf Hammock for the weekend. The camp was deep into the Hammock which took 30 minutes to drive from the paved road to the camp. That's where we parked the vehicles and then it took another two hours to actually get to the camp from there, either by swamp buggy, walking or horseback; it took the same amount of time because it was so rough and thick.

We didn't kill anything on our first trip but a few weeks later, Dad, Cande and I took a horse along with our cow dog, Tip, back to the camp. The first day, there was a man about my age named Richard, who knew the woods well so he took Cande and I hunting.

We had Tip with us trying to catch wild hogs, but all he would do was bay up cattle that day. The next morning we went out with Tip, who I had to get on to for baying up cattle again. But later in the afternoon Tip went to barking, like he did when he had cattle bayed up, so we went to him and found that he had a wild barr hog bayed.

I called Tip to back away and Richard shot the hog. He then handed Cande his gun while he walked over to cut the hog's throat. As he knelt down he pulled his knife out of the sheath and that's when the hog jumped up, though on wobbly legs, he started charging at Richard.

116

Richard was running backwards swinging his knife back and forth at the hog's nose trying to keep the hog from cutting his legs with his tusk. I raised my gun up as the hog was charging but Richard was in the way so I couldn't get a good shot. As Richard kept coming back towards me, he finally reached me but tripped over a vine and fell on his back.

As soon as Richard fell, I shot the hog in the head at Richard's feet. I handed Cande my gun and went over to cut the hog's throat. I was laughing at Richard because he was shaking like a leaf as he was getting up off the ground.

We were looking over the hog as Tip was trying to nip at his ear. I knew the hog was too big for us to drag back to camp so I ran back to camp to get the horse in order to drag it out of the woods. As I was saddling the horse, I told the other men about what happened with Richard and the hog, so Dad along with about four others, followed me back in the swamp buggy to the edge of the woods.

The horse didn't want the hog on its back so I took off my jacket to put over the horse's head to keep the horse still. We finally got the dead hog across the saddle to take the hog to the buggy so the men could take it back to camp. When all of a sudden Tip started barking again in some palmettos not 30 foot from where we just killed the hog.

I grabbed my gun to go check on Tip and saw another big hog that he had bayed up which I killed after calling Tip off. Those two hogs were the biggest barr hogs that I've ever killed with each weighing 220 pounds.

When hunting season was over that year, I killed 18 hogs with Tip and we decided to buy a membership share in the camp. The camp had a total of ten members, five from Manatee County and five from Levy County.

The membership share allowed the use of hunting on the property around the five acres that the members owned but you could only camp on the five acres that your membership owned. We built a small one room cabin to sleep in and the camp had a large building with a large kitchen for everyone to eat and cook in but everyone had their own cabin area to sleep in.

Our camp was soon known as "The Boar Hog Camp". Needless to say, we didn't go without meat, that's for sure!

We sure had a lot of fun at Gulf Hammock and had plenty of pork and deer through the years. But in 1970, the Paper Company started knocking down the Hammock, cutting pulp wood and building lime rock roads all through it. It changed everything and there were more hunters in the woods because you could drive cars right into camp and I couldn't get lost anymore.

I did mention before that Wendell never adapted to the "Clark" lifestyle, and our visit to Granddaddy Johnson's place was no different. One Sunday afternoon, Wendell, Sandra, Cande and I along with all of the kids stopped by Granddaddy's house in Brooksville for a visit on our way back from a weekend hunting trip.

Granddaddy Johnson lived in an old rough sawed board house with his son Alvie and his wife, Thelma. They lived quite primitive back in the woods and Wendell had never been there before. The wood walls throughout the house had cracks in them with newspaper stuffed in the cracks to keep out the cold wind. There were light bulbs hanging down from the ceiling with a pull cord. They had an outhouse for a toilet, a pitcher pump on the back porch that was used for washing and a big rain tank caught the rain water off the roof for drinking water.

It took all I could do to keep from laughing at the expression on Wendell's face while we were there. He obviously had never witnessed "back woods" living. As we were getting into our trucks to leave he said, "I never knew that I married into the "Clampett" family!"

In June of '65, Dad and I went into the seed business. Dad heard that Mr. Swift, from Sarasota, died and that his small seed operation was for sale through his estate. Neither of us knew much about a seed operation and actually I didn't know one seed from another or about how the entire seed operation worked.

Dad mentioned the seed business to me and told me to go take a look at it the next morning. So I met Olin Hawkins, who worked for Mr. Swift for many years, and he had a world of knowledge about the entire operation.

He showed me the combine first, which was my first sight of a combine up to that point. It was an old Massey Ferguson with a ten foot grain header on it. He really went into detail with me on the machine and the operation of it but I didn't pay close attention to him because I knew that I didn't have much time for it besides my interest wasn't there.

We then went to the seed barn to look at the seed dryer and seed cleaner. He, once again, went into detail on what was what and what did this or that. By the time we were finished talking, I was all confused on most all of it.

I stopped by Dad's house on the way home and he asked if Mr. Hawkins showed me everything and explained it all. I told him yes but I wasn't sure about it all, besides I didn't think that it was a good idea at the time.

Well Dad said it was too late for all of that now because while I was there talking with Mr. Hawkins he bought it all. Boy, then I got scared! But to top it all off, he then went on to tell me that Raleigh Edwards had 125 acres of Bahia seed ready to harvest and that I was to start harvesting it the next morning.

I tried to tell Dad that there was no way that I could do that, but Dad said that Olin would be there to help and teach me. And he wasn't kidding…the next morning Olin followed me on the combine in my truck to Mr. Edwards' field, which was on south side of SR70 just before Lorraine Road.

When we got there and Mr. Hawkins saw the field he said, "You're very lucky! You won't find many fields to combine as good of seed as what is in this field; most fields aren't half this good."

I didn't understand exactly what he was saying but I found out later what he meant. With a ten foot grain header, the most you can harvest is about 35 acres of Bahia seed per day. By the end of that day I had the hang of the combine and we had a full pickup load of seed in the bed of my truck.

We took the seed back to Mr. Swift's barn in Sarasota to unload it. The barn was located on Cattlemen's Road where the Stockyard Feed Store is now. I shoveled the seed into the small elevator that took the seed up into a small upright dryer. There were two of these dryers that dried the seed using LP gas at 130 degrees with a squirrel type air blower that blew the heat through the dryers. The seed was then sifted down through the dryer to the bottom and back into the elevators to take it back to the top to go through the process all over again. With this continual process, the seed would be dried by the time I brought another load the next afternoon.

The next day, Cande got a babysitter so she could go with me to the field. We went through the same process and had a full load in the truck at the end of the day. When we arrived at the seed barn to unload, Mr. Hawkins had the seed from the day before already moved to the holding hopper where the seed goes through a cleaning process.

After we got the seed unloaded and into the drying process, Mr. Hawkins showed us how the cleaning process worked. He showed us how to weigh the seed, put it in 100 pound burlap sacks and how to sew the bags with a needle and thick string.

From that point on we were on our own and in the "Clark Seed Company" business. Dad wasn't able to help much in the seed business because he was still County Commissioner at the time and had to look after the cattle due to the seed business taking all of my time.

We would clean and bag the seed at night, but not get home until close to midnight. Most of the time, I would leave around four in the morning because the old combine broke down a lot and needed repairing. I repaired it in the early morning so that the combine would be ready to roll by nine when the dew would be dried off. Cande got to the field about that time to take over the combining so that I could take a nap.

Within a few weeks, we hired a maid to clean the house, do the laundry, take care of the kids and have supper ready for us when we got home. The maid would leave at five when the babysitter would arrive who would stay until we got home.

Bahia seed was our biggest crop and by the end of 1965 the business was doing very well. With our first seed season over, we had more growers for the coming year that committed to having us harvest their seed. They were also willing to have more acreage for us to harvest than they originally had.

My third and last child, Donald Gary was born on September 11, 1965 and weighed nine pounds nine ounces. We were picking up a load of millet in Dade City when she went into labor, so we had to rush back. I told her that I could just drop her off at the hospital but she said no because she wanted to go home first to get her stuff. After getting her stuff, I took her back to Manatee Memorial and once they got her into a room I left to go unload the seed.

We started building a seed barn behind our house in Elwood Park in the winter of '65 with the help from Matt Miller. We installed six drying bins in the back of the barn. At the low end of the bins was a conveyor that took the seed to an elevator that then took the seed up to a holding grain tank for the seed cleaner to clean. The rest of the barn was used to stack the bags of seed.

We purchased another combine, which was a used Massey Ferguson with a 12 foot header. This combine allowed us to combine 45 acres with the extra two foot instead of 35 acres with the ten foot. We found a used two and a half ton truck that we built a plywood seed body attaching a tarp on it so that we could cover the seed when it rained. It wasn't the dump type so we still had to shovel the seed into the drying bins.

Matt worked in the seed barn after it was finished making sure the seed was dried, cleaned and bagged during the daylight hours. Dad, Momma, Cande and I would take turns running the barn at night. Varnell Green, Lee Sly and I would run the combines during the day.

With Lee working for me I picked him up in the mornings quite often and he was truly not a morning person. I normally would be there to pick him up around five. Lee's Momma had a hard time getting Lee out of bed and this one particular morning she told me she couldn't get him up. I said, "Well, I can get his ass out of that bed."

So I went back to my truck and got my hot shot and I walked around to his bedroom window. He normally left it open, without a screen in it, so that his horse could stick its head in to nudge him.

When I looked in the window, I saw Lee sleeping on his back without any covers on so I stuck that hot shot to his belly and pushed the button. Lee just wiggled at first, but then the wiggle got much faster. Suddenly, he reared up with his knees to his belly and started screaming.

Of course, I fell on the ground laughing as Lee came out of the window on top of me. He was pounding me the entire time I was laughing my ass off. From that point on, all his Mother had to say was Donnie's here and Lee was up putting on his clothes. Another one of them "Clark remedies" that actually worked.

Most of the time, we went to the Colonial Diner for breakfast. One morning the waitress waited on Lee first. After his plate was delivered with grits, eggs and bacon on it, I took my false tooth out and threw it into his grits. Lee grabbed the tooth and started scooping his grits into his mouth. I actually thought that this trick would tick Lee off but my trick backfired on me which was unusual.

We decided to use LP gas for the heating of the dryers because we were able to get a flat price of fourteen cents a gallon for the LP gas. We were still bagging the seed in 100 pound bags but we did buy a hand sewing machine to sew the bags.

In 1967, Manatee Fruit Company's lease was up and we were able to get the rest of the acreage at 34th Street. Only 1200 acres of it was farmable because the rest of it consisted of palmettos and pines where El Conquistador is now located. We built a small tractor shed at the end of the main road, along the south side of 53rd Avenue which was a dirt road back then, leading onto the property. Later on the shed ended up being our main operational point. We added a house trailer for a sod office, a shop and paint shop room. We also had four house trailers for workers to live in.

Dad and I were only in the cattle business a little over two years because neither of us had the time to check on the cattle. Dad was spending more time on the County Commissioners business having to go to Tallahassee and Washington, D.C. and I was getting busier with the seed business. It took most all morning to check on the different pastures so the cattle were not doing as good as they were before.

I had to quit butchering also due to the business taking all of my time. So Lee took it over. When I was butchering, I was on call 24 hours a day. Even the law enforcement would call when a vehicle hit someone's cow or horse.

Lee had been butchering for about a month or so, and he was starting to get calls from the law enforcement as well. So after learning that the law was now calling on Lee, I came up with an idea.

I called Lee late one night and disguised my voice telling him that I was Captain Tom with the FHP and there was an accident on 301 south of Oneco. I explained that someone had hit a cow and it was dead.

Lee drove up and down 301 looking for the accident. He finally called FHP and they said that there was no accident, and there was no one by the name of Captain Tom. So Lee called the Sheriff's

Department and they told him the same thing. The next morning I called Lee and said, "This is Captain Tom".

All I could do was laugh and of course, Lee started cussing me and calling me all kinds of names. Didn't I mention the fact that I could make the devil come out in Lee?

All of the seed we harvested, which was Bahia, Pensacola, Argentina and Paraguay, we did on halves which meant the grower got half of the money or half of the seed and Clark Seed Company got the other half. But we really did the hard part of harvesting, drying, cleaning, bagging, selling, delivering and making sure the seed passed the state seed test.

The Florida state seed test requires all seeds to have a new seed analysis test every six months in order to be sold via the seed industry. Seed testing is concerned with two primary test results; those results covering the seed purity and germination. All other items reported by a laboratory are derived from these two analysis areas, and further explains to the consumer the aspects of quality and dependability concerning one particular seed lot.

There were times that we would get a semi load of seed and we would sell the seed directly to a wholesale seed dealer, mostly to Hale Dean Seed Company in Orlando. They were the highest bidder because they knew we were guaranteeing the State of Florida seed test of 95% pure seed with 80% germination.

In 1967, after Lee's mother passed away, Lee married his first wife, Liz. They lived in the same house as Lee and his mother did and I still went by to pick him up for work sometimes. Most mornings when I drove up a light would come on in the house but when it didn't, I would go to the side door to go in to wake him up.

One morning I was almost to his bedroom when a light came on, so I stepped into the bathroom which was right outside of his bedroom. Lee came into the bathroom naked and I jumped out at him screaming. Of course this startled Lee and he asked, "How damn long have you been there?"

I didn't answer him because all I could do was laugh. Lee said, "I bet I go buy some damn locks to put on both doors so that you cannot get into this house!"

Most of the time, we ate lunch somewhere close to wherever we were working. A few weeks after Lee told me about getting the locks, I ate lunch with him and Liz at their house. As I followed Lee into the house he showed me all of the locks and chains that he had put on the doors.

While Liz was in the kitchen, I sat on the sofa in the living room. Lee went to the bathroom, so I reached around and turned the tabs down that held the screens in the awning style windows.

A few mornings later when I drove up no light came on. I walked around the house and noticed the windows were open. I pushed on the screen and laid it aside and rolled the window out as far as I could. I crawled through the window and then put the screen back in place.

I hollered for Lee to get up out of bed and he came running into the living room to see me standing there. He immediately went to the front door, then to the side door and noticed that all of the locks were in place. Of course, I was laughing so hard, I couldn't answer him when he asked how the hell I got into his house. He didn't think it was too funny though, imagine that!

One morning after breakfast, I was looking everywhere for my cowboy hat. A few days earlier, Lee and I both bought identical hats and all day that day I was complaining about losing my hat. When Lee got home that night he saw my hat on the dining room table. He started giving Liz hell about my hat being there, wanting to know when I was there, and what the hell was going on.

Luckily for Liz, Ross, Lee's brother, stopped by and heard Lee giving Liz hell about my hat. Ross told Lee that he was the one that brought the hat by his house because he found it at the diner. The waitress told Ross that it was Lee's that he had left at the diner from breakfast. Lee just knew that I had been to his house probably to have a rendezvous with Liz. I really can't blame him for thinking that because that was exactly the way I was in those days.

One of the funniest things that happened was when Lee bought a used GMC pickup truck that was in real good condition without a scratch on it. At the time, I had a stock rack made for pickups that was light and only required two people to lift onto a truck. Lee borrowed the rack to haul his horse somewhere and it was still on his truck at the time.

Lee and I were both disking the fields on 34th Street with each of us on a tractor. Lee had mentioned earlier in the morning that Liz was coming at lunch time to pick him up. So around lunch time, I saw Lee's red truck coming down the road and dust was just a flying with the stock rack at an angle. Liz didn't realize that by going that fast and hitting the dips or holes, the rack would come out of the holes especially because Lee didn't bolt the rack down.

Lee was about a quarter of a mile ahead of me in the field when Liz went flying by me. When Lee saw the truck, he stopped the tractor, shut it off and ran over to the truck. I could tell he was real mad when he snatched open the truck door for Liz to get out because he was throwing his arms in the air and pointing at the stock rack.

He and Liz put the rack back into the holes but the rack had already damaged the side of the truck bed pretty good. I could tell Lee was still raising hell with Liz as they both got into the truck with Lee driving.

There was a large rock that we had to disk around right near the road. It was sticking out of the ground about two feet and was real easy to see and it was the only rock in the entire field. Well, guess where Liz stopped? She actually stopped about 20 to 30 feet beyond the rock.

I was getting closer to them on the tractor and could see that he was still raising hell. With him being madder than hell, he backed the truck up into the disked field to turn around totally forgetting about the rock. His front left side, right behind the front wheel, smashed into the rock. The rock stopped the truck dead in its tracks and I believe Lee had to get out the passenger side of the truck because the driver's side door was jammed by the rock.

Now he was really mad and raising more hell! He and Liz got back into the truck and took off. Lee didn't even look my way because he knew that I would be laughing like hell at him, which I was!

When he came back to work after lunch in his truck he was alone but without the stock rack. The funniest part was now the cab of the truck and the hood was smashed to hell. I could tell he was still mad as hell but I asked him what the hell happened to the hood and cab of the truck. He told me that while he was driving home, he was still giving Liz hell and forgot about the stock rack and drove the truck right under the carport at his house which knocked part of the carport roof down onto his truck.

In less than one hour, Lee's nice truck was a wreck! I laughed and laughed at Lee and I still laugh when I tell someone about it. I can't believe he destroyed his truck the way he did in such a small amount of time. At least, Liz only did a small portion of the damage in the end.

In 1967, we traded the two Massey Ferguson combines for two new Case combines and had LP gas installed in both of them. We also bought a used flatbed Dodge dump truck to haul the seed in. James Meador and Tom Harrell started working for us, replacing Varnell Green, operating the combines and Dallas White also started. Grady Wilgus worked in the seed barn after school and in the summer time.

We added ten more drying bins which filled up the barn, so we built another barn in front of the first barn for seed cleaning and storage. With the business growing, we had to make adjustments so we also went to 50 pound paper bags that year as well.

When I first purchased the Case combines I thought they were great but our biggest problem was unloading the seed. The Bahia seed would bridge up in the grain tank and someone had to get into the grain tank with a wooden broom handle and make the seed go down to the bottom of the unloading auger. It was a big pain in the ass that we never had with any of the other combines.

The first year there wasn't many break downs and they had fans in the cabs which were better than the old combines where you had to sit in the hot sun. But after the first year it was hard to believe the problems that we had with them. By the end of the season, both combines rear ends broke and had to be welded back in order to finish the season. The bad part about it was the fact that the Case Company would not warranty any of the parts either.

Lee and I had to pick one of the combines up from a field at the Hi-Hat Ranch to bring back to the seed barn. Knowing it was faster to pull the combine than drive it, I decided to pull the combine with the truck using a chain with Lee steering it. The combine header was about 14 foot wide and the wooden bridges, on the dirt road part of Highway 70 were about 15 foot wide from railing to railing with railings on each side of the bridges.

Once we got on Highway 70, which was a dirt road, we came to the first wooden bridge. I was talking to the passenger not paying attention or thinking about the combine behind me and went across the first bridge doing about 30 MPH.

Suddenly I felt a hard jerk and realized immediately what happened. I looked in the rear view mirror only to see Lee standing up in the combine. He wasn't just standing there though! He was stomping on the brakes as hard as he could with a death grip on the steering wheel and his eyes were bugging out of his head. Of course, I immediately started laughing.

But it really wasn't funny because the combine did tear the railings off the bridge. With me going as fast as I was and the combine being as wide as it was, it ended up hitting both railings.

He would often do things that were not the smartest thing to do like the time he tried to throw spiders on Cande. Lee and I were catching banana spiders in some orange trees beside the seed barn. We had about a half of a quart jar full of these spiders and after a while, I talked Lee into putting the spiders on Cande. Now if there's one thing that Cande is scared of, and I knew this, are spiders.

I was carrying the jar of spiders when Cande came out of the barn. Lee walked up to her, casual like, then grabbed her and threw her on the ground straddling her. She was struggling to get up when I handed Lee the open jar of spiders and Lee shook the jar real hard for the spiders to come out. They came out alright, in one big wad, right on Cande's chest. Cande threw Lee off her, knocking the spiders off her as well, while running for the house.

She slammed the back door and locked it. We were laughing at her when Lee walked to the door and called for Cande. Cande opened the back door with a revolver in her hand. Lee was trying to apologize to her, but Cande kept the gun on Lee telling him to get away from her. Lee kept telling her he was sorry and kept walking towards Cande.

Cande wasn't kidding around because she started pulling on the trigger and the hammer was going back. Lee thought the gun was empty, but as he got closer he could see the bullets in the cylinder. All of a sudden, Lee turned around and took off, looking over his shoulder and saying "Damn she's going to shoot me".

Guess what I did? Of course, I hit the ground laughing! I'm surprised I wasn't the one being shot at because I was the one that handed him the jar.

Another funny episode was when there was a bunch of us at a birthday party somewhere in west Bradenton. Cande and I were in the kitchen, and someone began talking about smashing a cake into someone's face which reminded me that I had told Cande that I was going to smash a cake in her face one of these days.

Well, Cande had made a red velvet cake for this party and Cande saw me grab the cake so she took off out the kitchen door. Outside the building, she jumped over a small hedge near the sidewalk and took off running down the sidewalk. When I jumped over the hedge, the cake dumped onto the sidewalk.

Everyone was coming out of the building to see what was happening. Now it's a rare occasion for everyone to be laughing at me and I didn't like it very much! As I was putting the cake back onto the pan, Maxine Hooper came up to me laughing and asked, "What's the matter Donnie, you can't have your cake and eat it too?"

As I stood up with the cake back in the pan, I smashed the broken cake in Maxine's face. The first layer of the cake stuck to her face as the rest fell on the sidewalk. More than surprised, she leaned over to keep from any of the cake landing on her dress as she wiped the cake and icing from her face.

With most of the icing and cake...well...caked on her faced, all Maxine could do was make noises in shock as she tried to wipe it from her eyes and out of her nose. The look on Maxine's face was priceless, needless to say. If she wouldn't have said what she said, I probably would still be chasing Cande. But as I've always said, "It ain't any fun when the rabbits got the gun!"

Now I have seen Cande perturbed, annoyed and all that kind of stuff but I have never seen her so mad as the one time a lady tried to steal our cows. Cande and I had a small herd of cattle of our own beside what we had with Dad in a pasture just east of Oneco where Lion's Head subdivision is now.

A woman had just won a lawsuit and she was going to buy some cattle to keep on the pasture she rented from her attorney. This same attorney also owned the pasture we were keeping our cattle on and we were the only ones using the land at the time in order for him to be able to get the green belt.

One day, Cande and I were checking on the cows when the woman came over to the pasture to tell us she had rented the pasture. We knew then that we would have to move the cows to another pasture but knew that it would take a couple of days. While we were there, we noticed one of the cows was about to have a calf any time but we were too busy the next day to check on her.

This woman lived next door to James Meador and she told him that night that she had called the veterinarian out to the pasture to pull the calf from the cow. She also told him she put locks on the gates and informed him that she was going to keep the cows.

She didn't know that James worked for us at the time and he called me to tell me what the woman had said and done. I was mad but not near as mad as Cande was. She wanted to beat that woman's ass right then and there!

I told Cande not to worry about it because I planned to go get the cows out of the pasture at daylight the next morning. I had seen an old wire gate in the north east corner of the pasture before and thankfully it was almost hidden by some high palmettos.

The Gateway East pasture was only a half of a mile away from this pasture so at day break the next morning I opened the wire gate and began calling the cows. They always came running to my calls, "Come on bee, bees, come on".

I always had some feed for them when I called them. They could see me calling for them over the high palmettos and came running right through them as I poured some citrus pulp on the ground in small piles.

After the last cow was through the gate I closed the gate and then after the cows finished eating, they followed me in the truck to the Gateway pasture. The woman called the cops but they couldn't figure out how I got the cattle out of the pasture. The gates were still locked and no sign of cows being in the pens, or loaded in the loading chute, and no truck tracks.

In the latter part of 1968, Wendell and Sandra along with their two children, Penny and Wade, moved to Elwood Park from Belle Glade. Wendell was going to work at the seed company for me. So Wendell and I had to go to Gene Tomlinson's pasture to combine his Argentina Bahia seed one day. The pasture was a few miles east of Zolfo Springs on a dirt road called Ten Mile Grade. I was driving an old Dodge seed truck that was in pretty good shape except the hood wouldn't stay locked down at times.

We stopped to get something for lunch in Zolfo Springs and were headed east on SR66. Wendell was eating some grapes that he just bought and we were talking as I was driving.

I noticed a white semi-truck coming towards us pulling a livestock trailer. As soon as we passed one another, the wind from the semi blew the hood of the truck against the windshield. That's when Wendell let out a dying scream. The only other scream that I remember being that bad was when Fagan and I almost got killed by the train.

I had to literally stick my head out of the window of the door so that I could see where I could pull off. Of course, as I was doing so, I was laughing my ass off at Wendell. He had no idea about the hood not staying locked down. I looked over at him and he was leaning back in his seat with his head against the back window trying to get his breath back.

He told me that he saw the semi coming towards us but didn't think anything of it until he looked back up from getting some grapes. As he brought his handful of grapes up to his mouth, all he could see was something big and white hit the windshield. He just knew that we had hit the semi head-on and that's when he let out the blood curdling scream throwing his grapes all over the inside of the cab. That was a scary experience even though I knew it was the truck hood. I don't know if the hood scared me more or if it was Wendell's scream.

I said earlier that I quit bull riding and I did except for my encounter with a "Yankee bull" in Ohio. Sometime in 1969, I flew to Maryville, Ohio to look at a used seed cleaner that a grain elevator company had for sale because our small cleaner couldn't keep up with all of the extra seed coming in. After looking it over, I did buy it but I knew it would take a couple of days before the truck could pick it up to take it back to Florida so I stayed with the Elliott's which are some of Cande's relatives.

While I was there, I helped them with some of their farm work. Ralph, who was the oldest son and about three or four years older than me, was running the dairy and the farm. While he was milking one day, he and I started talking about rodeos, and he said that he would like to see me ride sometime.

For some reason, he thought of his 1300 pound steer that he had and he wanted me to try riding him. Though I didn't have my bull rope with me, I made do with a half inch rope knowing that there wouldn't be much to the steer.

Later that evening, we put the steer in a chute that he used for working his cows but it didn't have any side gate to it so we put a pole behind him that didn't allow him to move much. After I got seated on him they pulled the pole out and the steer backed out of the chute and bucked five or six times but then stopped. He was actually too big but mostly just fat and I was disappointed with him. So Ralph started thinking again and thought of his huge Holstein bull that weighed about 2300 pounds that was a pretty mean bull that would try to catch you.

I asked if I could ride him but it was too late to ride him that night so we decided that I would ride him the next day. The next morning we went to make certain that the seed cleaner was loaded and on its way and while we were in town I asked Ralph to take me by a Western Store. I wanted to buy a bull rope because I knew I would need one for this bigger bull.

Later in the evening there was about ten or so people there to watch me ride the bull. The bull was accustomed to being on the concrete floor with the milk cows so when we put him in the lot that was dirt and gravel you could tell he was glad to be off the concrete.

The lot was about 50 feet by 50 feet beside the milk parlor holding pen and as soon as he got into the lot he started jumping, bucking and pawing with his head in the dirt. Ralph knew that he would be hard to put into the chute so he went to get an aluminum ladder knowing the bull was afraid of the ladder. While Ralph was gone I thought I would show off by showing everyone how I could fight a bull. I had performed bull fighting at a few rodeos before so I picked up a two by four that was about two feet long and started running towards the bull.

He was pawing at the ground and shaking his head as I ran by and hit him across the nose. He just snorted and dropped his head like he was going to charge me. After the third time, he came after me so I dropped the board as he came closer. Keeping myself in a small circular motion with my right arm extended behind me on top of the bull's head, suddenly I knew I was in trouble.

I have done this many times before while fighting bulls but I had football cleats on in dirt not cowboy boots in gravel so I couldn't keep my footing. I was starting to fall so I took my hand from his head to catch myself but as I did his head hit me in the ass and threw me about 15 foot into the air.

In the beginning everyone was screaming and hollering but afterwards they said that my legs were going like I was running in air. As soon as I hit the ground I started running toward the board fence ahead of me. There was actually a four foot concrete wall at the bottom before the board fence started that was a holding pen for the cows going into the milk parlor.

I didn't look back until I was in the air jumping for the top board. When I did look back, I saw that his head was going to hit me square in the back. At that moment I thought I was dead because I knew if he hit me he would smash me into the concrete wall. Luckily, I turned just enough to keep him from crushing me into the wall. But the momentum of him hitting me knocked off two of the bottom boards.

My stomach and lower part of my abdomen got the worst of it and the bull crashed into the concrete wall beside me which knocked him to the ground. Once I realized I was still alive, I ran to the opposite fence where everyone was watching from. I jumped the fence and fell to the ground holding my stomach. I laid on the ground moaning and groaning because my stomach hurt so bad. Everyone said that the bull got up right after me and went the opposite direction looking for me.

About this time, Ralph came back with the ladder and put the bull back in with the cows. He took me to the hospital where I found out that I had three cracked ribs and was quite bruised in the stomach area. When I got up the next morning, I couldn't fasten the button on my jeans. By the time I boarded the airplane to go back home, my zipper was down and my shirt had to be left out to cover me. I actually looked like I was pregnant. The next day, I literally looked like I had stood in a barrel of ink from my chest down to my toes.

Now, I have gotten teased since then from everyone. The boys in Ohio would say, "These Yankee bulls are too rough for you Florida boys".

And after I told the people here in Florida what happened to me with a Holstein bull they would say, "A Holstein? Of all of the bulls that you have fought, you let a Yankee bull do that to you?!"

After my return from Ohio, we had a lot of seed customers with more acreage to harvest which meant more expansion to the business. We had to invest in more dryers, trucks, combines and added to the building again.

We ordered two New Holland 995 combines which was their biggest combine they made at the time and they were twice the size of our other combines. Each combine had two grain headers with one being 22 feet long and the other being 13 feet. The smaller headers were used for legumes and the bigger ones for the Bahia seeds. The bigger header could harvest 120 acres per day and the cabs were air conditioned.

Our competitors said that the 22 foot headers wouldn't work in Florida but the only trouble we had, at first, was the larger headers started bowing. The bowing was mainly due to the rough fields being rooted up by wilds hogs and the bull holes, so we built an arch support for them which stopped the bowing.

Even with the two new bigger combines we couldn't keep up with the seed harvest. So in the middle of the season, we decided to buy another combine. With the two that we already had and now with the third one, we still had to rent two combines.

There were several weeks we had five combines running, with more seed coming in than the dryers could hold. We even had to dump seed on the concrete floor, next to the dump pit, stirring the seed every hour with shovels, to keep the seed from getting too hot. If seed reaches over 130 degrees for a few hours, the germination of the seed will drop. Through all of this we were finally able to finish the season which ended up being the biggest season we ever made.

We built trailers to haul the headers on and pulled the trailers behind the combines. We also bought seven new GMC trucks all with different features. Four of them were the best three quarter ton pickups that GMC made at that time. We had LP gas installed in them as well, which we could run either LP or regular gasoline.

One of them had a tool box with side compartments that was equipped to carry all of the tools and parts to the field for repairs. We bought two dump trucks with a special seed body on them with tarps that ran only on LP gas.

We invested in a new American dryer which was an upright type dryer that stood about 40 feet high with a 70 foot elevator. We built a concrete pit with an auger in the bottom of the pit to feed the elevator. This allowed us to dump the seed into the pit instead of shoveling it.

We sold most of the seed right away but still had a warehouse full of seed. We harvested seed all over Central Florida that year but we also had more help.

Our next investment was the two-way radio system which we had installed in all of the trucks and combines. We installed a 160 foot radio tower between the seed barn and our house. We had the base station in the small office inside our house for a while, but later on we moved our office into the newer seed barn. I have to say that the radio system was the best investment that we ever made. It cut down wasted time by about 90% and the effectiveness went to 99% because this allowed everyone to know what was going on all of the time.

The company told us that they would install everything once we received our communication license, which normally takes about six months. Dad was in Washington on county business and was able to get them to rush our application for the license so within three weeks we had our license.

Aside from the jokes and pranks that I pulled on everyone, I worked my ass off in the '60s. Once the seed business got going, I really didn't have much time to play. With a family to provide for, my play was quite limited.

As you can see, my theory in life hasn't changed much even as I was getting older. Yeah, I got wiser about things but I still tried to have fun in everything that I did. If you learned anything about me in this chapter, hopefully it was the same as before... how to have fun, enjoy life and always be happy!

*One of Clark Seed Co. combines, harvesting Bahia seeds.*

*Back row: Wendell Cooper, Ralph Clark, Donnie Clark.*
*Middle Row: Wade Cooper, Duane Clark, Gary Clark.*
*Front Row: Sandra Cooper, Tammy Clark, Cande Clark,*
*Penny Cooper, Edna Clark.*

135

*Donnie, Tammy & Duane.*

*Riding a bull in 1969.*

## CHAPTER 4
# 1970 - 1980

The *Seventies*, in the United States, was still amid war and social realignment. Social movements, particularly the anti-war movement, were highly visible on college and university campuses along with the mandatory busing to achieve racial school integration. But in 1973, the Paris Peace Accords put an end to the U.S. military participation in the Vietnam War.

The country also went through some profound changes in the leadership of the Presidency. First in October of 1973, VP Spiro Agnew resigned from office amid charges of tax fraud and corruption which brought a Congressman of Michigan, Gerald Ford to become Vice President of the United States.

Then President Richard Nixon resigned from office in 1974 due to the Watergate scandal and his impeachment proceedings by the House Judiciary Committee making Gerald Ford our 38th President of the United States. After President Ford was sworn into office, he granted former President Nixon "full, free and absolute pardon" which most feel made him lose the 1976 election to Jimmy Carter.

The Arab Oil Embargo brought widespread panic in 1973 and 1974. It first started when Syria and Egypt launched a military attack on Israel which was the beginning of the Yom Kippur War in October of 1973. The U.S. supplied weapons and supplies to Israel during the conflict, which outraged the Shah of Iran, whose nation was the world's second largest exporter of oil and the closest ally to the U.S.

The U.S. was buying the crude oil from Iran and then selling it back to them as petrochemicals at a hundred times the price of buying it. So the angered Shah of Iran then placed the Arab Oil Embargo on the U.S. as punishment for its decision to supply Israel during the war.

With the oil embargo in place, the price of oil went from 38.5 cents in May of 1973 to 55.1 cents in June of 1974. The New York Stock

Exchange lost $97 billion in value in six weeks and politicians were calling for a national gas rationing program. The scarcity of oil created long lines at the pumps, especially when the Government mandated license plates with odd numbers as the last digit to purchase gas for their vehicles on odd numbered days and the same for the even numbers.

Through all of the crises in the U.S. in the '70s, the nation did celebrate the bicentennial in 1976. July 4, 1976 marked the 200th anniversary of the adoption of the Declaration of Independence.

You can see, things were changing nationwide and Manatee County also went through changes in the '70s. A second span was completed on the Sunshine Skyway Bridge allowing two lanes of traffic in each direction in 1971. Also in 1971, the De Soto Memorial Speedway opened the oval track for racers and the drag strip was opened two years later in 1973.

In November of 1974, the first sewage treatment plant was operating in Manatee County costing the county $47 million to complete. Connection was mandatory by the home owners if a collection line was made available to the property.

Tropicana entered into a business deal with CSX railroad to haul their famous juice north. Tropicana saved $40 million in fuel costs alone during the first ten years in operation.

In the latter part of the '70s, State Road 70 was paved from Linger Lodge road to Highway 675 which made a huge difference in commuting from town to Myakka City. The construction of Interstate 75 was started in 1979 with the Interstate opening from North Port to Ellenton in 1980.

We were still very busy with the seed business and the kids were getting older. We had to expand by adding a larger warehouse behind the seed barn. We changed over to a valve-pack bagging system which was a lot faster and didn't require sewing the bags or weighing the seed.

Dad lost his Commissioner seat and started selling the seed for us. We got the idea of selling the seed to ranchers in place of selling to other seed companies that we had been doing in the past. So we borrowed money on the seed for operating expenses which required us to put the seed in bonded warehouses.

Dad hired Richard Lamb not too long afterwards to help him do the selling because we were keeping most of the seed for them to sell.

But they were not selling the seed as fast as we needed it sold. Between the interest on the money, the insurance on the seed and the lack of seed sales, we lost money that year.

Needless to say with the overhead that we had, Dad and I had a falling out. The aeschynomene (pronounced ash-a-nom-ee) seed was the main cause of it because we really needed to get this seed sold. Dad was traveling and spending money left and right trying to sell it but we were not any closer to getting it sold.

This created friction between the two of us because we were not seeing eye-to-eye on things, so Cande and I bought him out. Momma and Dad divorced around this time and he moved to Okeechobee shortly afterwards to start another seed operation. It actually helped us with him moving to Okeechobee because we didn't have to travel so far to harvest seed in that area.

We got started in the sod business in the fall of 1970 because of an argument with M. O. Logue. He had been cutting sod off our fields at the Gateway pastures. M.O. had just bought two New Holland combines like ours only with 18 foot headers, and we were processing his seed for him.

One night when he brought his seed in for us to process, I asked M. O. when he was going to get back to cutting the sod at Gateway. One thing led to another but in the end I told him that if he didn't get back to cutting the sod soon, that I would invest in some equipment to start cutting it myself.

A few days went by, and there was still no sod being cut in the fields, so I decided to buy a Ryan sod cutter and a new forklift. I hired David DeSear to run the sod field and got him a truck with a two-way radio to help him run the wholesale sod business better.

We started cutting the sod at Gateway but were having problems getting help to stack the sod by hand. At first we were loading two to three semi loads a day, then after a couple of weeks we were loading five to six loads a day with the help from school boys that would work in the afternoons and on the weekends.

One evening while M. O. was unloading his seed at the barn, he and I started talking about the sod business and he said that he would buy all of the sod that we could stack. So I bought another sod cutter and started selling all of the sod to M. O.

After a few weeks we were up to ten to eleven loads a day and M. O. said that I needed to slow down because he couldn't handle all of the sod. I told him that I was just getting started and couldn't slow down. That's when I got on the phone to start getting more sod customers. In the end I was actually selling more sod than I could cut.

I was running into some trouble because the sod on 34th Street wasn't quite ready to be cut and I didn't want to lose my customers so we started cutting sod at Schroeder-Manatee off SR70. That field of sod was the best holding sod that I had ever cut.

We were selling the sod for two and a half cents per square foot in the wholesale fields and we were taking customers from our competitors who were getting two and three quarter cents per square foot. My competitors came to me and asked me to join them by going up on the price to three cents per square foot, which I agreed to do.

We didn't sell any sod for a week and I got suspicious so I decided I would go by some of my competitor's fields to see how they were doing. Surprisingly, they were moving sod just like I was a week before. That's when I decided to go back down to two and three quarters cents. After I went back down in price, we started selling sod again.

In 1971, we purchased two new combines with two 23 foot headers and two 15 foot headers. We used the two new combines along with our New Hollands to harvest the crops that year.

We also started installing sod along with the wholesale business that same year. Sandra moved back from Okeechobee after divorcing Wendell and I put her in charge of the installation business with a six man crew who were American Mexicans. The crew laid 500 pallets of sod per week.

Robert Hughes, my buddy from school, started working for me running the seed business and Dallas White was my general manager of the seed and sod business. We also hired Jesse Cabellero, who had two semi-trucks, to haul the sod for the installation business.

We had to invest in more two-way radios and another base station which we installed at the 34th Street office. By this time, we were cutting sod at 34th Street strictly for installation purposes. But we became so busy that we still didn't have enough sod for the installation business.

There were two times that I repossessed sod that we had installed. The first one was from a new builder from St. Pete. After Sandra's crew installed the sod at three different houses in Palma Sola, the builder told Sandra that he wasn't going to pay us.

The builder met me at the job when I went over to see what the problem was. We walked over the three yards and I immediately noticed the first two were brown and were on sugar sand but also neither had been watered. I told the man that all it needed was watering and that the sod was green when it was brought out.

The last yard was green because the people who bought the house had been watering the grass. He said that he wasn't watering the grass on the other two and he wasn't going to pay me for those two yards only the green one. I told him, "Fine, I would be bringing the crew back to pick up the sod from all three of the yards."

He tried to pay for the green one but I said if you don't pay for them all I'm not taking any money for one. The sod was good when it was laid and it wasn't my fault that it hadn't been watered.

The next morning I took the crew to the house with the green sod and took it up first before the roots took a good hold into the soil. I donated the sod to a church that was just built nearby.

I called all my competitors and told them about the builder and for them to watch out for him. I know that builder lost lots of money on those houses because it took him several months to find someone out of town to lay his sod.

The next repossession was a little later. This one wouldn't pay us because we installed Bahia grass sod instead of St. Augustine. I told him that we have never laid any St. Augustine before only Bahia grass.

Now this particular job had been installed for several weeks and had started growing together so it had to be cut with a sod cutter. I told him that we would pick up the sod the next morning.

The next morning I took three Mexicans with me and as I was cutting the sod with the sod cutter, the Mexicans were stacking the sod on pallets. I loaded four pallets on the sod truck and was still running the sod cutter when a Deputy drove up.

He went to the house and spoke to a woman and then came over to me. I showed him the unpaid bill and told him what I was doing. He went to his car and made a call, meanwhile I kept cutting. He came back and told me I had to stop, load up and leave and that I couldn't take the sod that was on the ground or on the pallets.

A week or so later, Dick Cummings, who was the constable at the time, called and said that he had a warrant for me. I asked, "What for?"

Dick said for trespassing but I couldn't figure out where I had trespassed. I asked for the name of who was making the file against me and it was the man with the yard I had repossessed.

After going downtown to sign some papers, I had to go upstairs and get finger printed. Man did that make me mad! I didn't know that trespassing was a felony. In the end, I finally agreed to not press charges on him for the sod if he wouldn't press charges on me for trespassing. You definitely learn something new every day in the business world.

We remodeled the old drying bins by adding block walls in place of the wood walls. The blocks helped stop the loss of air and heat, which made the seed dry faster.

There was lots of hours being spent driving pickup trucks to various fields tending to the harvest of the seed crops, such as fertilizing, knowing when to take cattle off the fields, mowing for weeds, and weekly check-ups on the maturity of the seed crops. So I got the idea of using an airplane for the seed business. In an airplane, all of this could be done in half a day when it took most of a week using a truck.

I started taking flying lessons at the Bradenton/Sarasota International Airport. Cande even came along on the third lesson so she could get the feel of flying and start taking lessons too; she had never been in a small airplane before.

I introduced her to the flight instructor and she climbed into the back seat of the plane. While climbing up to 2,000 feet, we looked out the window as I explained different locations and landmarks to her. She said nothing more than, "Uh huh...uh huh!"

I looked back and found she had her face covered with her handkerchief and could not see a thing. While I was laughing at her, I looked over to the instructor and told him she would be one of his students tomorrow morning.

A month later, after Cande had several flying lessons, I asked the instructor how she was doing which he said she was doing well and would soon be ready to solo. He also said she was his only student to always check his seatbelt, making sure it was securely fastened and that he didn't have any plans of jumping out in mid-flight. Cande never did solo as she was too afraid to fly by herself.

We also started going to ground school at night once a week. This is a class on weather, flight communication etc., but seed season came too quick for us to finish our classes. Once seed season was in full force, we had no more time for class.

In the beginning of seed season, I hired a pilot and his airplane to check on the seed fields. The fields were as far south as Immokolee, east to Palm Beach, and north to Yee-Haw junction. Dallas, my general manager, went with us in the airplane one morning to check on the seed fields. Our first field to check was in Palm Beach, but we landed and took off in a dozen or more fields that day. After leaving the Mormon ranch in Yee-haw Junction, we flew over the McClure fields off Buckeye road in north Manatee County and I told the pilot to drop down so I could see the approaching seed fields.

By flying 100 feet or less over the field, I could tell what stage of maturation the seed was in by their color. The pilot said we better keep going as there was a rain storm coming soon around the Bradenton/ Sarasota airport. I told him to go ahead and drop down because I needed to see the seed so we did.

As we were climbing back to 1,000 feet and approaching the Manatee River, the control tower at the airport would not give us clearance to land due to the rainstorm. By this time we were almost five miles from the airport and over our seed and pasture fields in the Gateway area. I told the pilot that those were our fields and that he could land there so that we could wait on the ground until the storm passed by.

We landed just before the storm came overhead and it rained hard for at least 45 minutes. When the rain finally quit, we taxied back to the east end of the field for our takeoff toward the west. The area we had to take off was only a quarter of a mile long before ending at a barbed-wire fence. The seed stems were so high that the prop was cutting some of the seed heads off and the ground was pretty wet as well. But with it being so wet that caused more drag on the three wheels and the fender skirt.

The pilot didn't say anything as we taxied to the east and we took off heading for the fence at the other end. Before we reached the fence I looked at the speedometer and it read 40 knots and holding. The fence was coming up fast and I thought the pilot would shut the plane down. Instead, he pulled back on the yoke and the stall indicator start-ed beeping. As we briefly lifted into the air, something caused the plane to shake suddenly.

I looked back out of the window to see if the plane caught the fence but couldn't see anything. I then turned back around to hear the pilot telling us to hang on as we were about to crash. All I could see in front of me was the ground coming up at us.

We were flung about, left to right, finally coming to a sudden stop. The pilot asked if we were alright and both of us said we were. That's when he said, "Let's get the hell out of here before the plane catches on fire."

The pilot turned the fuel pump and master switch off and we were out of there in no time. I unbuckled my seatbelt and jumped out of the door but I felt something move under my feet when I hit the ground. I looked down only to find a rattlesnake under my foot which made me immediately jumped straight up in the air.

This nearly knocked my head off because as I jumped up my head hit the mangled plane's wing. I fell to the ground on my back, away from the snake, with both hands holding my head. I then saw Dallas coming out of the plane in a big hurry, so I hollered at him to watch out for the snake. But he was so startled from the crash that he didn't pay any attention to the snake. He landed on the snake as he hit the ground but continued running about 200 hundred feet from the plane without even looking back.

I got up with my head and neck still hurting and saw the pilot about 200 feet on the other side of the plane. I had to go check out the snake and found it to be about five and an half feet long and real fat. Part of plane hit the snake as there was only a small piece of skin holding his head on. Due to the nerves in his body, he was still moving but dead.

The pilot caught my attention about this time because he was pitching quite a fit. I looked over at him to see him throwing his arms up and down in the air, kicking his legs as if he was kicking the ground and cursing the entire time. To keep from laughing out loud, I headed back towards the fence to see what we hit. Dallas came over to me and said he was going to over to the Forestry tower to call someone from the office to come pick us up.

I saw where the plane broke the top wire on the fence. Then I realized I hadn't even seen the plane and looked back at it for the first time since the crash. The nose was dug into the ground with both props bent back towards the engine. The tail was almost straight up into the air and twisted and turned 180 degrees. The wings were bent up over the cockpit and crossing over each other. The three wheels had broken completely off the plane and were scattered between it and the fence. The pilot's fit lasted about 20 minutes knowing he may lose his commercial pilot's license for landing a plane within five miles of an airport.

It was about that time that Robert Hughes drove up with Dallas. Dallas briefed Robert on what had happened when he called him but Robert could not believe it until he saw it. Robert said he still couldn't believe no one was hurt after looking at the wrecked plane.

We took the pilot back to the office so he could call his brother to inform him of what happened. His brother said not to worry that he would bring a mechanic to fix the plane and then fly it back to the airport. The pilot tried explaining that the plane was beyond repair however the brother remained insistent that the plane could be fixed; needless to say the plane was obviously a total loss. I paid the brothers for the rent of the plane but never saw them again.

After the seed season was over, I began my flying lessons again. I finally got to fly solo. I checked out a plane for a half-day session. I liked flying in the morning since it was much cooler. The instructor didn't tell me I was only to fly in the practice area which was east of the Braden River in the Lorraine Road area. So I flew out east and ended up in Arcadia landing at the grass airport.

Then I took off and flew over some familiar fields eventually coming back to our fields on 34th Street where I landed again shortly taking off for the Sarasota Airport. When I got to where the planes were to be parked, my instructor asked where I had been. He said they had been looking for me in the designated practice area and they were getting worried. I told him where I went which made him slightly mad; he told me I can't leave the practice zone until I accumulate enough cross-country time, so I flew in the practice area from then on.

I decided I was going to go ahead and buy a plane for the business. After careful consideration, I decided the Maul airplane would be a good for the business, because it could land and take off in small, rough areas. I found one in Wauchula and I took Robert Hughes with me to check it out. Robert was impressed by the plane and we ordered a new Maul from the Moultrie, GA factory by the end of the week. When the factory delivered it to Sarasota, my hired pilot, High Price, got checked out in the Maul so he could teach me how to fly it.

Mr. Price had to go away for a week so he checked out an instructor at the airport so I could get started while he was away. On the way to the airport where my new plane was being stored, I got a call on the two-way radio from the office telling me my plane had crashed. Apparently my to-be instructor decided to kill time while waiting for me by flying the Maul with his girlfriend without my permission.

When the plane was fixed, Mr. Price and I took it up and practiced touch-and-goes at the airport. When I came home I was disgusted because I couldn't figure out how to land or take off in the Maul. I kept over correcting the rudders; causing the plane to zig-zag on the runway which at times was so bad that High had to take over the controls.

It ended up taking me ten hours before I could fly the Maul solo. The whole time I was constantly teased by Robert, who was getting impatient as he was waiting for his chance to get checked out in the Maul. But I wasn't about to have him get checked out before me! He had a hard time believing the plane was that hard to fly.

We built a hangar for the plane at the farm on 34th Street. I also bought the top of the line walkie-talkies to keep in the plane which could transmit for many miles on our two-way radio system; the plane turned out to be very helpful for our business.

If Robert and I were too busy to retrieve or deliver parts, Mr. Price would use the Maul to get the parts and take them where they were needed. Many times during the seed season, Robert would fly the plane to Trenton, FL to pick up parts. The plane came in very handy for delivering parts to the sod fields as well.

The business was still doing good during this time; in fact, we were the biggest wholesale Bahia sod business on the West Coast of Florida. Some of our competitors were going out of business. Our lowest price on installation was five and a half cents per square foot and we were making a profit but our competitors were at six cents and losing money.

A couple of the competitors from St. Pete came to me because they knew that I knew most of the sod competitors and that I had an airplane to land in the sod fields. They want to meet about going up on the price and wanted me to get all of the competitors together for a big meeting. After about two months and two big meetings with all of the sod business leaders around, there was a lot of time and effort put into the agreement, but we agreed to go with the lowest price of installed sod to be eight cents per square foot and four cents in the field for wholesale sod.

With the new increase in price, I was making a lot more money. I was already making a profit at five and half cents and three cents for the wholesale sod. This was our biggest profitable year in the sod business. The sod and seed business worked well together because the sod gave us a steady a cash flow while the seed was only a seasonal cash flow.

We were having monthly financial statements done for us and the accountant said that if we show the next six months profit like the last six months he estimated our taxes to be $180,000. He also showed me that I was worth 2.5 million dollars and I asked, "Where the hell is the money because I'm not chewing any more tobacco than I did ten years ago?"

I soon found out that it was all on paper. The money tied up in equipment, trucks, land and everything together was where the money was. In the past I never paid taxes because I always borrowed more than what I was going to have to pay the IRS by year end. I would invest in 100% tax deductible things like spare parts for equipment, fertilizer, additional equipment, and etc.

So here I was, at the end of spring heading into summer with a big chunk of money to have to pay the IRS. Needless to say, my attitude wasn't the greatest because of all of the hard work that we put into the business just to turn around and have to pay Uncle Sam. I was devastated and mad at the same time because I did not want to pay the government that much money.

My first thought was to buy some acreage but I was leery that something might happen to the business and then I wouldn't be able to make the payments. Then I thought about farming which I always wanted to try but never did because of the money but now

I had the money and needed the tax write off.

I decided to bite the bullet and borrowed around $250,000 to invest in farm equipment, like tractors, spray machines and irrigation pumps. I bought everything that I thought it would take to start farming and put Terry White in charge. Terry didn't know much about farming and we didn't have a good crop the first time.

I knew I had a lot to learn so I racked my brain thinking of someone to farm with. That's when it dawned on me to go straight to the best there was, who was Herman Braimester. Oh, there were a lot of other good farmers but Herman didn't have a family and spent 90% of his time farming. Everyone knows that a good farmer is a farmer who devotes his life to farming, and he did that. I truly felt that Herman was the best, and I knew he would be a good teacher as well.

We had a real bad rainy season going on at the time and most all of the farm area out east was under water. There was a group of farmers that played poker when it rained, and I joined in on some of the poker games. My intention wasn't to play poker at all but to try to talk Herman into farming with me. It took about two weeks for Herman to finally agree to go with me to the sod field and look at the ground that I had ready to farm.

We had not been getting as much rain in town like they were getting out east, so the 75 acres at 34th Street was all prepared to farm. We looked over it together but he said it wasn't enough land for both of us, so we started getting the ground ready on another 30 acres along Sarasota Bay.

We agreed on a partnership with the agreement that each of us would put up $30,000 to cover the labor costs and other expenses. The fertilizer and spray material could be paid for after the crop came in. We didn't need papers drawn up, just a simple handshake. That's the way most good businesses were back then, a simple handshake with a whole lot of trust.

The field along the bay was a sod field that was just lifted with the sod strips still on the ground. We were too late on disking the sod strips and letting them rot so Herman put 600 pounds of ammonia-nitrate per acre on it to help rot the sod when it was disked. I had two tractors disking this field as Herman was getting some of his equipment moved to the sod field to start farming tomatoes.

Herman was dating Carlene at the time and Cande and I would go to dinner with the two of them often. About two weeks after our partnership, the four of us decided to go to Las Vegas for a quick weekend trip. None of us had ever been before and while the crew was getting the ground prepared around the bay, we decided this would be the best time to go.

Our stay was seeing the shows, touring the strip and playing the games. We had a good time but when we boarded the plane, I died. I never slept while we were there but I definitely slept the entire flight home.

After we got home, we started laying plastic for the tomatoes on the sod field. While the bay field was still being prepared I decided to get more fields ready for truck crops. Truck crops are normally small vegetable crops where the farmer has many different types of vegetables. After a while, Herman told me to stop disking because we were over 200 acres in field crops at that point.

Our sod farm was looking like a vegetable farm by this time. We grew corn, peas, beans squash, melons, cantaloupes, cucumbers, collards, greens, and eggplant. We used the wooden storage shed as a produce stand and set it up on the northeast corner of 34th and 53rd. We bought a refrigerated truck to keep the produce cool during the day and overnight as well. We installed electric to the shed and ran a water line from a well nearby. Herman said this was the best site for a produce stand.

It started raining before we left the field one day so we shut off the watering pumps and went home. That evening Cande and I went to Buck & Velma Godwin's house for a Tupperware party. Yes...a Tupperware party! That was my first "woman" party that I had been to.

It hadn't stopped raining since we left the fields earlier and I was getting very nervous while we were there. Around nine, I told Cande that we needed to go check the fields and Velma said, "You should stay a little longer; what's the big deal, you might win another prize."

I said, "Big deal? We stay here any longer to win a $25 prize when we could be losing thousands of dollars on our crops and you ask what the big deal is?"

When we got to the field there was water everywhere, almost up to the plastic and the plants. I immediately got on the backhoe to dig out the culverts and break-out risers with Cande following me in the truck for lighting. Within a few hours the water wasn't standing any longer. If we would have stayed at that party another hour, our entire crop would have been gone.

When the tomatoes were picked, they were dumped in large bins on the field trucks, but the tomatoes with color were separated from the others and put in boxes. All of the boxed tomatoes were going to be taken to the Tampa Produce Market with the bins being sent to the packing house. Prior to taking the boxed tomatoes to the market, they had to be graded by size and color, with the grading by color being reds, oranges, pinks and breakers.

Herman, Cande and I would leave for the market at 2AM in order to get a good spot on the outside sheds of the market. Farmers would back their trucks up to the concrete platform and set up their display of produce on the platform, behind their trucks. There was about a 12 to 15 foot wide walkway so that buyers could walk down and see both sides of the displayed produce.

At 5AM, the gates would open with a swarm of buyers coming, hurriedly down the aisle way, to buy what they needed for their produce stands, stores or restaurants. They all paid cash and they would direct us to where they were parked and I would deliver the tomatoes to their vehicle.

For the first week or so, we were the only sellers that had tomatoes and we sold out within the first hour. We were getting $20.00 per box until they got cheaper as more tomatoes came in. After we sold out of tomatoes, we would then go buy what we needed for the produce stand like bananas, apples, grapes and potatoes.

We also had first choice on the outside because while Cande and I were setting up our display, Herman would walk down the aisle and buy what vegetables we needed for the stand. He wasn't able to pay for them before five but the seller would put them aside for us to pick up before we left for the day.

One morning after we finished setting up our display, I went walking down the aisle to where Herman was. Most all of the sellers would be sitting by their displays waiting for the gates to open. Herman was always pulling up his pants so I decided to help him that morning and walked up behind him jerking his pants down to his ankles. There was a roar of laughter from all of the sellers sitting

150

around. He hurriedly pulled them back up and turned around with his face red saying, "What the hell's wrong with you?"

After I stopped laughing I told him, "I thought that you needed some help with your pants!"

I drove the truck back while Cande and Herman counted the money. We split the money three ways, a third to Herman, a third to Cande and I and a third to the IRS. When we arrived at the produce stand, we unloaded what we brought back and set up the stand for the day normally around 7:30 AM.

Herman and I went to the fields to start our day of picking. Most of the time, Herman would go home for a nap in the afternoons. I normally slept from 8PM to 1AM except for Saturday nights which I was able to sleep longer on Sundays because the market was closed. This was our hours and our life for about six to seven weeks.

The tomato market at the packing house was cheap and we lost money on them, but we made money with most everything else. After we finished picking tomatoes for the packing house, we opened the field for a u-pick which was crazy. There was a steady stream of cars coming and going most all of the time.

We had to put in another cash register to keep the flow of people going in and out of the produce stand and had to bring in one of the seed harvesting crews to help us with the u-pick. The produce stand and the u-pick did a great business with people waiting in lines.

For that first fall crop, in the long run, we lost money but we all had a good time and most importantly I learned more in that one crop than I would have learned farming by myself in five years or more. I learned every aspect of farming to marketing.

There are two main factors that I learned the most about farming. First, was to do it yourself. There is too much money at risk; it's like playing poker, you wouldn't give money to someone to play for you. And secondly was the processing and marketing. Though we lost money on the tomatoes going to the packing house, we made good money at the produce stand and the u-pick.

As we were finishing the crop, Herman was moving his equipment back to his farm on SR64 to get his spring crop ready. I had reviewed our records on the fall crop and said to Herman, "I see where you screwed me out of $30,000."

He didn't say a word just kept looking straight ahead while driving. So I proceeded to tell him what happened and how he did it. The way I saw it was that he drew a weekly salary out of the produce account and I was still being paid by Clark Seed Company. And the help that we used in the fields, at the stand and in the u-pick was employees of Clark Seed Company who were paid by Clark Seed Company.

He wrote all of his money off the produce business and I didn't really have that much of a write off. I guess he thought that I wouldn't find out about it and I could tell he was feeling bad.

After a few minutes of neither of us saying anything, I told Herman, "Don't feel bad about it; I'm not mad at you, just a little hurt. That $30,000 is nothing compared to what I learned from you in just one crop. Why did you think I spent weeks with you playing poker, trying to get you to farm with me? In my eyes you are the best farmer there is and $30,000 is very cheap for the lessons that I learned. I got to farm with the best and right now, I don't know if I'll farm again!

I could tell, now, Herman felt as though he got screwed because he thought that I was going to farm big time since I was so big in the sod and seed business. I did farm a spring crop of tomatoes with Alden Guillett doing the farming but lost money again and I didn't farm again until many years later.

But the way I looked at it was, yes I lost money farming but it was money that I would have had to pay the IRS but I learned a lot about farming so I really didn't lose anything. I had my farming lessons and the IRS didn't get my money!

Now it's 1974, and I'm just not the same person that I have been. The economy is going to hell, the news from my accountant is bad and prices are skyrocketing!

In '74, the U.S. had the oil embargo which started the economy going to hell. This got me to thinking about getting out of the seed business and there were several factors that really got me thinking long and hard about my decision. First, the cattle market went down the tubes, which meant that the ranchers wouldn't be able to fertilize their pastures for the seed crop the next year. Secondly, the gas price to heat the dryers in order to dry the seed went from 14 cents to 80 cents per gallon.

The fuel crunched really turned me upside down! It put me into another way of thinking; it seemed like everything was going to hell. Nearly everything was doubling in price. All the farm equipment I had bought, more than doubled in price and it took me some time selling it just so I wouldn't have to pay more income tax.

Mildred Cone bought some of the farm equipment for her two sons to farm. She and I got to talking about the fuel prices and she said it was a bunch of malarkey. She said we had a lot of oil in the United States and even told me about her oil wells out west.

She said for the last few years, they made her cap off her wells because they said they didn't need it. She said they did this to make it look like we were out of oil here so that we would have to pay higher prices for the Arab oil. The bottom line is that we, as a nation, accepted the foreign oil prices believing we were running out of oil in our own country.

Myself, I did not know anything about all of that or if anyone else did either. One thing, for sure, was the fact that I had never seen anything like this happen to our economy before and I did not like the looks of it. But something had to happen with the economy and I felt there was no way that it would be good.

After several months of thinking, I decided to get out of the seed business. I don't believe anyone agreed with me, including Cande. The first thing I did was sell the airplane. Then I shut down the seed business which really broke Robert Hughes' heart. He did a wonderful job running the seed business as most all of our employees did their jobs well.

I can't really explain my actions or my thoughts but my gut feeling was that the bottom would soon fall out. I had no more interest in the business or in making money. Not only was I getting tired of all of the hassles of the business, we had over 100 people on the payroll. But the biggest let down was the news from our accountant about the taxes. I got the feeling that I was working for the government.

There I was, 35 years old and had the world by the tail…now what? '*What*' seemed to be the word.

"*What* was going to happen?"

"*What* was going to happen if the bottom falls out in the economy?"

"*What* am I going to do to get motivated again?"

"*What* could possibly get me motivated when I'm feeling this way?"

"*What* about all my dreams of having a ranch and a farm paid in full by my forties?"

"*What* about my family and my children's future?"

It took me a few months of talking to myself and trying to decide what life was all about. What would I do with the rest of my life? Am I going to do what most people do like working to save for the future of their children and their children and for *what*?

This got me thinking about some ranchers and farmers that I had known all of my life in regards to when they died. I thought they did all they could for the future of their children and all of them that I knew personally, most were worth millions. They lived simple lives, doing without for their children. Some of them died without a good will or a good accountant so the government and attorneys got most of their wealth. So they died working for the government and attorneys. I decided I would not work and waste my life away for the government or any attorney. Life is too short for that!

All my life, I have enjoyed doing exciting things! This was mostly because I found most everything challenging but once I conquered one thing, I was ready to move on to something else.

I never did take anything seriously until Cande and I got married. From 1962 to 1974 I worked long and hard hours. So when all of this started weighing on me all those ideas and goals were destroyed.

I had a habit of making money but a worse habit of not keeping it. From 1974 on, I did half or less than what I was capable of. It seemed I had no more goals to strive for.

In 1974 I bought the Grand Champion steer at the Manatee County Fair. I divided the meat among Clark Seed Company management employees. In 1975 I got this idea of having a raffle for the steer quarters with the money from the raffle going to the 4-H Club and for the Future Farmers of America. All of the clubs in Manatee County sold tickets at a dollar for each ticket and each club was to keep the money that they got.

I thought that this was a better way for all the kids in the clubs to earn money for their own clubs. Not only did the steer owner get money from Clark Seed Co. but others benefited from the sale. Bill Roberts, a local land surveyor, thought it was a great idea also and he donated his two steers for the raffle. I did buy the Grand Champion, as well as another steer this year. Of the four steers we had 16 ticket winners, 16 quarters of beef from the four steers. The clubs total was over $30,000 off the raffle.

But that was my last year of buying steers because the Fair Association said that we couldn't do the raffle anymore because it was against their rules of no gambling at the fair. I was very disappointed with their decision and quit buying steers.

I still worked the sod business after shutting down the seed business. I bought a Preston sod harvester that year which took a crew of four men who could do the same job as 15 men hand stacking. We ended up buying two more machines later on which meant no more hand stacking at all.

One time while cleaning ditches at Schroeder-Manatee Ranch, I almost got my ass bit by a gator. The boys and I were using two backhoes with Gary and Duane on one and I was operating the other. We had to clean out the ditches so the rain water would drain off the grass field, before we started cutting the sod.

Gary saw a six foot gator in a pond near the spot they were working and he ran over to tell me about it. He wanted to shoot the gator but I told Gary to get back to work and we'd get it later. A few hours later, it began to rain real hard so we got into the truck and parked it on the edge of the pond. Soon after the rain stopped, the gator came up to the water's surface and I grabbed my .22 rifle. I set my sight on the gators head and pulled the trigger shooting the gator dead in the water.

The gator rolled over, sank, and looked to be dead. Before we got out of the truck, I reached in the console to get my .22 Ruger pistol. The three of us started wading in about two foot of water near where the gator sank.

When I got to where we saw the gator sink, my foot bumped into what I assumed was the dead gator. With the pistol in my left hand, I reached down into the water to grab its tail which my foot had bumped. I pulled him up to the top of the water so we could have a look at it.

With Duane on one side of me and Gary on the other the gator swung around at me snapping its jaws. His sudden jerk caused me to lose my grip on his tail and I jumped back quickly, moving backwards as fast as I could, the gator started coming at me.

All I could see was the white, inner part of his mouth chomping at me as I struggled to back away. I started shooting into his wide open mouth with most of the bullets hitting inside his open jaws. But before he sank back below the water's surface, I was able to get a few gunshots between its eyes which finished him off for good.

After things finally calmed a bit, I looked to see where the boys had gone. I turned around to find them looking at me while standing on top of the truck! That was a hell of a note, so much for their help!

With my attitude going sour about the economy and the business, my drive to keep working hard started going sour as well. So I started playing instead of working long hours. I would go out at night dancing and partying and not come home until early morning.

I first started smoking marijuana around 1975 while dancing with some women at the Village Barn and at the Grapevine, but it was commercial pot which wasn't very good. Several months later, I smoked some of Mark Massey's homegrown pot. I argued with Mark about the pot that I bought from him for $100 an ounce because I had been paying $25 an ounce for the commercial pot.

But after smoking Mark's pot, I realized the definite difference so from then on I smoked only the homegrown pot. The difference was I could smoke an entire joint of commercial pot with barely getting a buzz on but take two tokes of the homegrown pot and I was buzzed immediately.

One day while getting some of Mark's pot, I asked him about growing marijuana. Mark told me what and how to grow it and gave me a book called "The Marijuana Grower's Guide". I just wanted to grow enough for myself and experiment with the growing part of it.

Believe it or not, the Sheriff's Department gave me the idea to grow marijuana at the sod farm. This was because after several times of them having to come to the farm to check out plants that we found in different places, they said to just pull them up if there weren't more than 20 plants. So I got the idea that I could plant no more than 20 plants and they wouldn't bother me.

I decided to grow some at the 34th Street farm along the Sarasota Bay. I started with planting about 100 seeds in some Styrofoam cups, to get them going. And then I started turning the dirt over in the woods, as if breaking the ground for planting. In doing so I mixed lime and dolomite in the dirt to bring the pH up.

Each mound was on the south side of a tree or a big bush which the reason for planting on the south side was in order for the plant to get enough sunlight in the fall. Also planting around bushes or trees would help camouflage the plants. The woods were not very wide but were long around the bay. Mark also told me to put some small wire mesh around the plants to keep the varmints out.

When the plants were about six inches tall in the cups, I took them to the woods and planted them in the wire mesh mounds. I was still busy with the sod business during the day and could only work with them in the early mornings and late afternoons and only two to three days a week.

One afternoon, without seeing the plants for three to four days, I drove to the bay to check on them. I noticed that Manatee Fruit Company had disked about 400 hundred acres of land in front of the woods where I had the plants planted. The marijuana had grown about two and a half foot tall and was looking good until I saw them that day.

With the disking being done on the land in front of the woods, this drove the rats, which were in the fields, into the woods and all of the plants but about 15 were eaten to the ground. The rats had climbed over the wire and ate the plants down to a stub.

I immediately bought some rat poison to put on the outside of the wire mesh. The poison did help but I had to keep doing it, because there were a lot of rats and it didn't take long before I was down to eight plants.

One afternoon, after working some of the cattle at 34th Street, one of the guys wanted to see my marijuana plants. I took him to see them but when we got there they were gone! That's when I noticed a Deputy's card inside the wire mesh. We both jumped when we saw the card and immediately went back to the truck to get the hell out of there. After that, I didn't harvest any marijuana for a few years due to being too busy with the business to take care of them.

While I was partying, I would be out dancing, chasing women, smoking marijuana and getting home at daylight. My favorite spots were the Village Barn and the Grape Vine which were only two miles apart. When the band took a break at one bar, I would drive to the other bar and dance until that band took a break.

My first trip to the Keys was the first day of lobster season in the summer of 1975. I wouldn't have gone then but Sam Boyette, Robert Keen, Doug Gross, and Tommy Metcalf talked me into going with them. I rode with Sammy and Robert in Roberts's pickup truck with me sitting in the middle. Tommy rode with Doug in his van.

I hadn't been smoking marijuana but a few months before the trip but I did take four commercial joints with me. We left on a Friday morning and when we reached Myakka City on SR 70 Sammy took out a big bag of home grown stuff and started rolling a joint.

I asked Sammy, "You're not going to smoke that now are you?"

I asked him this because I had never smoked in the daytime before, only at night while dancing. Sammy and Robert started laughing at me. At first, I wouldn't take a toke off it, but soon with the windows rolled up and the air on, I was getting a buzz anyway.

It wasn't long before Sammy started rolling another joint. By the time we got to the Bears Den on Highway 27 and heading south towards Palm Dale I was already screwed up and it wasn't even noon yet. We got to Homestead in the middle of the afternoon and got a few rooms at a motel. While we were at supper that night we heard there was a good band playing at a bar called Big Daddies.

The five of us went to the bar in Doug's van after eating dinner because the boat and trailer was still hooked up to Roberts truck at the motel. I felt uneasy about going there in a strange town, but also because I was still screwed up from smoking all day.

When we first got there I wouldn't get out of the van. I told them to go ahead and go in, I would be alright. Finally, Sammy, Doug, and Tommy went in, but Robert stayed with me. About 30 minutes later he talked me into going inside the bar.

We walked in and it was so packed we had to stand along the wall. I was freaking out because I thought everyone was looking at me. I stood under a picture that was hanging on the wall just above my head and felt a little better. This made me think that they were looking at the picture instead of me. I was really screwed up and knew that I needed to get to dancing to get the buzz off.

So I told Robert that I was going to dance and headed towards the bar. I saw this blonde haired person and tapped on their shoulder to ask if they wanted to dance. The person looked around at me and I saw that it was Doug. He was laughing at me and said, "No Donnie I'm not going to dance with you."

After asking about four or five women, I finally got one to dance with me. After dancing the first dance, I didn't need to ask anymore because they were all asking me to dance. This Negro woman kept asking me to dance more than the other women and she actually danced pretty good. She told me that I danced more like a black person then a white person.

I barely got to sleep when everyone got up to go eat breakfast and diving for lobsters for the day. We went to Key Largo the next morning to a marina called Alabama Jack. We met up with Charles Coker and Tom Parks. Charles was from Manatee County and I went to school with him, but he worked at the power plant in Key Largo. He knew the water well and where to catch lobster. Tom was from Oneco and I knew him and his family.

We left the marina in two boats following Charles in his boat. We were headed to a sunken barge that he knew had some lobster. Robert and I already had our fins, masks and snorkel on when we reached the barge. Once we got there, we dropped anchor and Robert and I swam over to the barge, which was in ten feet of water.

Robert and I dove down and grabbed the side of it to pull ourselves on down to get a good look underneath for lobsters. What a shock we had...we came face to face with a six foot sand shark. The sight of the shark scared us at first until we realized it didn't move.

We had to go back up to the surface to get air. As we surfaced we pulled our masks up so that we could talk. We saw Sammy swimming towards us and I hollered real loud to Sammy so that everyone heard, "There are lots of lobsters down here".

Sammy pulled his mask down and swam down to the barge. Robert and I did the same, but stayed on top of the water just to watch Sammy when he looked under the barge to see the lobster only to see the shark. As his head went under the barge, there was an explosion of bubbles coming up at us from Sammy's obvious shock when he saw the shark.

We immediately saw Sammy swimming up to the surface as fast as he could and as soon as he got to the surface he jerked off his mask and yelled "Shark!"

He was swimming towards the boat as fast as he could. Tom was in the water also and was swimming towards us when Sammy yelled. But he turned back towards the boat and jumped back into it throwing his mask off saying, "That's it! I'm not going back into that water again".

Robert and I had to lie on our back to keep from swallowing a lot of water because we were laughing at them so hard. Sand sharks are not aggressive but that didn't matter to the rest of them. All they knew was that a shark was there and that scared the shit out of them.

All day we dove, smoked joints and ate all the food we brought with us. We stayed out on the water all day Saturday until almost dark because we were heading back home on Sunday. We didn't get a lot of lobster that day but Doug was able to get quite a few fish for his aquarium.

We left the next morning to go home and I was completely exhausted from the lack of sleep and smoking too much marijuana. What a short but long weekend we had. Of course, they all got a lot more sleep than I did.

We went scalloping a few times over the summer at Tarpon Springs and rented a boat. After renting one several times, I decided I would like to have my own boat. So in the late summer of 1975, I bought a new Dyno-Glass 22 foot tri-hull with a 185 horsepower inboard-outboard motor. The first week I had it, I went through five propellers from hitting sand bars. After two weeks of owning it, I soon learned how to operate it and learned which side of the channel markers to be on.

I installed one of our company's two way radios so when we were out I could keep up with what was going on in the business. The boat also had a dive platform on the back for scuba diving which we did a lot in the keys.

The first time I took the family to the Keys was around 1976 on the first day of lobster season. We stayed at efficiencies on Marathon Island that had a dock for boats. We stayed two weeks and had a really good time. We fished on both sides of Marathon, the Atlantic and the Gulf. We dove with scuba gear for lobster on the Gulf side and snorkeled on the Atlantic side. We looked at coral reefs, spear fished hog snapper and caught queen conks to make conk chowder.

The boat lasted better than two years and was something that the whole family enjoyed. In the end the boat definitely looked used with dents, scrapes and totally worn out.

Even though I tried to take time to play or relax, the sod business was still going. From 1974 to 1979, the 34th Street property was mostly used to grow sod. With me being burnt out on the economy and in the back of my mind wanting to retire in my forties with my own ranch, I was able to get an opportunity when John Anderson visited us from Ohio. He was in real estate and asked if I knew where he might be able to buy some property.

Mr. Homer Hyatt, who was working for us in the sod business, was rotovating the fields of sod that we had already cut. At times when I would stop to talk to him, he would bring up the subject about me buying his ranch in Myakka City. I kept telling him that I didn't have enough capital to take on the ranch and all of the expenses.

But when John came looking for property, I thought of Mr. Hyatt. So I called him one night and told him that I had someone who would like to look at the ranch and asked if he could meet us there the next morning.

Mr. Hyatt was from South Dakota and bought the ranch in 1969 but made several mistakes with it. He didn't have any income coming in off it and also had his wife and mother who were both bed-ridden at his home in Sarasota. He was working for us to try to make ends meet. He needed to get rid of the ranch and expenses.

We rode over the ranch knowing we didn't have the money to purchase it. But I said that I could put money into the ranch using it as a sod farm and be able to pay for it with the money from the sod. Mr. Hyatt said that he would sell us the 638 acres with a lease option.

The terms were that I would give him $1,000 to start with and make his annual bank payments of $5,700 plus the ranch taxes every year. It was a 15 year lease option with no interest at a $1,000 per acre. Also Mr. Hyatt was to get $1.00 per pallet of sod that was cut from the ranch, which was to be applied to the purchase price; the annual bank payment was also applied to the purchase price.

In other words, all monies paid to Mr. Hyatt went toward the purchase price, except the ranch taxes and his weekly wages. John drew up the contract on the lease option and within a few days was signed by all parties. Cande and I were fifty-fifty with John on the ranch deal. If it wasn't for John we wouldn't have known how to go about purchasing the land with hardly any money down.

I put Mr. Hyatt in charge of preparing the land for growing the sod. It took several months of disking to kill all of the existing grasses before planting the Argentina Bahia grass seed for sod. We spent a lot of weekends picking up palmetto roots, lighter knots and pulling up the pine trees and burning it all.

I had a dragline dig a small pond about 250 feet long by 60 feet wide and about 15 foot deep. I also had three drainage ditches dug with each being about ¾ mile long running north and south. I had to stop on the third ditch because I had already spent $30,000 that first year and only planted 100 acres of seed.

After several of months of working on the Myakka ranch, Cande bought two double wide house trailers that were more hulls. We put one at the Myakka ranch to store the seed in for planting the sod fields, with the other one taken to 34th street for a bigger office.

Varnell and Yvonne Green drilled a four inch well and installed an electrical pump for the well for the double-wide at the ranch. It wasn't until after we had constructed the tall barn south of the trailer at the Myakka ranch that we moved the other trailer from 34th to Myakka alongside of the sister trailer. I then had a hallway built to connect the two trailers.

It was starting to look like home with two trailers 40 feet by 60 feet each. One had bedrooms, a bathroom, and a pool table with the other having a back bathroom, large kitchen, and a living room. Then a porch was added on the front that was 20 feet by 60 feet with a four foot overhang and a back porch that was 20 feet by 20 feet complete with picnic benches along the outside. The trailer setup made for good ranch-style living.

In the summer of 1978, there was an increase in the building trade but a steady decrease in the cattle market. With the decrease in sales at the cattle markets, the sod on the ranches was getting bad as well. Due to the lack of fertilizer on the Bahia pastures, the sod would not lift. I always kept about 500 or 600 acres of sod that was ready to lift at any time. This was because if a field that we may have lifting problems, such as mole crickets, field being too wet or too dry; I would have other fields ready to lift. I always tried to have sod for the customers.

I started thinking and came up with an idea of preparing the ranches Bahia grass for sod. The cattle market was starting to rise again so the ranchers had the funds to buy the fertilizers and I put my plan in motion to start doing some research with the ranchers, the builders and other sod competitors.

My idea was to control the market of Bahia sod over the next one and a half to two years by getting the ranchers to agree to fertilize their pastures to enhance the lifting of the sod with an agreement to pay them a half of a cent more than my competitors were willing to pay. At the time, everyone was paying one and a half cent per square foot so with me being willing to pay the extra to the ranchers sounded good to them.

I began talking to attorneys and bankers to help me look for loop holes in my plan because I felt like this plan was too good to be true. Then I started talking with the builders and explained the sod situation being so bad due to the depressed cattle market but that I was getting enough sod ready to supply the builders for the next one to two years. The builder's concern was the price because they were not willing to pay an increase for the sod.

But with FHA doing most of the financing at the time and their requirements of sod being laid in the front yard, the sides and about ten foot of the back before a final inspection is issued, I knew that the builders would have to pay whatever the prices were for the sod or they wouldn't get the final inspection. My only answer to the builders regarding the cost of sod was that it all depended on how much the building was going to increase the supply and demand.

Next I began making deals with the ranchers in four counties, Manatee, Sarasota, Hardee and DeSota. The way my plan was to work was if a rancher had 100 acres already being lifted by one of my competitors I had the rancher fertilize an additional 100 acres for me to lift when it was ready. My competitors didn't realize that the other acreage was for me. So with me doing this with some of the ranchers in the four counties, I had quite a bit of land being prepared.

For my plan to work, the sod had to be ready for the market in a short time so I spent most of my time during the day working the four counties making sure the sod was being prepared. Timing was critical for what needed to be done and I needed to be available at all times.

So I placed an order for a four wheel drive van that Ford just came out with for me to use as a mobile office. I had it customized by having the roof raised three feet so that I could stand up in it with a bedroom in the back. Between the bedroom and the rear bucket seats was a sink and refrigerator with cabinets overhead and below. Between the rear seats and the front bucket seats were roll up maps of the four counties attached to the ceiling of the van. There was also an electric winch mounted on the front end, our two-way radio system and a telephone installed.

The entire time that all of my plans were going in motion I was still searching for any information or reason why this plan wouldn't work. This was the only idea that I ever had that everyone who I talked to couldn't find a flaw in. I was getting a lot offers for partnerships but I turned them all down by simply saying that I was going to ride this bull by myself. I felt like this plan was like riding a bull to me, real exciting but dangerous! If I made the whistle I could make around $30-$50 million dollars but if I got bucked off I could lose probably $250,000.

On top of all of this, came the equipment that was needed to harvest the sod so I started with renting a vibrator roller to smooth out the fields running 24 hours a day. I signed a contract with a deposit on eight new sod harvesters to be delivered, two at a time, with Preston Manufacturing Company out of Ohio. Then I ordered 15 Case forklifts without a contract or deposit to be picked up on certain dates.

I had options to buy two ranches which had over 60% Bahia grass on them already and I thought I would save this sod for when the prices were at their peak. Once at their peak, I would sell the ranches as sod investments after I lifted the sod and had it replanted.

I also kept a close eye on my competitor's sod fields knowing that when the time came they would have to buy sod from us. Because they didn't know of the deal that I had with the ranchers where they were cutting sod at, they would be out of sod.

There wasn't a day that went by that I didn't think of what could happen to my plan. I never had an idea that didn't fail somewhere, but everything was going along as planned. Some of the fields were almost ready to harvest and some of my competitors were running out of sod, so they had to come to me to buy my sod, just as I thought.

Just weeks before the delivery of the first two sod harvesters, the company called me to tell me that the harvesters were ready for delivery except for the three-way hydraulic control valves. There were three valves that were involved in the hydraulic control panel. One ran the sod cutter, another ran the cutter head lift up and down and the third one started and stopped the elevator that carried the sod to the pallet. They told me that there weren't any valves to be found and that the manufacturer of the valves said it would take a month or more to make more.

My first thought was, "This is it! This is what was going to go wrong with my plan!"

Then my second thought was about the ranchers who, from the beginning, I wanted to make sure they didn't lose also. I had three harvesters but there was no way I could harvest all the sod that needed harvesting with just three.

Looking back now, I should have got an attorney and sued the Preston Company for breach of contract. Then I should have bought some Brower harvesters which were cheaper but couldn't produce what the Preston's could have.

So in the long run, I lost control of the sod deal and everyone made out but me. But I didn't lose much money and it was the most exciting business adventure that I had gotten into. Excitement and having fun has always cost me through the years; some more than others. The bottom line is I bucked off the bull before the whistle but had a great ride!

In '79 we quit the installation business and sold the sod harvesters and forklifts to Desoto Sod Company in Arcadia. I did keep one forklift and the sod cutters for the Myakka ranch. I was burnt out and didn't want to work for the government anymore.

I started cutting sod at the Myakka ranch, where I was living at the time, and started about another 100 marijuana seeds in cups. The only place to plant them was just south of the trailers where there was a small sand scrub with palmettos and taller scrub oaks.

I had a lot of trouble with these plants due to the lack of sunshine because I had to plant them in areas where there were trees to keep them hid. And I had to water them every day due to the sandy soil. The lack of sunshine made the plants grow tall and straggly but I did get to harvest the first set of plants. Because of the conditions only 15 out of the 100 survived, which reaped only three and a half pounds of good pot.

Somewhere in the summer of 1979, Mark Massey asked if he could use my farm for his pilots to practice taking off and landing with his twin engine airplane as well as practice parachuting. The purpose for his practice was for smuggling cocaine in from other countries.

I was told that parachuting was hard to do without having a side door on an airplane. The plan was for the parachutist to practice jumping out as if he had fifty pounds of cocaine on his back before the plane landed and went through customs in Tampa. They packed him with fifty pounds of weight when he did his practice jump.

I wasn't at the farm the day the two pilots, who were also parachutists, did their practice jumps but was told later what happened. The two pilots were taking turns jumping, so when one of them jumped and was free-falling, the other one was preparing to land the plane. On the last attempt, after the one jumped, the pilot forgot to put the landing gear down and he landed the plane on its belly and bent the two props.

Mark had to have a crane brought out to lift the plane up in order to get the landing gear down but had to wait several days for the new props to arrive. While waiting on the props, it started raining and rained for several days so we had water standing all over the farm.

There was only one dry spot on the air strip which was about 600 to 700 feet long. After replacing the props, they tried taking off in the plane but couldn't because of the lack of runway without water.

Somehow the FAA found out about a plane crashing in the Myakka area and was looking for the plane. I was leaving one of our sod fields off Sugar Bowl Road at the IMC Ranch, when the FAA people stopped me to ask if I had seen a plane go down around the area.

Like a dummy, I said no but there was one that went down at my farm on Wauchula Road. They asked how to get there and, again like a dummy, I told them to follow me. I was in one of our transport trucks hauling sod equipment back to the farm and while I was driving with them following me, I got to thinking about what I just did.

Here I was bringing the FAA and the law back to the farm where I had all of the marijuana seedlings in pots as well as a six foot tall marijuana plant in the front yard right beside a huge rock that I hauled in from the 34th Street sod fields.

Eva, Grady Wilgus' wife, was at the trailer, so I called her on the two-way to have her hide the plants that were in the pots and explained that the law was following me back to the farm.

When we arrived at the trailer, the men started going over the plane, which was parked between the trailer and the barn. They were so focused on the plane that they never looked in the direction of the big marijuana plant. For several weeks after that, the law staked out the farm thinking that I was landing drugs. I never got involved in the drug smuggling business but they sure thought that I was.

On a hot summer afternoon in '78, Cande and the kids were swimming in the pond at the farm. I was mowing the sod fields when I decided I'd join them for a swim. I parked the tractor on the opposite bank from them, took off my boots and clothes, and dove into the water naked.

After playing around with them for about half an hour, I cooled off and swam back to the other bank to go back mowing again. As I was about to reach the bank, I felt something brush my back. I looked backwards and immediately counted the heads to find they were all there as I thought Gary or Duane was messing with me.

I felt the bottom and started wading up the slope of the bank and felt the same thing brush along my back once more. I had both my arms behind me feeling for whatever it was and then it hit me. Something grabbed my little peter and was pulling and shaking on it and then I started feeling its teeth.

Boy did I come out of that water fast and whatever it was finally let go. As I was holding little 'pete', yelling, hollering and running around in circles, the others jumped out of the pond and ran over to me. I finally stopped running around in circles so we could get a look at what happened.

There was a small bit of blood oozing from the bite and they all started laughing at me. If it hadn't happened to me, I'd be laughing up a storm too. I think it was either a bass or a catfish, but for sure it was a peter eater. That was the last time I went skinny dipping.

We had several family reunions at the farm probably starting around 1978. With the ponds and all of the land this made for a lot of room for everyone to have a good time.

During this Thanksgiving gathering Cande was talking with my cousin, Donna Lou's husband, Johnny Jones about growing watermelons. He and his family grew melons in Trenton, FL. And he was looking to grow a crop further south and I had just lifted sod from forty acres around the pond which was all the ground that I had that could be farmed.

Cande asked me if they could use the acreage to grow melons on which I told her yes but there wasn't a well to use for water and the pond didn't have enough water for the forty acre crop. But Johnny said that they had grown melons up in their neck of the woods without water. I always learned through Herman that you couldn't grow a good crop without water so I was against the idea of growing the crop with the Jones' altogether.

With Cande being insistent, I told her that I wasn't having anything to do with the farming part of it but if they actually produced a crop that I would help harvest it. So their plan was for the Jones' to come down after the first of the year to start preparing the ground.

Unlike the previous years, I did work a lot in the beginning of the '70s but I took more time to vacation, relax and always had good times. But during these years I also had a lot of melt downs. The fuel crisis really hit me hard and then the IRS tax bullshit really put me in a tailspin.

I didn't have the drive anymore to do anything other than destroy myself and my future. Oh, I still had good times no matter what I did and definitely no matter what the cost was. I made a lot of money in these years but lost it and most everything else because of my lack of motivation.

I was definitely on the wrong track from here on but I couldn't get myself back to where I needed to be or where I could have been. From working long hours to partying all night, I was on the fast track to self-destruction but, as you know by now, I always had a good time!

*Donnie buying the Grand Champion Steer from Connie Bailey.*

*Donnie and Cande Clark with*
*Herman and Carleen Brameister in Las Vegas.*

*Donnie's mobile 4 X 4 van.*

*Sandra & Duane Rawls wedding.*
*Back Row: Ralph Clark, Duane Rawls, Donnie Clark.*
*Middle Row: Edna Clark, Sandra Rawls, Cande Clark.*
*Front Row: Gary Clark, Wade Cooper, Penny Cooper,*
*Tammy Clark, Duane Clark.*

170

*Priscilla Whisenant, Grand Champion Steer bought by Clark Seed Co., Donnie Clark.*

## CHAPTER 5
# 1980 - 1990

The **Eighties** in the United States, saw social, economic and general change. A lot of countries faced economic and social difficulties as they suffered multiple debt crises requiring many to apply for financial assistance. Major civil discontent and violence occurred in the Middle East including the Iran-Iraq War.

The '80s signaled the start of the computer age with the birth of the IBM Personal Computer (PC) and with this came video games. Another technology that was just starting was the cellular mobile phones. In the beginning the phones were big and heavy and hit and miss for signal strength. But in time, as with the computers, it evolved into a much larger and stronger way of life.

More research was being done on the effects of global warming through population growth and land clearing of rain forests for agriculture and logging. They also were looking at the increased use of fossil fuel for power generation.

A sad day in our history was, January 28, 1986, when the shuttle Challenger exploded 74 seconds after liftoff at Cape Canaveral killing all seven astronauts on board. Christa McAuliffe, who was to be the first teacher in space, was one of the seven on board.

The Reagan Administration accelerated the War on Drugs. Drugs became a serious problem with cocaine being most popular with celebrities and the young. Crack, a cheaper and more potent offshoot of cocaine, turned the inner cities into war zones.

Manatee County was growing in population with subdivisions being built east of the interstate. Braden Woods and Braden Pines were the beginning of the country out east disappearing. A lot of the roads were being widened and/or paved due to the population growth. Interstate 75 opened from Ellenton north to SR672 in 1982 allowing further interstate traveling.

On May 9, 1980 a freightliner rammed into the Sunshine Skyway bridge during a blinding spring storm. The accident knocked out a 1200 foot length of the bridge across the mouth of Tampa Bay. Thirty-five people, most of them in a Greyhound Bus, plunged 150 feet to their deaths. The accident was one of the worst bridge accidents in U.S. history. Construction of the current bridge began in 1982 and was completed on February 7, 1987.

With Tropicana being sold in the '70s to Beatrice Foods, they had more financial resources to develop more products. In 1985, Tropicana debuted their pure premium Home Style juice which featured added pulp.

I was still living at the ranch in Myakka and still on a self-destruction path. I spent a lot of time partying and dipping into more drugs. I just couldn't seem to get my life back on track.

With that said, a few years are left out here and there in this chapter. This wasn't intentional; it was simply because I can't remember what happened, due to the intensive amount of partying and drugs.

But the boys and I did some type of farming all throughout the '80s like sod, hay, watermelons, tomatoes, cabbage and cucumbers. At times I leased some pasture land to Farren Dakin, Danny Overstreet and Dewey Oren for their cattle.

At the end of 1979, I started to build a dirt bike and three-wheeler track at the ranch. Shortly afterwards, I got to thinking about making an entertainment park. It would be something that I hadn't done before and at the time it seemed like it would be fun and make some money also.

My thought was with the bike tracks there, I would then have a sky-diving area, then a hog catch and later on a rodeo, a mud-bogging track with maybe an airboat track. My plan was to do a little at a time because most of the ranch was planted in Argentina-Bahia grass for the sod farm.

In January, the Jones' came down, as planned, to get the ground prepared and brought their semis pulling flatbed trailers loaded with their equipment. I was busy getting the entertainment park going, so I really didn't help other than building a dirt ramp for them to unload their tractors and other equipment.

By the time they planted the melons, I was finished with the park and it was getting real dry. The melons were not looking very good due to the lack of water. It wasn't long before the Jones' brought a walking water gun with a trailer load of irrigation pipe down from Trenton to water the melons using the pond water.

I went to my attorney to get some advice from him on building the park. First, there was the insurance which would be very high. Then I asked him about having everyone sign a release form that stated that they were entering the park at their own risk. He told me that the form would not hold up in court if someone got hurt and sued me.

Then I told him of my idea of having the hog catch which was something that hadn't been done before. He said that, in the beginning, I would probably be okay but after a while I could possibly be arrested because of it being inhumane to do something like this.

So, all in all, he advised me not to do what I was planning with the risk and without insurance. But everyone who knows me knows that when I make up my mind to do something, that I'm going to do it, regardless of the cost. And I did just that.

I got a group of people from the Myakka area together who were catching wild boar hogs in the woods and selling them to a man who resold them to wild game hunts in the northern states. We had several meetings at the farm and planned out the hog catches.

The plan was to have the hog catches every Sunday until I got word that the law may be coming out. I had a good friend of mine who had inside information as to when the law would be coming out. So if I was informed about the law, we would stop using the dogs and we would then use another person in the dogs place.

I wanted to start off charging $5.00 for an admission fee per person but everyone thought that was too high so we settled for $1.00 per person. The hog-catch drew the biggest crowds because no one that I knew of had ever tried it before I did. Most of the hogs weighed around 100 to 250 pounds.

At the beginning of the hog catch, a man and a dog were a team. With each team was a $10.00 entry fee. The wild boar was put into a chute smaller than a calf roping chute with the catch dog and the contestant standing off to the side of the chute.

A flag-man was about ten feet in front of the chute off to the side holding up the start flag. When the boar hog was released and crossed the ten foot line, the flag-man would drop the flag. The time would start at this point and the man and his catch dog could go catch the hog.

Most of the time the hog made it to the other end of the arena and started back before the dog could catch up to the hog. The majority of the dogs caught the hogs by their ear, holding the hog as the man grabbed the hog by its hind legs making it easier to throw them on their side.

With the hog on its side, the man would tie its three legs together like a calf-roper does a calf in a rodeo. Time stopped when the legs were tied and the dog let go of the hog. There were two classes of competitors; first was the teenagers followed by the twenty and up. The top three places for each class with the fastest times won the money.

One of the best dogs that we used a lot was Tammy's dog, Whiskey. He stayed right around the arena at all times and some of the guys would use him if they didn't have a dog of their own because he was so good. A lot of dogs wouldn't let go of the hog's ears when you told them to, but Whiskey would.

Whiskey liked to get high on pot too. Whenever he saw me rolling a joint or smoking one, he would come right over so I could blow some smoke in his nose. As he started getting high, he would run around jumping up and down acting crazy. It was funny watching him. Not long afterwards, he would lie down and roll over on his back with all four paws in the air. Sometime later he would roll back over with his head between his front legs and pass out.

We started our first show with the hog-catch, sky-diving, and dirt bikes. Later additions included bar-b-q, drinks, and bull riding by day with a bull-bucking machine and dancing at night. We ran eleven shows straight every Sunday with the last show being a full rodeo as the big finale.

The main problem was that I didn't charge enough per person and soon found I couldn't keep it going. Probably 80% of the people were from in town and would have gladly paid the five dollars that I thought of charging. My thinking was that this would be something I could have a lot of fun at while profiting from it, but it turned out to be all work on my end with little fun to be had. Everyone else seemed to have had a good time though!

Just before our third hog catch, there was quite a few of us on site, but I only remember Drew Duncan and Bushrod Teuton being there. We had a lot of work left to do on the arena. I had to go into town to pick up the public address system which was in the shop being repaired, but before I left I told everyone not to smoke any marijuana while I was gone. I knew they would not get any work done if they did.

When I got back, I started setting up the P.A. system to make sure it would work and used one of the flat-bed trucks as the announcer's stand. But it didn't take me long to see that they had not got much done while I was gone.

By the time I got finished checking out everything, I was mad because I could tell they had been smoking marijuana. Drew walked by and I said, "I told you guys not to smoke any marijuana while I was gone."

Drew remarked, "We ain't been smoking."

I said, "Like hell, you're all f***** up!"

Drew tried telling me again that they didn't smoke anything. I asked him why he was f***** up then. Drew said the crew had been taking Quaaludes.

Before that point in my life, I never seen, taken, or really even heard of Quaaludes. I told Drew he sure seemed to be stoned on pot to me. Drew brought out a Quaalude for me to see and said I should try it. I told him that I wasn't about to try that. He pushed a little harder saying that it was better than pot. To me, there was nothing better than pot so I took the Quaalude and swallowed it.

I then went back to working on the P.A. system as Drew went back to working with the crew. It didn't take long at all for the Quaalude to hit me. I started feeling dizzy and nauseous. I climbed down from the truck, hopped on a three-wheeler, and headed for the trailers. I went inside to lie on the couch as everything seemed to be going in circles.

I talked with this leather man to construct a leather vest which would wrap from the hog's belly all the way up to its head along with leather ears for the dogs to grab. The hog vest was something that I thought should help keep the hog-catch alive because I didn't want any problems with it being inhumane. With the vest covering most of the hog's body, I felt this should remedy my problems.

It wasn't long before Drew came in to tell me that the leather man was there. I told Drew that they would have to help the man and to tell the man I was sick and could not come out. The man left and some of the crew came back into the trailer to give me an update. They said they had a hard time putting the vest on the hog. When the hog was released out of the chute, it came out just a bucking like a bull. But the dog didn't want anything to do with a bucking hog. That was my first and last time that I ever did Quaaludes.

At the third show of the hog catch, we had three dogs that got cut by the boars' sharp tusks with all three having to get stitches. One dog got his throat cut causing blood to spew into the crowd of people. Several women vomited at the sight of the blood and from being sprayed with it.

So on the fourth show, we took a metal hand-grinder and ground down the sharp pointed tusks to try to keep the dogs from being cut anymore. But then we had problems with the dogs because some of them were city dogs that were not used to such confrontations. They really didn't know what to do with a hog because they would grab the hogs by their balls.

We had a total of eleven hog catches but on the eighth or ninth catch, I got word of the law coming out with an arrest warrant. So I told all of the guys not to have the dogs at the ranch and that we would be using people in their place.

The law did come out and was asking why the dogs were not there and left without arresting me. So from then on we used men in the place of the dogs. We only had a few more hog catches after that because using the men wasn't as exciting as the dogs and took more time catching the hog.

While the hog catches were going on, Cande and the Jones' were still working on the melon crop. We probably ended the hog catches around the first of March and they harvested the crop in May. They were only able to water about twenty acres of the crop so with only half of the crop watered that was all that was harvested. I did help them with the harvesting and they actually made money. I also learned that you could grow a crop of melons on very little water but you couldn't expect a real good crop if it got real dry.

It was around November of this same year that I decided to grow a crop of marijuana. Mark Massey, along with some other guys, grew a large crop of marijuana. They had harvested the crop early due to a freeze coming and since the buds didn't fully mature, the crop wasn't very good.

While I was at Mark's house, on Erie Road, he showed me his drying room that he built out of two by fours and plywood without flooring with only the walls and roof. He then stacked some square bales of hay around the room which made it look as though it was just a large stack of hay with visqueen covering the hay to keep it dry. You were even able to enter the room through a hidden door in the haystack.

Mark already had marijuana hanging from the ceiling drying with the bottom ends of the plants at the top of the ceiling and using two dehumidifiers to draw the moisture out of the plants. He used electricity from a nearby service pole to run the lights and humidifiers with. There was a large table with a lot of chairs for people to clean and bag the marijuana.

Mark asked me if I would help him clean the pot and I said that I would. So the next morning, me and some other people were there cleaning and bagging the marijuana. It wasn't long before someone who was cleaning some of the pot wanted to smoke some to see how good it was.

The room was warm and stuffy with the smell of hay, drying marijuana plants and then adding the smoke of marijuana made the room that much stuffier. Just breathing inside the room would get you high and there were several of us who had to go outside to get fresh air including me. I only worked for two days because of the conditions in that room. I liked getting high but not all day long.

In those two days, I got the idea of growing a big marijuana crop. In the few years that I had grown marijuana, I only grew about three to five pounds or just enough to last me and some friends a year. I had never sold any up to this point just smoked it. After thinking it over in the next few weeks, realizing what it would take to grow a large crop, I decided to grow a crop of marijuana in the three acres of swampy area on the southwest corner of the ranch.

Though I had never heard of anyone growing a crop of marijuana in a swamp other than Mark, I went into the swamp area several times and came up with a plan of how to go about doing it. The area that I was planning to grow in had a lot of big bay trees and with it being

December the trees were bare of leaves. This made it a good time to cut the trees down because it wouldn't be as noticeable from the air.

So Duane and I cut the trees down and I flew over the swamp afterwards to check it out. I was only able to see the sawed off stumps so we put mud, leaves and moss on the stumps or anything to hide the stumps. There was about two foot of water in the swamp so we dropped the trees as best as we could and cut the limbs off in order to walk on the tree trunks to keep from having to wade in the water.

The stumps were cut about two foot above the water so that we could put tubs or drums on them without them being in the water. After we did all that we thought we could do, I flew over the swamp again and saw that there was no sign of any trees being cut down.

Next I gathered 25 fifty-five gallon oil drums from a local farmer and we cut them in half giving us a total of 50 drums to grow the marijuana in. After the drums were cut in half we painted them camouflage and cut holes in the bottom of the drums for drainage. It took us awhile to tote all of the drums into the swamp because we were always tripping over vines or limbs and falling off the logs. I also got a truck load of cow manure from Farren Dakin to add to the soil.

The hardest part was digging the holes because I knew there would come a time that the swamp would dry up. So we dug holes beside the drums so that we would have water in the holes to dip out of to help with watering the plants. Although the water had dropped down about a foot in the swamp, it was still hard digging.

We put the soil from the holes into the drums mixing with the manure and lime and dolomite up to four inches from the top of the drum. The holes had to be dug big enough so that the soil from the holes would fill up the drums. Because we were digging right at the tree stump meant that we had to dig in and around roots and some roots had to be cut with an ax. We then put dead leaves on top of the soil so that it couldn't be seen from the air.

We planted a few seeds in January in quart cups and put them in the barn when it was cold at night. Because of the short days, the plants flowered when they were small and we pulled all of the male plants out because it isn't good to have the male plants pollinating the female plants hairy buds. There is very little THC in the male leaves. THC is the active ingredient in marijuana that relaxes you and can heighten your senses. The more potent the THC is the better the marijuana is.

In April, we brought twelve female plants into the swamp to prepare for the larger crop in August. As the twelve plants grew, we pinched off the top part of the plants in order for the plant to split in two. Once that split started to grow, we would then pinch it off in order for it to split again. This would insure us of having multiple female cuttings for the bigger crop later in the year.

The first cuttings, about 300, I took was somewhere in June. I cut them about six to seven inches long and broke the leaves off the stems all but the tops. I dipped about two and a half inches of the stem into root tone then poked them into the soil cups and kept the plants in a shaded bedroom.

I wasn't successful with the cuttings at first, because I was impatient and pushed them so they all died. Sometime around late June, I was at Mark's house discussing my problems with the cuttings. While sitting in the living room, Mark threw a big bud over to me out of a paper bag as he was laughing saying, "That's the way I grow big buds".

I was holding and looking at the biggest marijuana bud that I had ever seen. It looked and smelled different than any marijuana that I had ever seen also. Mark told me that a friend of his had grown it in the mountains of Colorado and that it was an Afghan type.

We smoked a joint from the bud and I liked the taste of it. The big bud had seeds in it which Mark gave me 50 or so seeds which were bigger than the sativa seeds. The Afghan seeds were grey with dark stripes looking somewhat like a striped watermelon.

I planted the seeds in a Styrofoam tray and put the tray on the edge of a sandy scrub. When the plants sprouted, a rat ate all but twelve of the plants so I put the plants in a quart cup for them to grow bigger in. Once they got bigger, I planted them in the drums in the swamp and it wasn't long before they sexed but only four were females. I pulled out all the males and took them to the cow pens that were about a half mile away from the swamp, so that the pollen from the Afghan males would not pollinate the females in the swamp.

Over a week, I pollinated the Afghan females by taking cotton balls and rubbing them over the male flowers which put yellow pollen on the cotton. I would then put the cotton balls in baggies to take them to the Afghan female plants that were in the swamp to rub the pollinated cotton balls all over the white hairs on the female buds.

It was just over three months from when I planted the seeds that they were ready to harvest. My main purpose was to grow the plants for some Afghan seeds which I got a little over a pound of good seeds.

I believe it was the middle of August when we planted the sativa cuttings and boy did they take root and grow fast. The August crop came from the twelve female cuttings which makes better marijuana in the end because if you start with seeds, you will have both sexes and normally in a 50-50 ratio. So by using female cuttings, you are guaranteed female plants with the exception of a few limbs going morphodite.

We drove tomato stakes into the soil beside the plants and tied the plants with string for extra support in case of high winds and heavy rains. Several months before we planted the cuttings, there were a lot of young bay tree sprouts shooting up all around in the swamp. This was really good for hiding the marijuana plants because they were the same color green as the marijuana plants. I had to go into the swamp at different times of the day to trim back some of the fast growing bay trees sprouts in order for the sunlight to get to the marijuana because sunlight is a must for marijuana to do well.

Somewhere in the middle of September, we had a heavy wind and rain storm one night and I was very concerned about the plants during the storm. The twelve older plants were already ten to twelve foot tall by now, so I was in the swamp at daybreak the next morning.

The water was almost to the top of the stumps and almost thigh high on me so I waded mostly because I couldn't see the log path under the water. There was little damage to the smaller plants but when I got to the twelve bigger plants they were in bad shape.

Two were broken in half with only a small amount of bark holding them together. The rest were leaning to one side about to break as well and a few of them had broken limbs. I went back to the trailer to call a good friend of mine to ask him to bring six rolls of duct tape with some heavy duty string as soon as possible. While waiting him to bring the tape and string, I went to a farmer friend to get 20 six foot cherry tomato stakes

Once my friend arrived, we went into the swamp to fix the larger plants. I wanted to try to save the two broken plants so we straightened one of the plants up and duct taped the area that was broken. We then put a large tomato stake alongside of the trunk of the plant and duct taped the stake to the plant. We then fixed the second one and put stakes beside the other ten plants and duct taped them to the stakes as well. I never thought that the two worst plants would survive, but they did.

The next day, I was able to tie the hanging limbs up to where they should be by tying them to the small bay trees that were much higher than the marijuana plants. This took better than two weeks to do by myself.

I was taking a break and smoking a joint when I looked back over the stringing of the plants to notice the white string looked as if there was a huge spider web everywhere. I went to the trailer to get some cotton balls and black shoe polish and I spent the rest of the day painting the string black. The swamp was very hot and humid and several times during the day I would have to walk out of the swamp to cool off. I always had a jug of water to drink and some joints to smoke.

One day while taking a break, I was sitting on a log in the shade of the small bay trees smoking a joint when I heard a helicopter coming over the swamp. I didn't try to move because I felt that I was hid well. It came down over the plants and the bay trees almost touching them. The wind from the helicopter was bending the small bay trees and pot plants over. I could see the pilot very good because he was only 30 foot from where I was sitting. He was looking real hard for the marijuana and moved the chopper all over the swamp and then took off.

Around this same time, Linda Coker moved in with me shortly after her divorce but her ex-husband, Philip, didn't like it a bit. Cande and I separated and she was filing for divorce. She did not want to be any part of me and growing marijuana.

We got some much needed rain around the first of October of 1981. It had just started raining and I was watching the six o'clock evening news. An airplane flew over the trailer sounding very low to the ground. I didn't pay much attention to it at first, but I heard it again a few minutes later. I then went to the back porch to take a look but all I could see was the black rain clouds that were only about 200 feet from the ground.

For the third time, the plane circled very low and looking up from the eaves of the porch I could see the green and white flashing lights of the plane. As the plane circled towards the east, I heard a sudden increase in the engine's power. I then saw the plane come out of the clouds and disappear behind the line of trees at a 45 degree angle.

All of a sudden there was a sudden flash of light, like a bomb exploded, lighting up the nearly dark sky. In a few seconds, all was dark again. I then heard a final big boom. At first, I didn't know what to do thinking I was probably the only one to see the crash.

It was about that time that I saw Linda's car lights coming up to the trailer. I asked Linda if she had seen the plane crash but she only saw the big flash and thought it was lightning. I started to call the sheriff's department when I saw the lights of two different vehicles approaching what seemed to be the scene of the crash.

One vehicle was coming from the south in DeRossi's pasture with the other coming from the east from the Bass pasture. Surprisingly, they soon turned around heading back to their houses. So I called each of their wives to tell them that I had seen a plane crash. I told them to watch for my headlights as I would be heading their way soon.

After fifteen minutes of talking with the sheriff's department and trying to explain where I lived, I finally told them to call Deputy Donald Roland in Myakka because he knew where to find me. Deputy Roland and I stopped at David Park's house to pick him up along with the keys to the Bass' property.

We met up with the other two trucks in the rain and by this time it was pretty dark outside as well. So we lined our three trucks up about 300 feet apart pointing into the pasture area in order for our headlights to shine over the area.

It didn't take long before we spotted what looked like an engine on the other side of the canal. I got out of the truck and crossed the canal and saw it was in fact an engine. About 200 feet away, one of the other trucks found the actual airplane or what was left of it. I started walking towards the plane when I tripped over something. I shined my light back down to see what it was and noticed what looked like a big baby doll without a head, but it was a dead baby.

Then I heard another man at the plane say he found some bodies in the plane. Continuing on towards the plane, I found a woman's body without a head and only stubs where her legs once were. By this time David and Deputy Roland had caught up with me and we found a small boy that looked to be about seven years old. Though he still had his head, the top of it was split open.

We found a total of six bodies; a man, a woman, and four children. As soon as we found the plane, Deputy Roland called the findings in to the sheriff's department. Within 30 minutes, there was a Coast Guard helicopter flying over us.

The plane made a three foot hole in the ground and what was left of it came to rest about 30 feet from the hole. The engine was the furthest away from the crash site, about 200 feet from the impact sight. In the plane, there were only the bodies of a man and two children with the other three scattered about the area.

I left with Deputy Roland as he was going to the gate to pick up a Lieutenant from the Sheriff's department. We were about two miles from the gate and only a four-wheel drive vehicle could get to the crash site. It was about 11 o'clock by that time and I wanted to get home. I really didn't want the law around the farm because of the marijuana crop in the swamp nearby and it was soon due to be harvested.

Early the next morning I checked the marijuana plants in the swamp. They didn't need any water because of the all-night drizzling rain. As I went back to the trailers I could see helicopters flying over the crash site. I decided to ride the three-wheeler over to investigate.

About noon that day, the FAA officials had me report what I had seen since I was the only one who witnessed the crash. They told me it was a young doctor and his family who were leaving Kissimmee back for their home in Fort Myers.

I told them they were circling for a bit which helped the FAA conclude they must have been lost in the rain storm. It was obvious the doctor forgot to set the altimeter before leaving for home. The doctor thought he was at 2,500 feet instead of 500 feet and going lower in the clouds when he crashed. They said his wife was afraid to fly and that this was her first time flying with her husband.

That was the worst sight that I have seen and it was really a sad thing with those little kids and such a young family. But as a pilot, you always have to pay special attention to the weather and definitely have all of your systems set properly.

From the first part of November on, it was very dry and the plants were in the middle part of their budding stage which is when they needed lots of water. The only water around was in the holes by each drum that we had dug and some of the holes we had to dig deeper to get more water.

We had to water the plants twice a day towards the end of harvest time because they were heavy with buds and sweet smell of the buds was in the swamp. The swamp was also very hot to work in and there were times that I had to walk out of the swamp just to get a cool breeze.

In late October, I air-laid about 20 marijuana plants by taking a two foot long limb from the bottom of a plant very close to the main trunk. The limb was covered with half matured marijuana buds. I scratched the bark all the way around the limb about two inches long and then I put root tone on the scratched off bark.

With a piece of cling-wrap in the palm of my hand, I put about a half of a handful of dark wet soil onto the cling-wrap and then put the limb with the root tone on the cling-wrap. I wrapped the soil and cling-wrap around the scratched limb and used a twist tie to secure each of the cling-wrap ends.

Within a few weeks I could see the roots in the cling-wrap of the twenty plants that I air-laid. I knew that the plants wouldn't grow much being it was late into the year, so I planted them along a big ditch where the dirt was in piles along one side. I remember watering them several times from the water in the ditch.

In November and throughout December, the swamp became drier and drier. As the buds grew bigger the plants needed a lot more water. I was watering them and checking the sativa plants real close for male balls.

I don't believe I enjoyed growing anything more than I did when I grew marijuana. The work was hard but to smell the buds was something else. The swamp had a sweet smell to it from October on and each plant had a different smell to it.

One day, Gary was riding up to the barn on the three-wheeler with his nose all black with rosin off the marijuana buds. I said to Gary, "You've been in the swamp, haven't you?"

He said, "How do you know?"

I told him to go look in the mirror because his nose was black.

The family was planning to have Thanksgiving at the farm, but this year was a difficult one. On November 25, 1981, Uncle Donald, my dad's younger brother for whom I was named after, was killed in an automobile accident in Myakka City. He and his family were living in Arcadia and he was working for Yancey's Dairy. He was heading west on SR70 when a tractor trailer pulled into the first store, where Suzy Q's is now, in front of him, killing him on impact.

With Thanksgiving being planned to be at the ranch, this sad news had a lot of family feeling that we shouldn't go through with it but Aunt Mary, Uncle Donald's wife, insisted. She said, "We will have Thanksgiving at the ranch because Donald would have been here."

So we did have Thanksgiving there and for the most part it was a good day. After all, that's what Thanksgiving's about, family gathering together to be thankful of each other.

Uncle Donald and Aunt Mary had seven children at the time of his death with the oldest being 28 and the youngest being 17 and a senior in high school. The family pulled together to help all of them out as much as we could.

By the first of December, we continued to have problems with the water drying up in the swamp. Not seeing any white hairs on the big swollen buds, I thought the plants were ready to harvest so I called Mark to come over the next morning to take a look at them. Mark was very surprised to see what we had accomplished and said that we would reap over a hundred pounds of pot.

He checked every plant and marked the plants he wanted and he agreed that they were ready to harvest. As Mark and I were leaving the swamp, we walked around a tree and walked by a big rattlesnake that jumped into a coil, with his rattlers just a buzzing. Mark tripped and fell down when he saw the snake and I got a big stick to kill the snake with.

Mark left around noon so I went back to the swamp to start cutting the plants, and carried them to the edge of the swamp so they could be hauled away that night. That evening, we had the back bedroom full of plants hanging upside down from the ceiling with two dehumidifiers running to take the moisture out of the plants.

I then remembered the rattlesnake and told Linda that I must think I'm rich for leaving that rattlesnake in the swamp. So I took a three-wheeler with a headlight back to the swamp to get the snake. I skinned it and we had it for supper the next day.

It took us over two weeks to clean and bag the pot in quarter pound seal-a-meal bags. We then put about ten pounds in PVC pipes and buried them but we were hardly finished cleaning the pot when I sold about 50 pounds which was the largest amount of pot that I ever sold. The rest of the pot was sold in quarter pound bags.

At harvest time, the pot usually brought about $1800 to $2000 per pound but if I buried it until June it brought around $2500 to $3000. By June most of the pot was gone.

Mark came by to pick up his pot and left me an ounce of cocaine. It was the first that I ever had it but then I got hooked on it for over three years. Later I bought more from Mark to sell and to support my habit and this screwed up my marijuana growing from then on.

After we harvested the swamp crop, I forgot about the air-laid plants that I had growing along the ditch. Sometime in early January, I was on a three wheeler going alongside of the big ditch when I remembered them. I got off the three-wheeler and crossed the ditch to find the first plant looked strange.

It almost looked white or like white sand had blown onto the brown buds. Without my glasses I couldn't tell what it was and saw that all of the rest of the plants looked the same way. They hadn't grown anymore since I planted them but the buds definitely got bigger.

I cut them all and headed to the trailer and laid them on a large table in the kitchen. I got my glasses to check them out to find that it wasn't sand after all. It was rosin from the buds that had crystallized but still sticky so I put them in a room with a dehumidifier running.

We had two different hard frosts about three weeks apart. Being that the plants were on high ground and in the open, the first frost froze the THC in the buds. Then the buds cracked open and the THC oozed out from the buds as they thawed but then dried up covering the buds as white crystals.

After the second frost the same thing happened again. That was the best marijuana that I ever smoked. One toke and I would cough my head off and after that I had a big buzz. I named this pot "The Myakkie Wacky" because it was so potent. I only got about a quarter of a pound from those limbs and I kept that for myself. I never did get the chance to try that again to see if it could be duplicated.

At the beginning of 1982, we started building a grow room in the loft of the barn to start a spring Afghan crop. It amazed me how you could grow plants in a controlled environment, which I had never tried before. We never grew the plants to total maturity; we just grew them in the grow room to get them started.

The room was 20 feet wide and 40 feet long with nine grow lights that I ordered from the High Time Magazine. Each light cost over $300.00 and drew a lot of electricity, so I had to rent a portable generator to use in order to keep the electric bill down. Normally, the monthly electric bill ran around $300.00 for the house trailers and barn, but if I would have run the lights on top of that the monthly bill would have jumped to $2500.00. So the generator was a must because if law enforcement ever suspected someone of growing inside, the first thing they look at is the power bill records.

After installing the lights, we built long tables in the room in order to put styrofoam seed trays on. Each tray held 250 plants and I had enough trays for 30,000 plants. We lined the walls with tin foil to reflect the lights and damn it was bright with all the high powered lights. We even wore sunglasses if we were in the room for a long period of time. Due to the heat from the lights, we installed a wall-unit air conditioner to run while the lights were on and it was still hot and humid inside there.

We put a 55 gallon drum on top of the grow room filled with a mixture of gas and diesel fuel. I took off the propane gas igniter from the upright seed dryer at the seed barn in town and put an electric pump on the drum to discharge the fuel through poly-pipe. We put holes in the poly-pipe about one foot apart that would spray the fuel all over the grow room. A timer was set for one minute to ignite a ball of fire to go off once the fuel was sprayed. We had a hidden switch down below in the barn that would set all of this in motion to burn the barn down.

My idea was to burn the barn down and get rid of all of the evidence if we knew the law was coming. We tried this experiment outside of the barn and it worked good.

It took several people to put seeds in the trays in one day. With 120 trays and 250 seeds per tray, the tables were loaded by the time nightfall came. We left the lights on, day and night, for a week. At the end of the week the plants were six to seven inches tall. I never saw plants grow so fast, but then again plants normally do not get 24 hours of light for a solid week.

We then switched to ten hours of light and 14 hours of darkness for about ten days. When all of the plants started showing their sexes, we pulled the males out and put the females in quart cups. Those female plants were the best looking plants that I ever saw. They were real bushy and stocky. I think, in the end, we had around 15,000 female plants.

That was the most plants that we grew in the grow room. I ended up selling some of the plants but gave most of them away with the exception of about 2500 plants. After that we grew mostly vegetables plants in the grow room.

I did, however, grow about 2000 of the plants in the drums that we had in the swamp. My original plan was to grow some in different areas in Myakka but getting the ground ready in those areas was a lot of work. I also planned to set up some growers on a fifty-fifty basis with me furnishing everything but the work. The first and last two growers that I started with didn't do what I told them to and the crops were a failure.

Before I planted the plants in the drums, I put vapam in the soil to kill any soil-borne diseases. I waited two weeks before planting and when I did plant, a week later the plants died because the vapam was still in the soil.

I could actually still smell the vapam in the soil when I dug into the soil. So I stirred the soil up and kept pouring water on it until the smell was gone. By this time I only had about 500 plants left.

So other than what I sold and gave away, I failed with the spring Afghan crop, mainly because I was doing too much cocaine and partying. I believe, maybe, 20 pounds of pot was all that I harvested after the big crop.

I did learn a little about Afghan plants in the short time that I fooled with them. I learned that they would mature within 90 to 100 days and not get very tall, only about three to four foot. The other thing was that when planted in the summer, they would get bud rot which is when the bud would get real big and tight.

The lease was up at the 34th Street property this same year and the owners wanted about three times as much as we were paying in the past with a year to year lease option, so needless to say that was our last year there.

Around this same time, I bought 50 pounds of aqua-sorb which was something new to help retain water in soil. It was small particles that looked like sawdust and would absorbed water 100 times its size. The first time I used it was in several one quart potting cups and didn't know how much to use per cup so I put a tablespoon full mixing into the potting soil of each cup.

Several weeks later, I saw something that looked like a blob that was expanding every time it was watered and pushing the plant out of the cup. The main reason I bought it was to help store water within the soil of the plants that I planted on some sandy scrub land.

When some of my friends were at the ranch, I would show them the plants in the swamp. Cande warned me if I didn't stop messing with marijuana that I would end up going to jail and our divorce was final in April of 1982 because of it.

When I was growing marijuana, up to the mid '80s, it was like a slap on the wrist if you got caught growing marijuana. But in 1986 to 1987 with the new drug laws, it was a different story.

In the fall of this same year, I worked for Robbie Brameister, Herman's son, at the packing house on SR64. I was responsible for overseeing the packing house operation, mainly grading, packing, and the inventory of the incoming and outgoing vegetables.

I worked 90 to 100 hours for several weeks and at one point I worked 132 hours in one week which was the most hours I had ever worked and got paid for. I never left the packing house that week except to take a shower and change clothes. What sleep I got was on the couch in Robbie's office and he brought my meals to me that week.

In the early morning hours, after all of the crew was gone, I would start cleaning the machines while waiting on some late semis coming in for produce. I do remember one morning, around four after loading a semi, the driver was in the office getting his receipt and he told me that I needed something to keep me awake which I agreed. He then handed me a handful of black beauties and I took one. It didn't take long after he left that I was working like hell. During this time frame, I know I was doing cocaine pretty heavy but I don't remember ever doing any while working at the packing house, just marijuana and those black beauties.

It was April or May of 1983 when I went to Costa Rica with Bill and Robert Kipp along with Bill Britt. Bill Kipp had been going to Costa Rica a lot because he was looking for investments in that country. He would take others along with him most of the time and Bill Britt was looking for some beach resort possibilities on the Pacific side.

We left Miami and flew to San Jose, the capital of Costa Rica. We stayed in one of their best hotels that first night. The two Bill's stayed in a room and Robert and I shared another room with two hookers who tried taking all our money but they couldn't find it.

Bill Kipp had bought a Toyota Land Cruiser on one of his earlier trips to Costa Rica so that he would have some kind of transportation. We left San Jose somewhere around two that next afternoon going to John Hull's ranch in San Carlos, which was about a 50 mile drive that took about an hour and a half. The four of us were crowded in the vehicle because we also had our luggage with us.

It was dark and raining when we reached San Carlos. It was at this time that Bill realized that he forgot to make our reservations at this one particular hotel. So here we were with no hotel room and no place to stay.

That's when Bill said that we would have to drive back to San Jose. But I said that I could get us a room somewhere in this town because I sure didn't want to make the long drive back to San Jose. I felt like I could speak enough Spanish to get us a room.

As we drove through the town of San Carlos we saw what looked like a boarding house. I went inside and got us a room with four cot-like beds in it. As we brought our luggage in, we found out that the walls didn't reach all the way to the ceiling. You could hear other people talking in the next rooms. All of the rooms shared the bathroom that was located down the hallway.

Bill Britt got his shower first and Robert said that he was going to walk around town a little. After Bill came back from the shower he went to sleep right away and Bill Kipp went for his shower. I was lying on my back on the cot, when I saw these large rats looking down at me from the rafters overhead. One of them actually came running down a bedpost right next to Bill Britt's head.

Robert came into the room about this same time and I asked him why he came back so soon. He said that it didn't look too safe walking down the streets and it was still drizzling rain. Then I told Robert about the rats up in the rafters but they were nowhere in sight as I was pointing up to where they were.

Bill Kipp came back from his shower and went right to sleep as well. As it got somewhat quieter from the surrounding rooms, Robert yelled for me to look at the rat overhead. I was laughing when I said, "I told you that there are rats in here and one already ran down that post by Bill Britt's head."

The next morning Robert looked like he needed some sleep. He said that he couldn't sleep for the rats and he watched them all night long. The best part about our room was that it only cost me five dollars that night for the four of us along with a $2.50 charge for someone to watch the vehicle. Compared to $75.00 a night in San Carlos that wasn't too bad even if it was rat infested.

After we ate breakfast we headed to the ranch. There were no bridges across the river so one of John's workers came in a boat to take us to the other side of the river where his ranch was. John's house wasn't big, but it was a well-built house with an open patio overlooking the river.

John was going to take us to the Pacific side of Costa Rica in his airplane to look at a beach resort that Bill Britt was interested in. But our first stop was to run off some squatters who were living on a ranch that John was overseeing. As we landed at that ranch, the Costa Rican military landed there as well with guns to run off the squatters. Lots of Americans have lost their land to these invaders. If a squatter lives on a piece of land for five years and has cleared a 20 foot boundary around that piece of property, then he can claim the property as his.

Afterwards, we flew on to the beach resort which had a small airstrip next to it. It was kind of excluded from the other buildings along the beach and the hotel was full of hookers and military soldiers. The beach looked good but not up to American standards. We there an hour or so and took off back to John's ranch. After visiting a while, we got back into the boat and crossed the river back to Bill's vehicle.

If you were to ask about John Hull you would get many mixed replies. He now lives in Indiana on his family's farm with extradition papers on him from the Costa Rican government. John and his airstrip got caught up in the politics during the Reagan administration in early 1982.

Allegedly the CIA had embarked upon a covert military operation to bring down the communist government in Nicaragua. John's airstrip was used from 1983 until sometime in 1985. In 1984, in a hotel lobby in the middle of a press conference, a bomb exploded and killed three journalists including U.S. citizen, Linda Frazier, who worked with the Tico Times, the Costa Rica Newspaper.

From that time on, John has had to fight to clear his name. John has consistently argued that he was never involved in any illegal drug trafficking in Costa Rica. Evidently, there were drugs for weapons exchanges made that possibly involved the CIA.

Costa Rican officials based John's arrest upon statements presented by two convicted drug dealers. John was released on $37,500 bond that was raised by local ranchers and their workers. The locals wanted to have a parade and a celebration when he was released from prison, but the police asked that they not do anything for fear of retaliation.

We then went to see a sawmill operation that was partly owned by Bill Crone. Bill was also from Indiana, but Bill sold his farm in Indiana and moved to Costa Rica. He bought an interest in a saw mill and it was the biggest sawmill I had ever seen as were the logs.

Bill Crone and I hit it off when we first met and I agreed to go with him the next day into the jungle to load some logs on a semi-trailer. He wanted to get the load of logs out of the jungle because the semis couldn't travel on the dirt roads once the rainy season started.

The next morning the guys dropped me off at the saw mill as they were heading back to San Jose. Bill Crone and I were going to fly back in his airplane after we came back from the jungle. The plan was for all of us to meet in San Jose for supper that night.

So we headed for the jungle, and the further we went, the dirt roads got smaller. Once we arrived, there was definitely nothing but jungle. There were a pile of logs at the edge of the jungle in front of the house. Bill had, 1200 acres of jungle that he was getting the logs out of and his acreage ended at the river that separates Costa Rica from Nicaragua.

Bill asked if I could operate the bull dozer that was parked there and I said sure. Bill got the chain saw out of his car and with some help from his workers, they marked the length that he wanted the logs to be. Bill sawed them with me pushing the logs up the dirt ramp and onto a flat-bed log trailer.

Bill saw that I was having trouble getting the logs up the ramp, so he showed me how to do it. There were two workers with log hooks that helped me straighten the logs in place on the trailer. We got the logs cut and loaded on the trailer around noon time.

We ate sandwiches that we brought with us and the workers cut some pineapples for us to eat. Those were some of the best pineapples that I had eaten because they were so ripe. Now that the equipment was not running, you could hear monkeys howling in the jungle along with parrots and other birds.

When we were getting ready to leave, Bill gave his men orders on what he wanted them to do. After leaving to go to his airplane and taking off, Bill said that he was going to fly over the house to see if they were working on what he wanted them to do. As we flew over the house his workers were sitting on the porch not doing anything. Bill said they were good workers when he was with them but they didn't do anything with him gone.

That's when he made me an offer to come down to work for him. Because he needed someone to work with his men when he wasn't around, he was going to give me half on the logs that I could get out of the jungle. His biggest problem was getting the logs out of the jungle and keeping the men working.

We ate supper together that night and the next morning we were heading back to Miami. It was a short three or four day trip but it was fun and quite a learning experience. The biggest lesson was that if you don't want to sleep with rats you better make sure you have reservations in a nice hotel.

I was going to take Bill up on his offer if the ranch sold. At that time, Val Massey was going to buy it but the deal fell through so I didn't go back to Costa Rica.

In December of 1983, Dad was diagnosed with cancer. He cut out a small purple pimple-like boil that was in the center chest bone area. After going to see Dr. Joe Ganey, he was told that cancer had spread all over his body by him cutting into the boil like he did.

Dad was like that though; always doing his own doctoring like he had done most of his life on the livestock. He rarely went to a doctor, but after his diagnosis he started radiation treatments. The treatments really didn't seem to help because he was told that he had a brain tumor just after Christmas. Dad was sick most of the time due to his treatments and had lost all of his hair.

Though he was not feeling very well, Dad wanted me to plant a melon crop so that he could help us with it. After the sod was lifted from an area, I normally started preparing the ground for planting melons. I wasn't planning on growing a crop that year because I didn't have any ground ready. And I was still on cocaine and partying all of the time so I didn't care.

I ended up using 40 acres of the Stanfield property that joined our farm, knowing Dad really wanted me to grow a crop. I had the Jones' come down to help on a fifty-fifty basis since they had most of the equipment. They are all good people and we worked very well together.

When they arrived, they had their equipment with them loaded on semi-trailers and their camper was behind the pickup. As they had done in the past, they parked the camper beside the barn so they could hook up to the water and electric.

But this time I told Mr. Jones not to park beside the barn and he asked why. So I told him to come with me and I would show him. They all followed me up to the loft and I showed them the grow room where we had some young marijuana plants growing.

Needless to say, that shook them up quite a bit but not near as much as when I started showing them what I had rigged up to burn the barn down. I didn't need to say anything else or show them anything else because Mr. Jones was moving his trailer away from the barn in no time.

One day Grady and I were packing melons into a semi-trailer. After loading the trailer, I went into the office to give Linda the information on the trailer, so she could make out the invoice for the load. Not long after I was inside, Grady came into the trailer in somewhat of a panic saying that a deputy had just driven up in a county pick-up truck and parked beside the barn.

He immediately asked me if I wanted him to flip the switch in the barn in order to burn it down. I said, "No, just let me go out there to see what is going on."

The deputy was Richard Walker and all he wanted was some melons. So I gave him several and he was on his way. Needless to say, the Jones' were real nervous that year while growing melons knowing that I had marijuana growing.

Dad went to stay at Sandra and Duane's around early spring of 1984 until he died on July 6, 1984. Dad was buried in Okeechobee where he had lived for the last 14 years. He never did get to help or see the melon crop get harvested and it was the biggest yielding melon crop that I was ever involved in; over a semi load of melons per acre.

Though Dad killed himself by doing his own doctoring, he was no different than the other Clarks; you can't tell a Clark what to do. Dad was a good man and was well liked by everyone. Probably his biggest accomplishment was getting the Manatee County Dam built.

On February 19, 1985, I was at Bob Murphy's house with a girl who overdosed on cocaine. I didn't know what to do and hollered for Bob to call an ambulance. While waiting, I rolled the girl on her stomach to push down on her back and some fluid came out of her mouth so I rolled her over on her back to blow in her mouth to try to get her breathing. I kept working on her until the paramedics arrived.

When they arrived, they told me to get off her and grabbed a sheet for me to wrap around myself because both of us were naked. I was soaked with sweat from trying to do CPR. Her face was blue and I didn't think she was going to make it. I started telling them to do something and that's when they made me leave the room.

By this time, there were deputies looking around the house and asking me questions. I was so shook up that I don't remember what I told them. There wasn't anything wrong with me, but when the ambulance left with her they made me get into another ambulance to go to the hospital as well.

They wouldn't let me get dressed so I went to the hospital with the sheet still wrapped around me. I ended up staying there for about five days. The only thing that they could find wrong with me was an erratic heartbeat which was due to the cocaine use. I really thought the girl was dead and I had never been so disgusted with myself in all of my life. I felt so ashamed of myself that I didn't want to see anyone.

A few days later, that same girl came to my hospital bed pushing her IV pole and said that her boyfriend had brought her some cocaine and asked if I wanted any. I told her, "Hell no!"

I never wanted to do any more cocaine at all. When I got ready to leave the hospital, they informed me that I had a $7000.00 bill. I informed them that I wasn't paying it because I was fine when the paramedics arrived at the house but the deputies made me get into the ambulance. I never did pay that bill.

Sandra took me to her house for a few days after my release from the hospital. I obtained an attorney in order to retrieve my money and wallet from the Sheriff's Department. The attorney told me to go to the Sheriff's Department and that they would give my personal belongings back to me.

When I arrived there, they started questioning me and showed me photos of the bedroom with drugs in the photos. Like a fool, I admitted that they were all mine because they told me that I would not be arrested.

A couple of months after my cocaine incident, Herman Brameister called me and asked if I would help him with his spring crop. His farm foreman quit and he needed someone to help him harvest the crop. Knowing that I had a good time ten years earlier farming with Herman, I accepted the job.

For several years, all I was doing was drugs, dancing, and chasing women, but farming with Herman was like old times again. At least working with him would keep me more occupied with work instead of partying.

Herman's farm was just past the power plant on SR 62 in between Parrish and Duette and we were in the field at daylight. The crops looked the best in the morning, but the worst time was in the heat of the day. If there were any problems with the crop, it was more noticeable in the early morning. We would start at the farthest end of the fields and work our way back to the front. Going up and down the rows we looked for any signs of trouble.

We found small problems, not bad ones, but problems that would soon lead to worse ones if not corrected. Usually by the time we made it to the front, the crews were coming in and we would tell them what to do for the day.

On the first day that I started working, I was in charge of a big tomato field. My job was checking on the field picking crews and making out tickets for the amount of tomato bins on the trucks going to the packing house.

The next day I brought one of the three-wheelers from the ranch to ride around the farm which was better than driving a pick-up. The only problem was that Herman couldn't find me because the tomato plants were taller than the three-wheeler. So I decided to put a fiberglass pole with a red flag on it and attach it to the three-wheeler so I could be seen in the fields.

In the late '70s, Herman was diagnosed with diabetes and had both of his legs amputated several years later. He had two Jeep Wagoneer's with handicap leavers for the brakes and the gas. Both of them had the same setup with two-way radios, four-wheel drive and all the extras. He had the extra one because one was always in the shop getting detailed. Within two weeks one would be filthy and every month or so each one's brakes would be shot from Herman going in and out of water all day long.

Herman had several testers with him in the jeeps because he was always testing the plant beds. One was a pH tester, which is a moisture tester and the other a nitrate tester. He would pull the jeep almost on the side on the bed, so that he could open his door and lean down to the plants and inspect them.

One day I found Herman lying on a bed because he had fallen out of his Jeep and couldn't get back up. I was on the three-wheeler coming around a curve when I saw him on the ground. I was intentionally looking the other way when I went by him and heard him yelling at me to stop. After a few minutes I went back to help him into his Jeep. I was laughing as I lifted him up and he was cussing me for ignoring him when I went by.

Herman had a restaurant and a produce stand built on S.R. 64 at the corner of 27$^{th}$ Street just before the Braden River. His wife, Carlene, ran the restaurant while Herman ran the produce stand. Both the restaurant and produce stand was called Farmer Johns with the stand also having a Deli in it.

We would eat breakfast at the restaurant around five in the morning in the Jeep because of Herman's condition. Most days, Herman would leave me at the field and go back to the produce stand and would usually come back around noon with my lunch. It wasn't long before Herman had me going to the Tampa market to sell some of his produce and to bring back other produce that he didn't grow for his produce stand.

I didn't get much sleep in the weeks of harvesting that crop. There were times when I had lots of money on me from the sale of drugs that

I carried with me in brown paper bags. I would put the bag in the rear seat of Herman's Jeep so no one would steal my money.

One day, Mark gave me another big marijuana afghan bud that someone grew in Colorado and again it was the biggest bud that I had ever seen. I put it in the bag with the money in the back seat of the Jeep. Later that afternoon, while riding with Herman, I reached back to get the paper bag and took out the bud. Knowing that he didn't know what marijuana looked like, I asked him if he had ever seen a bud that big before. He flew off the handle! Saying "What are you doing putting that stuff in my Jeep? What would have happened to me if they searched my Jeep and found that marijuana in here?"

He was so upset because earlier that day as he was leaving the produce stand and headed back to the field on CR 62, he was stopped in a line of traffic by the law who were checking driver's licenses. I asked Herman, "You didn't know the marijuana was in your Jeep, did you?"

"No" Herman said.

I then asked "You would have had to say it was mine, wouldn't you?" He said "Yes".

So I asked him "Then why are you getting so upset?"

He told me "I just don't want you to ever have that shit in my vehicle again."

From that day on, every time I threw anything in the back seat he wanted to look to see what was inside of it.

On May 24, 1985, I was arrested at the ranch. I remember it was a Friday afternoon when I had two Mexican boys with me, who worked for Herman. We were going to the ranch to check things out because I hadn't been there in quite a while.

I rode over the ranch before going to the trailer and I stopped at the elephant trailer (a semi-trailer for hauling elephants) to see if Gary had removed his marijuana out of the trailer. He had been drying it in there, but Gary had not removed it yet, which made me mad.

As I got back into Herman's Jeep, I asked the two Mexicans if they wanted to see some marijuana drying, so we went inside the trailer. All of a sudden, someone yelled, "Sheriff's Department... freeze, don't move!"

I thought it was one of the boys playing a joke on me, but as I turned around I noticed it was two men with pistols in their hands.

They yelled again, "Don't move or we'll shoot!"

The two Mexicans were scared shitless and said, "Don't shoot... we're not moving!"

They ended up being plain clothes deputies and one of them came up and handcuffed all three of us. Apparently, they had been at the farm for three days waiting for me. That was when I was informed that I was being arrested for the cocaine, marijuana and paraphernalia incident at Bob Murphy's house when the girl overdosed.

One of the deputies started talking over the walkie-talkie and soon the ranch was overrun with cops. We were waiting on the porch for a deputy to bring a search warrant out when one of the deputy's asked me what was in the paper sacks on the dining room table and I said, "It's flour".

They didn't believe me and told me that they had a portable lab coming out to check it. I know they thought it was cocaine in the bags but a few weeks earlier I bought four 25 pound bags of flour and wrapped them in Visqueen to keep the weevils out. For over a year I had been stocking up on food because I thought the bottom was going to fall out of the economy and therefore, food would be in short supply.

After the search warrant was read, the cops scattered all over the ranch with some going to the swamp, some searching the barn, while others searched the trailer with the rest tearing into the four flour bags. After about 30 minutes, a deputy came onto the porch and asked, "What are you doing with all of that flour?"

I told him that I had some Mexican girls coming to make some flour tortillas for me and he said, "You're quite the smartass, aren't you!"

I told him, "I already told y'all that it was flour and there's about 2000 pounds more of it in the barn!"

The captain came to me very concerned holding his walkie-talkie while talking to his deputies who were in the swamp area and stated that the deputies were afraid of some booby-traps. He said, "If any of my deputies get hurt in that swamp, you are going to be in big trouble!"

I told him, "The only way they will get hurt is if they should fall into one of the holes that are beside the tubs that I used to water the marijuana plants with."

It was getting dark, so they couldn't get into the swamp where the marijuana was until the next morning. I only had about 15 female plants that I was taking cuttings off before I started working with Herman. I already had my mind made up before I started working for Herman that I wasn't going to grow anymore marijuana.

I was charged with having 900 marijuana plants but only had 15 big plants in the swamp and 200 cuttings in cups and most of them were dead, but in the end I was charged with seven felonies. Two for cocaine, two for marijuana, two on paraphernalia and one on manufacturing of marijuana.

I bonded out on my own recognizance and I told them that the two Mexican boys had nothing to do with the marijuana so they were released as well. It was really late in the morning before I got out so I went on to work with Herman. Herman couldn't believe what happened to me that night until he saw it on the television and on the front page of the Bradenton Herald.

A few days later, David Young, a friend of mine, who works for the Manatee County Sheriff's Department called me and said that he had a subpoena to serve on me. I asked him to meet me at the Farmer's Inn, early the next morning.

When he served me the subpoena, he said that he had never served a subpoena like this before. Herman and I both were shocked when we read it. It was from an attorney, Dick Lee, hired by Homer Hyatt. He was suing me for not having marijuana insurance on the ranch.

A few days later, I took the subpoena to the Farm Bureau office where I had my insurance. When I sat down at the agent's desk I told him that I needed some more insurance on the ranch, and handed him the subpoena. After he read it he said to me, "Isn't marijuana illegal?"

I said "I think it is; I did get arrested for it, didn't I?"

Richard said laughing, "I can't give you any insurance on marijuana."

I had been to court twice before with Mr. Hyatt. He was trying to get out of the contract on the ranch but lost each time and he also lost on the marijuana case. The judge threw out the complaint saying that I had complied with the contract which required liability insurance that I had.

After my arrest, Herman wanted me to continue working with him on the fall crop.

I retained an attorney from Sarasota who was recommended to me. When I first met with him he said that the report stated that my pot was very potent and I said, "I haven't seen any better yet."

He then said that he smoked marijuana but didn't have any at the time, so he asked if I would be willing to pay half of my attorney fees in exchange for some pot. His fee was $5000.00, so half of that equaled a pound of pot.

A few days later I returned to his office with four quarter pound bags of pot stuffed inside my shirt. As I entered his office, I walked up to his desk, pulled my shirt up and the bags landed on his desk. He freaked out and said, "I didn't mean for you to bring the shit to my office."

I went to court on December 10, 1985. My attorney got the court to withhold adjudication on growing marijuana, but I pled guilty to the six other counts; two were marijuana, two were cocaine, and two were paraphernalia. I received two years of community control or house arrest. I didn't want the marijuana growing charges because I would probably lose the ranch.

Because I had to work for someone while I was on house arrest, I planned on continuing to work for Herman. Herman planted almost every vegetable that there was to be planted for his fall crop. He even planted twenty acres of strawberries at the CR62 farm and 35 acres at the packing house on SR64. I didn't like growing strawberries especially when it would freeze.

One night it froze at both farms and I was the only one at the CR62 farm. I started the pump so the sprinklers would keep the berries from freezing. The water was being pumped out of a holding pond for the berries. After I got the pump going, I drove through the field to make sure the sprinklers were all working and there were a bunch that weren't.

So I had to get a stiff wire to ram into the sprinkler nozzles to clean them out. All of the stopped up ones were blocked from a small catfish in the nozzle tip. The wire would break up the catfish to allow the water to come out.

I stayed pretty busy farming with Herman. I wasn't partying at all, just dipping into cocaine at times even though I said that I wasn't ever doing any more. I normally had a little bit with me in a snuff can at all times.

One afternoon I stopped a tractor driver to adjust the cultivator. I parked the pick-up truck at the end of the rows. Before I stopped the truck, I noticed a field truck coming towards me with a load of cherry tomatoes heading to the packing house.

The Mexican boy stopped beside my pickup and got out of his truck. I wasn't paying attention to him because I was working on the cultivators but I did hear him leave. After I was satisfied that the cultivator was working okay, I got back into my truck and I noticed that my snuff can was gone which had about 3.5 grams of cocaine in it.

This particular Mexican boy, who happened to be one of the boys who was with me when I got arrested, knew I kept the cocaine in a snuff can. I got back out of the truck and walked around the truck to the passenger side and saw his foot prints beside the door leading back to his truck.

About two hours later, when he came back to the farm, I met him back at the tractor shed. I told him to get into my truck, which he did. I was headed to the furthest end of the farm when I said to him, "You look real high on my cocaine. I know you stole it out of my truck while I was working on the cultivators."

He swore to me on his mother's grave that he didn't take it. When he said that, I had second thoughts about him stealing it. But then I remembered his footprints so I didn't say anything, I just kept driving. He asked me where we were going and I said, "To the end of the farm where I'm going to beat the crap out of you for stealing my cocaine."

He said, "Turn the truck around because I hid it in the tractor shed."

That's when I stopped giving any dope to the two Mexican boys.

In early April of 1986, we got a heavy rain and Herman's bell peppers got real wet. The field was new ground, in a low area, where water would stand between the rows. The pepper wasn't planted on plastic, so with the ground being so wet, the field needed help getting dried out quickly otherwise the peppers would die.

With the rain water gone, it left a crust of mud on the top layer not allowing the rows to dry out. It was getting late in the evening when I started cultivating the dirt between the rows which allowed the ground to dry out quicker. I told Herman that I would work through the night to get the field dry. I got finished around 3AM and went to my girlfriend's house to get some much needed sleep. I hardly got to sleep when Herman's son, Robbie, drove up to tell me that Herman had died in his sleep.

The day was April 7, 1986, and boy did that shake me up. I knew I had to go back to the fields and oversee the crews. It was a long and tiring day mostly because of the loss of Herman. We were so different in many ways, yet we sure did enjoy each other's company and we both liked farming.

After Herman's funeral, Robbie took over managing of the farm. Since I didn't have the experience to run the farm, Robbie hired Daryl Parks to run the farm a few days after Herman died.

Daryl was a good farmer and had years of experience. I've known Daryl and his twin brother David for a long time. When they were in high school they stacked sod for me when I first started the sod business.

I helped Daryl finish that spring crop and helped get the ground ready for the fall crop. On August 23rd, while the crew was laying plastic on the rows, Daryl and I drove up. The tractor was doing a 180 degree turn at the end of the row and starting back down another row when we noticed one of the tanks had twisted around and was about to break a gas line.

The tanks were putting gas into the beds while also pressing the beds with a bed press. The gas was Methyl-Bromide and Chloropicrin to help kill the weed seeds and soil-borne diseases. So we stopped the tractor and both of us jumped onto the bed press to straighten the tank back to where it was supposed to be. I made the mistake of grabbing the valve to help turn the tank around and as I did the line broke.

The gas hit me in the chest but luckily I was wearing a cap, sunglasses, jean shorts and a t-shirt. But unfortunately, Daryl was behind me when it broke and some of the gas went in his eyes. I did get some of the gas into my eyes but my sunglasses kept most of it out of my eyes.

I got some of it in my lungs though and remembered from a safety meeting that I had to stand on my head to get the gas out of my lungs which I did. Daryl was flushing his eyes as much as he could and I splashed some in my eyes as well. I could see more than Daryl could so I ran to shut off the gas which was still spraying out of the broken line. The field crew had already run away from the gas.

Daryl couldn't see anything so I took him to Dr. Bobbie King, the eye doctor. Daryl's eyes were bad and he ended up having to wear patches over them for about two weeks.

I quit working for Robbie after Daryl's eyes were better. They didn't really need me anymore because Daryl could do it all by himself. So I went to Roger Harloff's packing house to see if he needed any help until my probation was up.

Roger said the only help he needed was for someone to run his bell pepper and cucumber machine. I had the experience because I had helped Robbie, so I took the job. But I only worked there for about a week because my feet got real sore from walking on the concrete floor all day.

Roger then sent me to work with Paul Gilmore at his farm in Myakka City. I only worked with Paul for a few weeks until I talked Roger into farming at the ranch with me doing the work not charging him for the land use.

First I planted about 100 acres of cabbage on the same ground that Duane had just harvested melons on that spring. Then I started disking another 125 acres of ground where sod was just lifted from. I used Roger's laser to level the ground which helped keep the water flowing from one end to the other without problems. Duane had a twelve inch well drilled when he grew the melons but didn't lay any PVC pipe. So Roger bought the pipe in order to get water to the crops.

On February 27, 1987, I was arrested for violation of probation. On the night of my arrest, I worked on a busted PVC water pipe at the cabbage field until around 11PM and had just gotten to bed when the dogs started barking. I looked out of the window to see cop cars without their headlights on going by.

I went to the back door and there stood my probation officer with a bunch of deputies. He told me that they knew that I had marijuana in the house and that it would be better for me to give it to them. Like a dummy, I lead them to the bedroom and handed them two joints that were in a baggy. It's amazing how pot can grow because that baggy grew in the arrest report into a half pound.

With my probation officer standing there, the cops said that they were told that I had 100 pounds in my deep freeze but I told them that this was all of the marijuana that they would find. They searched everywhere and they found no more than what I gave them.

But there were also guns in the barn, as well as a gun left by the pool table inside the trailer by Gary. I wasn't to have guns or be around guns or have any drugs in my possession. So with that said I went to jail that night and bonded out the next morning.

While I was in the holding cell, I was lying on a bench along with some other inmates who were sitting around talking. I was listening to them talk when one of them said, "I heard they put Donnie Clark on the 6$^{th}$ floor."

Then that guy started telling the other inmates all about me; like how he knew me and had bought marijuana from me. But the funny thing was I had never seen this guy in my life.

This was the first time that I had been able to listen to someone talk about me and not know who the person was and he not know that I was there. About an hour later, a guard came to the cell and said, "Don Clark, come with me."

You should have seen their faces. All of them looked at me with their mouths open not believing it was me in there with them the entire time they were talking.

After bonding out, I continued working with Roger awaiting my court date. I wasn't sure what would happen, but knew that I needed to keep busy and try to stay out of trouble with the law.

I went to court on July 27, 1987. I plead guilty and was put in the Manatee County jail. I was then taken to the laundry area to get my inmate clothes. I told them that my pants size was 44 instead of 34. The next morning I was hand-cuffed together with six other inmates with me in the middle trying to hold up my pants. This was hard because I had an inmate in front of me, who I was cuffed to and another one behind me that I was cuff to also.

I was going in front of the judge for my sentence and ended up being sentenced to 18 months in state prison. I was taken to Lake Butler with seven other inmates the following morning. We arrived around noon with about 200 other inmates who came there from other areas. They made us take off all of our clothes and sent us to the showers, where the guards sprayed us down to kill any bugs that we may have had, which is when they issued us more inmate clothes.

It took the rest of the day waiting in lines for shots, medical evaluations etc. We were put into a cell block, called the Charley House. It was a very hot place with no trees and no A/C in the cells. The guards were rough and were always getting on someone for something.

After a few days of orientation, I was sent to New River East in Lake City, which did have big oak trees. There were 40 inmate beds in wood barrack buildings. The inner buildings housed the commissary, TV rooms, game rooms, shower buildings and toilets, but the buildings were hot day and night.

The building where the toilets were had about 15 to 20 toilets that were lined around the four walls without any partitions for privacy. I remember the first time going to the john, the toilets were almost full with inmates and when I took a crap, the Negro that was sitting next to me said, "Man, put some water on it!"

That's when I learned that when I first dump, I should flush the toilet to keep the smell down.

When we went to chow, we had to wait in lines in military form. While reaching for the meal trays, the guards would look at the inmates for any whiskers on their face and if it wasn't clean shaven they were sent back to the barracks to shave. A guard would stand over you while you ate and we only had five minutes to eat.

Everyone is given an ID number when sent to prison. I don't remember the number that I was given, but I do know that it started with an "A" followed by numbers. Every time an inmate returns to prison the numbers stay the same but the alpha letter changes to "B" for the second return, "C" for the third return, and so on. I remember seeing some inmates with the letter "M" followed by numbers.

When the bus arrived at New River East, almost all of the inmates went straight to the work shack to sign up for work detail after unloading. Since I didn't know how the system worked, I didn't sign up until a few days later. I was in the rec yard when an inmate who was working asked me why I wasn't working. I told him that I only had 18 months to do and with only 60% of that to do, I would be out in no time.

He then said that if I got a job that I would be out in six to seven weeks earlier than that. So I went to the work shack and signed up for work the next day. I got a job pulling weeds from the flower beds along the buildings.

On the third day, of my first week working, I was sent to the sod fields to work. I was getting on the bus with about 20 other inmates and I asked the guard about the sod cutters. I mentioned that I knew how to work them so he told me to go with the other guard who was driving the van that was carrying the sod cutter, water cooler, and the bush hooks.

We went to the shop and I picked out a sod cutter that I thought was the best out of the three that were there. I had to replace the cam bearings in it as well as sharpen the blades because they were so dull.

I got back on the bus with the rest of the inmates and we all headed to the field. Once we reached the sod field, there were two other institutions, New River West and Raiford, which had sent inmates there to work. The fields were a mile behind Raiford and were planted in Bahia grass.

When we drove up, there were two inmates from the other prisons cutting sod with their sod cutters. They had to push their sod cutters because the blades were so dull. If they didn't push on the cutter, all it would do would stop moving forward with the wheel spinning in the grass. And the rest of the inmates were all standing around talking, waiting on the sod to be cut so a few could start cutting it in one to two foot lengths. Once the sod was cut into lengths, the rest would load the sod onto the trucks by hand.

Once our sod cutter got unloaded, I started it up and adjusted the depth in which to cut the sod. I was able to cut the sod about one and a half inches thick where the others had to cut almost double that because they were not able to lift the sod without it breaking into smaller pieces due to their dull blade. When I was in the sod business we always had 10 to 15 sharp extra blades that we changed every 45 minutes to an hour.

Our sod weighed half as much as theirs because we didn't have all of the extra thickness or roots. When I got started cutting the sod, I was able to cut six rounds before the other inmates could cut one. The other two sod cutters were ahead of me but over in another area of the field pushing hard on their cutters. But I was able to just walk on pass them cutting the sod like pushing a lawn mower. It wasn't long before the guards made them stop using their cutters and had them start with the bush hooks to cut the sod into one foot lengths.

Within an hour, all of the inmates were busy working with no one standing around. Three black inmates walked over to me asking me what I was doing. I said, "I'm cutting sod."

One of them even told me that I wouldn't get any more of my time cut by going so fast and that I needed to slow down. I said, "No, ya'll need to speed up."

That really pissed them off. About that time, two guards came over and told them to get back to work and asked me why I stopped. I told them that the other inmates were telling me to slow down. One of the guards told me that I was doing just fine and to keep cutting.

Another guard asked me how I got my sod cutters to cut so much better than the others. I told him what I did to the sod cutter and I then asked him why no one ever sharpened the blades. He told me that no one ever told them about sharpening the blades and that they had been cutting sod for many years without sharpening any blades.

I found out that it normally took them all day to cut and load three trucks of sod which took us a half of a day to do. Needless to say, I had all of the inmates mad at me because they had to work hard that morning.

At noon when we came back to New River for lunch, one of the guards told me that I was to report to the work office. There I was told that I was made a permanent, which is an inmate who is given a permanent job. I worked there for two weeks as a utility man who was someone who cleaned up everyone's messes.

One morning they had me dipping bread into an egg mixture for french toast. About halfway through, one of the cooks asked if I was taking out the molded bread, and I said that I hadn't seen any. Then he showed me some that I had already dipped, but I told him that no one would know the difference. He said, "But we do and we have to eat it too."

My last week at New River, my money finally caught up with me. I bought four cans of snuff, some ice cream and a soda. That afternoon I took a shower and I laid my clothes out to where I could see them while showering. While I was rinsing the shampoo out of my hair, I looked to see that my clothes were gone. I ran out of the shower to find my clothes with all of my money gone. I have lost lots of money before but I never got as mad as when the inmates stole my $15.

I was then sent to Avon Park for three days and then on to Bradenton Work Release center around the first of September where I stayed until the middle of December. My work release stipulations were that I had to work for someone during the day.

So I worked for Roger again baling hay. I mowed, raked and baled round bales by myself. Floyd was Roger's cow man back then and would pick me up in the mornings dropping me off at the fields. My girlfriend at the time, Teresa, would pick me up in the evenings and take me back to the Center.

One evening when I got back to Work Release after dark, the officer saw me coming in all dirty and asked me to come to his office. When I sat down in front of him all he did was look at me, actually kind of stared at me. He then started shaking his head and said, "You know you're not supposed to be drinking".

I just started laughing at him and told him that I had not been drinking. So he asked me why my eyes were so red and I told him that I had been raking hay all day. He then said, "What is hay?"

I was shocked and couldn't believe my ears and have often wondered how many other people were like him. I had no idea that there were actually people who didn't know what hay was. I thought everyone knew what hay was and what it's used for.

After serving my time with the State of Florida, I was back at the ranch at the end of 1987. I never grew anymore marijuana, but I did smoke it. I told everyone that I wasn't going back to prison...ever! I was done with marijuana and the business part of it.

Duane and I decided to plant a watermelon crop in February of 1988 on the 125 acres that Roger grew tomatoes on in the fall. This was the most acreage that we had ever planted and was going to be the first time that we grew on plastic or even used plastic. We didn't have much ground work to do just spraying roundup to kill the weeds and grass. We sprayed two weeks before planting, which was around the end of February.

Someone in St. Pete had a used 80 foot truck scale for sale which we bought. And Jerry Holder, from Trenton who was growing melons up the road from us, installed the scales. We installed them on the south side of our pond along with a small office and scale house.

This was a big help for us because before we had the scales, the trucks had to get weighed in Arcadia. And most of the time, they were a little over or under weight so they would, at times, have to come back to the ranch to load or unload the melons to get the correct weight.

During this same time, the Jones' were in partnership with Max Cohen on a melon crop on Hi-Hat Ranch in Sarasota. They were preparing the ground in early January. Grady Jones came by the ranch telling Duane and I about a used melon machine for sale in Lake City. It needed some work done on it, but he thought that we should take a look at it.

I told Grady, right away, that I wasn't going back to Lake City again. I had just come from there and I didn't have a need to go back. So we gave Grady the money for the machine and he picked it up for us. Duane and Robert Keen worked on fixing it for several weeks. The machine ran on electric motors that ran the conveyors.

Once the machine was running, we could load three semi-trailers at the same time, as well as weigh them right at the farm. This made it so much better for the truckers because they didn't have to wait so long to get loaded.

We ordered the plants Max and Wendy Cohen with backup plants in case the first planting died from a freeze. We planted 50 acres of Crimson watermelons, which are the round striped melons, and 75 acres of Jubilees, which are the long striped melons. We fertilized by injecting liquid fertilizer into the beds.

We started harvesting the melons in May and made a good profit on them because we didn't have a lot of money invested in them. With the melon machine and the truck scales being our only investment without a partnership with anyone else, this allowed us more money in the end.

This same year Duane bought a large lot that had a small house on it along the Braden River in the northeast side of Elwood Park. Duane was going to build a larger house for his family to live in, so instead of tearing it down he got a house mover to move it to the Myakka ranch.

The plan was to move it to the ranch for Cande to live in whenever she was there. It was set up in a small oak scrub area in the northeast corner of the farm. We also had a two-mile dirt road to maintain that led to the ranch. We were always having shell and gravel hauled in to fill the holes that the sod and melon trucks made with their heavy loads. Each year the road washed away in some places when we had our summer rains until we installed three large culverts. This allowed the water run off much faster.

We had around 200 acres of sod left to cut. We stopped mowing it because I wanted it to grow thick and tall so that we could bale it into big round bales of hay. We paid Harold Wright to bale it for us. He ended up baling over 600 round bales. I thought this would be enough for my new idea.

My idea was trying to burn the hay bales during a bad freeze which would keep the crop from freezing. By having the big round bales around the field burning, running water down the irrigation ditches, this would, in turn, create warmth from the running water under the smoke or a greenhouse effect, which would save our melons from any freeze that might come.

I planned to plant an early spring melon crop that could be harvested about the same time Immokalee harvested theirs. They normally got a higher price for their melons and usually started picking in April. The Arcadia area usually started in May, but with a much lower price. So we kept the bales of hay around the north and west sides of the fields until winter came to use in case of a freeze since I was planting earlier.

We laid plastic in October on 150 acres on the southwest corner of the ranch. In the dry ditch we planted two small rows of rye grass on each side of the ditch to help protect the melon vines on windy days. If you get windy days, the wind blows the small vines around, twists the plant off at the roots killing them. Three to four foot tall rye helps keep the wind from blowing the vines around.

We started planting the early crop of melons in November of 1988 in order to get an early harvest. Planting early was risky because of the possibility of a freeze, but we had the hay bales as backup hoping my idea would work. We usually planted our melons in January or early February for a Memorial Day harvest.

Again we bought our melon plants from Max and Wendy and ordered enough plants to plant 50 acres of Crimsons and 100 acres of Jubilees. And again backup plants were ordered in case my idea didn't work and a freeze killed the first plants. Once the plants got planted, they took off really good and the rye grass was growing taller.

The melons were growing and looking real good. The vines were four to four and a half foot long in late December when the first freeze came. The weather bureau said that there was to be two days of freezing temperatures. We took the forklift and started placing the bales of hay along the dirt road on the north end of the field ten feet apart. The north end was three quarters of a mile long and on the northwest end we did the same with the bales but it was only a thousand feet long. I also put thermometers in several different spots in the field.

Duane and Tammy's husband, Chad Lowe, along with some of their buddies were going to help with burning the hay. The night of the first freeze, I would go to the field and check the reading on the thermometers every 30 minutes.

Around midnight the temperature read 34 degrees and I said that we better get the bales on fire. I had already bought a bunch of cigarette lighters for us to use so I scattered everyone along the long row of hay to light the hay on fire.

Our first problem was a slight breeze and that the hay was old which made it very hard to get the fire started. When we finally got all the hay on fire the temperature was reading 31 degrees. It took two hours to get the bales burning. There was burnt ash all around the bales but no smoke.

I took a shovel and started stoking all around the bales. Sparks with lots of smoke were going up in the air over the fields when the slight breeze took the smoke south with a little heading over to the east.

Around 3AM the temperature came back up to 36 degrees but each bale had to be stoked every five to ten minutes to keep enough smoke over the fields. I could see where everyone was by the sparks that flared up.

We kept this up until daylight since the temperature was climbing. We all slept until mid-afternoon. Not long after I woke up I went over to Glen Parks to borrow his forestry fire pot to light the other bales.

The freeze did some burn damage on the melon leaves that were on the plastic but the leaves on the dirt were okay. Everything went well on the second night with the fire pot dripping a mixture of gas and diesel fuel along with the fire. In less than 30 minutes all the bales were on fire. We did the stoking again until daylight.

On the first night we lit every other bale every 20 feet. The rest of the bales were lit the second night. I later found out that there was smoke in Myakka City and in spots on State Road 72. The smoke helped save the Woodson Farm's tomatoes that were just south of us. We also found out that the bales would last ten hours before they turned to ash.

Around noon, after the second freeze, Max and I were riding in his Jeep looking over the melons. Just as we neared the swamp, where I had grown the marijuana crop, a loud noise was hovering over us. It was coming from a coast guard helicopter that was about 100 foot in the air with two men standing in the open door looking at our fields.

It sure scared the shit out of Max when he saw it and he looked over at me with a scared look on his face and said, "You still got marijuana in that swamp?"

That got me laughing like hell but I said no. Then Max said, "What the hell are they doing here then?"

Still laughing like hell at the scared look on Max's face, I said "Look, they're looking at our melon crop. That's probably the only green they have seen all morning other than the Woodson's tomatoes."

About that time the helicopter pulled up and headed west and Max began to settle down some.

In April, Immokalee melons came in and a week later ours were about ready to harvest. I started calling some brokers in Immokalee about buying our melons. None of the brokers believed that I had melons in the Arcadia area. Even after I told them what I did for the freeze, they came to look and couldn't believe what they saw.

Melons at the time were $0.18 per pound in Immokalee. I was trying to get $0.20 for our melons because our field was 125 miles closer than the Immokalee fields. Each of the five brokers said that they would call me back the next day on the price that they could offer me.

Boy did I screw up big time for calling the brokers. I should have only called one of them because when they got on the phones to call their buyers about paying $0.20 for melons in the Arcadia area the price on melons dropped. The $0.18 a pound that the melons were selling for that day dropped to $0.14 a pound by the end of the day.

The buyer thought that it was a big lie because the freeze didn't get the Arcadia area and when they found out that it was only one farm the prices never did get back to $0.18 again. Even though I killed the $0.18 market, we still made good money on the $0.14 market. So you see...I can screw up a steel ball with a rubber hammer.

After that crop of watermelons, Duane and I decided to plant 40 acres of pumpkins to sell in October for Halloween. We bought the seeds and started planting in July. We also borrowed a seed planter to plant the seeds on the plastic from the melons. We had some trouble with white flies and disease, but the biggest problem was that we planted seeds that were 90 day seeds instead of a 120 day seeds. So our pumpkins were ready to harvest the first week of September instead of in October. What a waste of time and money, but that was just another one of my many mistakes.

After the pumpkin patch was a big flop, Duane and I decided to get the ground ready for yet another spring melon crop. So we spent the rest of the year pulling up plastic, disking the ground and making sure all of the machinery was working properly.

The last time I remember seeing David DeSear was when he came by the farm when we were preparing the ground for the next melon crop. I was standing at the pond where we shipped out the melons when David drove up. He was in his Sunday best, as usual, as we were shaking hands.

David said as he pointed behind me, "Looks like you got a fire starting."

I turned around and saw Duane and Robert Keen trying to put out a fire, but it was getting away from them. They were doing some welding on the pump about half mile from us and a spark caught the dry grass on fire. I told David to jump into my truck to go help them.

As we got closer I could see that we needed something else to help them so I drove to our shop to get a 55 gallon barrel. I ran water into the barrel while I got some croker sacks and threw them into the barrel. When we got back to the fire, the four of us started fighting the fire with the water soaked sacks.

A slight eastern wind was blowing the fire which made it even bigger. Chad was disking a field close to the pond, so I jumped in the truck to get him to disk a fire lane on the property line at the western end. I was hoping that would stop the fire from spreading. It did, but the fire burnt up more than 100 acres of grass.

As I got back to where Duane, Robert and David were, I saw Duane and Robert kneeling over David. He was lying on the ground, exhausted and covered with black ashes. Once again, his Sunday best was a mess.

I asked David if he was alright and replied, "No, I need something to drink."

So we went to the trailers to get something to drink. I got some ice water and handed it to David. He said, "I don't want water! I want something to drink."

I said, "You mean whiskey?"

David replied "Yes!"

So I handed him a bottle of vodka and he dumped out the ice water filling the glass full of vodka. He drank it down like most people drank water.

About a month later I heard that David was in the hospital dying. Duane and I went to see him but he was unconscious. His skin had a yellow tint to it and his belly was bloated. This was my first time seeing anybody looking like that. He died two days later. David really was a good person and one of my best friends but the heavy drinking had done him in.

So for this era, you have learned that I spent a lot of time having fun. From the hog catches to growing marijuana to going to jail it was all in fun. I do, however, know one thing...I do not want to go back to prison. I was okay with growing my melons and other veggies without any trouble with the law.

*The Hog Catch*

*Trailers & barns at the Myakka Ranch.*

*Watermelon fields. The swamp in the top right hand corner is where I grew marijuana.*

*Loading melons next to our field.*

*Gary is bringing in some of his pot on his shoulder smoking a joint and with a Gator tail over his left shoulder.*

*Duane, showing how big the mother plant is.*

*Gary, harvesting some of his pot.*

*Gary, hiding behind a stack of marijuana.*

*One of the big buds.*

*Gary, in our grow room.*

*Gary looks like he's watching the pot grow.*

## CHAPTER 6
# 1990 - 2000

The *Nineties* seemed to be filled with violence in our country as well as abroad. The United States played a role of "world policeman", sometimes alone but often in alliances. The decade began with Saddam Hussein's invasion of Kuwait which resulted in the Gulf War. There was war in Somalia and troops were sent to Haiti, as well as to Bosnia with air strikes against Yugoslavia.

In the United States, there was the beating of Rodney King in Los Angeles in which four white policemen were acquitted. A bomb was detonated in the garage of the World Trade Center. O.J. Simpson went on trial for the murder of his ex-wife and her friend, Ron Goldman. Timothy McVeigh bombed a Federal building in Oklahoma City. Fourteen students and one teacher died in the Columbine High School shooting which also left 23 wounded.

In 1991, the "World Wide Web" or www first became available for public use. By 1994, three million people were online with an increase to 100 million by 1998. Yahoo was introduced in 1994 and quickly expanded to become one of the Internet's most popular search engines.

Manatee County was changing as well with the east part of the county growing by leaps and bounds. In 1992, there were 728 farms in the county totaling almost 300,000 acres or 63% of the land. In late 1994, Lakewood Ranch development was introduced to Manatee County with plans of great American family lifestyle. The first subdivision of Lakewood Ranch was Summerfield that was developed in 1995.

As for me, we were still preparing the ground for the next melon crop in the early part of the year. We started planting in February with hopes of harvesting by the first of May.

We built a barn and a loading ramp to pack the melons and put them into cardboard bins which would then be loaded into the

222

semi-trailers. I told the builders not to worry about putting on the truss straps, sometimes called hurricane straps, because we would do it ourselves. This was a big mistake on my part because we got busy with the melon crop and forgot all about doing that.

We were picking watermelons one day and a storm quickly came up and everyone ran for cover. I drove my pick-up underneath the barn where two other field trucks with melons were already parked. With the wind and rain blowing hard, the Negroes, who were driving the field trucks, jumped out and ran for their crew buses.

About this time the barn started shaking really bad due to the heavy winds. I fell to the floorboard of my truck not knowing what was going to happen. Suddenly, it seemed like all hell was breaking loose and then it became light again. I sat back up in my truck seat to find the barn's roof completely gone and electrical wires hanging around my truck.

I started my truck and backed it out of the barn. That is when I saw the roof which had flown 300 feet into the nearby melon field in several hundred pieces. We were right in the middle of harvesting the melons, so there was no way we could do any repairs right then.

While we were working on the melon crop, the law was working on a huge drug case in the Myakka area that we would all come to know as "The Myakka Gold Case". Apparently it all started when Bruce Hendry and Gary Huffman were arrested in late 1989.

Around October or November of 1989, Bruce Hendry and Gary Huffman were illegally hunting on the Lykes Brothers property in Hendry County. They were caught and arrested for armed trespassing. After being arrested they were released on bond but their guns were confiscated.

I have personally spoken with Gary in regards to their arrests, their indictments and how things took place. Gary seems to think that the law officials must have had the guns tested for prints and other matters because several months later the trespassing charges were dropped but a Federal indictment was served to both of them.

According to Gary that's when all hell broke loose. Their Federal indictment came around March of 1990. The indictment was for the cultivation of marijuana and they were put in Morgan Street jail without bond.

They were often questioned by government attorneys as to what they knew and who they knew in regards to the "Myakka Gold" drug ring. At first neither of them told anything. But Bruce finally broke down and told everything that he knew and then some.

Gary stated that he felt as though the government was getting antsy and was willing to try anything to get them to talk. He recalls Bruce telling him that they threatened to have his entire family locked up and all of their property seized. So Gary thinks that's why Bruce finally cracked.

Though Gary was not a part of Bruce's debrief with the government, I have a copy of Bruce's debrief and have read all of the interviews. Boy, what a liar he was! I believe he made up shit just to make everyone else look worse than him.

Bruce first debriefed with the government on June 6, 1990, and Gary debriefed a few weeks later. Gary states that he did not give them all of the information that he knew and that's why he received a slightly longer sentence.

Due to their cooperation with the government on the "Myakka Gold" case, they were both given lighter sentences. Bruce was sentenced to around four years, but only served two and a half. Gary, however, was sentenced to five years and served three and a half.

So with the information from Bruce and Gary, all the law had to do now was get Federal indictments on the rest of the clan. Now we must enter the days prior to the arrest and Federal Trial of the "Myakka Gold" members.

In late May or early June of 1990, Johnny Potts, who was a Lieutenant for the Manatee County Sheriff's Department, came to the Myakka Farm to serve me and my sons, Duane and Gary, a subpoena to appear before a Federal Grand Jury in Tampa, Florida. Johnny informed us that in 1987 Congress passed new drug laws that a person could get 25 years to life for growing marijuana.

I was laughing at him when I said, "Johnny, I could shoot you dead and not get that much time!"

Johnny said, "Donnie, I'm telling you that these new drug laws are very tough."

He also stated that they knew that I had not been doing anything since the last arrest with time served. He said, "We want you to go before the Grand Jury and tell all that you know."

I knew that my sons were still in the marijuana business but didn't know any of the details because I told them after my release from State prison that I was through and that I did not want any part of the marijuana except to smoke it. I told them not to bring any marijuana to the ranch or to conduct any business around me because I did not want to go back to prison again.

When I was busted in 1985, the laws were lenient, but the new drug laws that were passed in 1986 to 1987 were a different story. None of us knew about the laws at the time until Johnny stated that the laws had changed; I just knew that I did not want any part of jail again.

Congress enacted mandatory minimum sentencing laws, which forces judges to deliver fixed sentences to individuals convicted of a crime, regardless of culpability or other mitigating factors. Federal mandatory drug sentences are determined based on three factors, the type of drug, weight of the drug mixture (or alleged weight in conspiracy cases), and the number of prior convictions.

Judges are unable to consider other important factors such as the offender's role, motivation and the likelihood of a relapse. Only by providing the prosecutor with "substantial assistance", (information that aids the government in prosecuting other offenders) may defendants reduce their mandatory sentences.

A week or so later, the three of us, along with Cande, went to the Federal Courthouse to go before the Grand Jury. Duane and Cande had attorneys with them, but Gary and I didn't. There were several other people waiting to go before the Grand Jury, also.

As we were waiting, Duane's attorney, Norman, advised me to plead the fifth amendment because he felt as though I would be tricked into answering a question or say something detrimental to me since I did not have an attorney advising me. After being questioned three times and pleading the fifth, I was excused and the Prosecuting Attorney made a statement that I would be made a target. I think they really wanted me to testify against my two sons.

While Cande and I were sitting outside the Grand Jury room, Johnny Potts exited the courtroom with a file folder under his arm and entered a room right outside where we were sitting. He did not close the door as he entered it and we were able to witness him banging his head on the wall several times. I told Cande, "Look at him…he must be crazy!"

Several weeks went by and we all were living normal lives. We were busy at the ranch cleaning up after the watermelon crop. We had to bust the watermelon beds back down with a bog-disk and prepare the fields back to level ground again before the rainy season began. We also had to clean up the field that had the metal roofing and lumber scattered all over it from the barn roof.

Gary and Duane had been talking about getting the hell out of Florida. They were both trying to sell their stuff to go on the run. Gary told me, "Dad, you need to get rid of everything, get some cash and go!"

I told him, "I am not going to do anything because nothing is going to happen. I haven't done anything for anything to happen to me."

All of us spent the 4th of July weekend at Steinhatchee scalloping and had a real good time. Gary and his girlfriend, Diane, left on the run shortly afterwards. Duane and his wife, Judy was still making their plans to go.

My last day in the outside world was July 24, 1990. On July 23, 1990, Cande and I were in the gulf fishing when everyone was arrested. We spent the night with some friends after fishing that day. The next morning, I was on my way back to the ranch when Perry Taylor flagged me down to ask me if I got arrested yesterday morning with the rest of them. I said no and he proceeded to tell me that there was a big bust the morning before. He really didn't know how many people were arrested but he knew there was a bunch. I told him that this was the first that I had heard of it and thanked him for the information and headed on to the farm.

When I got to the trailer, I noticed Duane's driver side door of his van was open so I shut it and went inside the trailer. I didn't notice anything out of the ordinary except when I passed by the pool table I noticed a sheriff's deputy's card left on the table.

It was David Livingston's card, who was a Manatee County Sheriff's Deputy at the time, with a note telling me to call him. I locked the gate and went to my girlfriend, Teresa's house, who then took me to the sheriff's substation in Parrish. Upon my arrival, a deputy took me to the main office in downtown Bradenton.

Deputy Johnny Potts and David Livingston took me to the Marshall's office in Tampa from there where I was taken to the Federal courthouse to go before the Magistrate, Judge Elizabeth Jenkins. She set a detention hearing for me the following day. After the detention hearing, I was ordered to be held without bail because I was a threat to society and a flight risk. What a laugh! I turned myself in but I'm a flight risk?! At this time is when I first heard that our case was called the "Myakka Gold".

I was then taken by the Marshall to Morgan Street county jail and put in a Federal cell which was supposed to hold 24 inmates. There were 12 double bunks but there were about 20 or more that had to sleep on floor mats. The cell was loaded with roaches and the next morning I was killing them with my flip flops. When I rolled up my mat, there must have been 20 to 30 roaches under it.

It wasn't until I got to Morgan Street jail that I actually found out about the huge bust that included most of Myakka. They made 27 arrests in all. I did later learn that the law shot my daughter, Tammy, and son-in-law, Chad's dog when they busted into their house thinking they were arresting my son, Gary. Tammy and Chad bought Gary's house a couple of months before the arrest so when the law came to "Gary's" house to arrest him, they threw Chad down and cuffed him.

It took me several months before I could get accustomed to sleeping in a county jail because I was used to sleeping without lights on and noise free. But after a year in the county jail, I found that I could sleep in the middle of a football game with the lights on and the crowd screaming.

While in Morgan Street, Mark Massey was in the same cell as I was and a few days later Brian Coker was put in with us as well. Brian was having a hard time being incarcerated and was crying, so I was trying to comfort him by saying that they didn't have anything on us and to not worry because we would be out soon. It didn't take long for me to realize just how wrong I was because Johnny Potts was correct about one thing…the new drug laws were tough.

After a few court appearances, we were transferred from Morgan Street to Springhill County Jail in Brooksville. They put all of us, Mark Massey, Duane Clark, Danny Godwin, Brian Coker, Brian Alday,

Timmy Young and I, in different cells blocks without bond with the other 20 or so, indicted co-defendants, out on bond.

The indicted co-defendants were Glen Gavel, Trey Ness, Luke Brindel, Kenneth Harwick, Bucklin (Bucky) Godwin, Bobby Royce Maddox, Rodney (Bushrod) Teuton, Arthur Ness, Phil Harris, Marvin Bentley, Steven Arbuckle, Judy Clark, Robert Arbuckle, Tracey Shirling, Kayus Harwick, Matt Godwin, William Owen Bartruff, Anthony (Tony) Charles Lee, Jack Bentley Jr. and Ed (last name unknown). All of these people were out on bond until the trial and each of them received jail time but they all received different sentences.

Mark and Duane were my celly's with our cell block being next to the women's cell block. The men and women could talk to each other through the showers. We were only together for about three to four weeks until they moved us around. They finally put all of us in different cell blocks which the cell blocks housed about 60 or so inmates per cell block.

It was around this time that Gary showed up in Springhill. He was finally arrested after being on the run on September 19, 1990. He was arrested at a Tampa motel while only being in town overnight getting another vehicle to leave in again.

Apparently this particular motel was having problems with vehicle break-ins so the Sheriff's Department was patrolling the area and running the registered guest's name in the computers. This was Gary's first time of using his own name or showing a driver's license. All the times before he used bogus names, even registering under the name of Johnny Potts one time and David Livingston another time.

They put Duane by himself and Gary by himself in different cell blocks. Mark and Brian Alday were in one cell block and Brian Coker, Danny Godwin, Timmy Young and I in another cell block.

Springhill was the best county jail that I had been in. The food was good and there weren't any roaches or mice. They allowed contact visits which most jails do not allow. I spent most of my days playing poker and we used commissary for money. All of us did different things to pass the time. With weather permitting, we were allowed one hour of rec everyday together and we would discuss our cases then.

In our cell block, we had two different inmates that kept us awake at night. One was a black man from Palmetto, who snored really loud and was my celly. He slept on the bottom bunk and inmates would holler at me to throw something at him to get him to stop. When I would throw something at him, he would get out of his bunk; kneel down on his knees beside his bed with his head resting on the bed. This was the only way he could sleep without snoring.

The other inmate was a weekend inmate who had state charges and he would come in on Friday night and leave Sunday night. I don't remember his real name but his inmate name was Hiccup because he hiccupped all of the time. We found out later that he was born like that and at night it was almost impossible to sleep because he always had the hiccups. He told us that his wife bought a waterbed one time but they had to get rid of it because his hiccups would make waves in the bed.

Timmy's prison nickname was Possum because he slept all of the time. I cannot remember anyone that could tell lies with a straight face other than Timmy. One time there were five black inmates in Timmy's cell listening to his lies. If I didn't know Timmy better, I would have believed his lies as well.

My favorite was the one about him being the quarterback for the University of Myakka and the other one was about him being a champion bull rider. And then to top it off, he tried to get me to back him on up his lies.

To hear Timmy tell it, there was no one that could do anything better than him and if you don't believe it…just ask him. Before we were arrested, I didn't really know Timmy, I just knew of him and that he was a great poacher as well as a good hunter.

The four of us always ate our meals together and the day that we had fried chicken was the same day that Brian Coker left. In all county jails, they bring the food trays to the cell blocks and you eat in the cell blocks instead of a chow hall. We just sat down to eat when a guard came to the cell and said, "Brian Coker…B&B" (which means bag and baggage or get all of your stuff bagged and bring your baggage…meaning that you will be leaving the cell block or possibly that particular jail).

Danny asked Brian where was he going and Brian told him that he was going to Sarasota to be closer to his family. Since I didn't know how long he would be traveling, I offered him my quarter of chicken to eat. As Brian was leaving, as a joke, I told him to go by Duane and Gary's cell block to tell them that he was going back on the "rule 35". Everyone knew that was exactly what Brian did except me.

Brian did not go to Sarasota instead he was transferred to Kissimmee where they put all of the rats. A few weeks before Brian left, Bucky Godwin was put in our cell block. He was actually out on bond with the rest of the indicted co-conspirators, but because he kept failing his urine test they locked him up with us. After Brian left, all of us agreed to not take a plea agreement unless all of us were willing to plea, with the exception of me because I was not ever going to take a plea agreement.

There was an inmate in Duane's cell block who told Duane that he needed a real good lawyer for himself or "a smoking gun" as he called it. So Duane, Gary and I arranged to have a meeting with him at an attorney visit and afterwards he was willing to represent all three of us.

Smoking gun stated that Duane's case was going to be the toughest but he felt that he could still get him off and Gary's would be the easiest. As for me, he said that he could "walk" my case right out of court, so Duane hired him to represent all of us.

The trial was originally supposed to start in January, but was delayed until April due to the judge breaking her wrist. She stated that she would rather delay the trial than transfer the case to another judge or starting the trial and later having to abort it if complications arise with possible surgery to her wrist. So it was postponed until April.

On April 29, 1991, we were moved back to Morgan Street jail. Just before we left Springhill, Timmy, Bucky and I put together several bags of loose tobacco to take with us to sell at Morgan Street. There was no smoking allowed there, but you could get $1.50 for one rolled cigarette. Instead of being sent to Morgan Street, we were sent to the new jail on Orient Road and processed there. Since there were eight of us, they only processed two at a time, so we were able to pass the tobacco back and forth amongst us without the guards finding it.

After being processed, we were then bused to Morgan Street and put in different cell blocks. Duane, Mark, Bucky and I were in the same cell block and we put Bucky in charge of getting our commissary and selling the tobacco.

Our families brought our suits to us that we had to wear during the trial. We were taken to the laundry room at 5AM to get dressed for trial and then taken to the holding cell until the Marshall's came for us at seven. The Marshall's then took us to a Federal holding cell located under the courthouse where we stayed until eight-thirty at which time we were taken to the courtroom to wait for the Judge's arrival at nine.

The indicted co-defendant's attorneys, the ones that were out on bond, asked the judge to severance their clients from the eight of us, but the judge denied it. The first day wasn't that long because the judge was upset due to the lack of space in the courtroom. It was packed because of the amount of people with 28 defendants and 31 attorneys. With the large group of people and small courtroom, she delayed the trial until a larger courtroom could be used which was the next day.

That evening, after we got back to our cells, we all talked to our families and we received word that Timmy and Brian Alday were debriefing with the law. Boy was I pissed! The next morning when I saw them in the laundry room, I jumped them about the debriefing and reminded them of our agreement about no one pleading unless everyone plead. They told me that the law informed them that both of their parents would be put in jail unless they entered a plea agreement.

After all of us discussing everything again, everyone, except for me, agreed again that no one would enter a plea agreement unless everyone did. But no one was going to even think about it unless the judge would drop the points so that the most any one would get sentenced would be 15 years. As soon as the Marshalls brought us into the courtroom, Brian and Timmy told their attorneys to withdraw their pleas.

After the judge was seated, she asked the prosecutor if he had any new information for the court and his answer was no. I could tell the judge was pissed since no one was willing to go for a plea deal. I think the prosecutor had already mentioned to her that two defendants were willing to take a plea. What she wanted was for all of the defendants to plea because she really didn't want a lengthy trial.

She then said, "Alright, folks, I am going to severance the two groups."

She went on to say that the eight of us would be tried first and all of the attorneys objected so she called them to the side bar. It was quite the sight to see with 31 attorneys at the side bar with those in the rear trying to hear her. After about 30 minutes at the side bar, our attorneys came to all of us stating that she did indeed drop the points so the most anyone would receive would be ten years.

The eight of us looked at each other and all of them shook their heads in agreement except for me. All of the attorneys were shaking hands with everyone and each other as if they really did something. Duane's attorney had a big unlit cigar in his mouth and walked over to me trying to shake my hand and said, "Donnie, we did a good job for you all."

I did not shake his hand but said, "All I have seen that you all did was got a bunch of money for doing nothing!"

That was the end of court for the day, May 13, 1991, when the seven defendants along with the 20 indicted co-defendants went off with their attorneys and the government agencies for their debriefing about their plea agreements. For some reason, Duane's plea agreement in front of the judge was on May 15, 1991 by himself with Timmy and Gary entering their plea on May 16, 1991. The other four had their pleas entered in front of the judge on Friday, May 17, 1991. After entering their plea deals, they were all sent to Sarasota County jail.

On Tuesday, May 21, 1991, while the judge was preparing for the other indicted co-defendants to enter their pleas, there was yet another delay. The judge announced that everyone in the courtroom had been exposed to a contagious and potentially dangerous disease – tuberculosis.

The trial was postponed for two days while defense attorneys, prosecutors, court employees, witnesses, defendants, law enforcement officials, reporters and the judge were tested for the disease. Apparently Timmy Young tested positive on Friday. About 75 people were tested in all. The potential jurors were kept in another part of the building and were not exposed. At this point, 11 out of the 28 people had entered plea agreements.

On Thursday, May 23, 1991, in court, it was reported that none of the dozens of people that were tested on Tuesday and Wednesday tested positive. In fact, they determined that the positive testing on Timmy was not positive after all, so all of that time was wasted in my opinion.

The trial was ready to move forward once again, but it was

postponed until the following week to allow more time for plea agreements to be made with the remaining people. Of course, that did not include me, because I was not going to plea to anything.

On Friday, May 24, 1991, the rest of them entered their pleas with my trial set to begin on Tuesday after the Memorial Day weekend. The seven defendants received the following sentences:

| Defendant | Time sentenced | Time served |
|---|---|---|
| Duane Clark | 9 years | 8 years 4 months |
| Gary Clark | 7 years | 6 years |
| Mark Massey | 11 years | 9.5 years |
| Brian Alday | 9 years | 7.5 years |
| Timmy Young | 11 years 3 months | 5 years 4 months |
| Danny Godwin | 9 years | 7 years 10 months |
| Bucky Godwin | 20 months | 5 years 5 months |

As you recall, Bucky was originally one of the indicted co-conspirators who was out on bond until the main defendants plead but because he couldn't stay clean he was put in with the rest of us as a major defendant.

Brian Coker was one of the original major defendants in this case, but since he turned into a rat, his time was cut. His file is sealed by court order so therefore no one really knows how much time he served.

My trial started on May 28, 1991. A week or so before my trial started, my sister, Sandra went to Johnny Potts' house to talk to him about me. At the time, Sandra's daughters were real good friends with Johnny's daughter. My sister is a very religious person and Sandra told me what Johnny told her that day. He said, "I like Donnie, except for his criminal activity."

Then he asked Sandra if she believed in God and she said, "Sure."

Johnny raised his right hand, and then said, "I swear to you, before God, that I will never testify against Donnie at trial."

That sworn statement didn't last long. He did indeed testify and boy was Sandra fuming.

The judge presiding over the trial was Elizabeth Kovachevich, the government's attorneys were Walter Furr and Edward Page with my attorneys being Thomas Ostrander and Smoking Gun. It was a known fact that the judge did not like to go to trial. She always wanted the defendants to take pleas and I was no different.

On a daily basis, she instructed my attorneys to take me into the side room during the recess periods to talk to me about taking a plea agreement. At first, I was furious about it because I wasn't guilty and I was going to fight until the end no matter what the end brought.

My attorneys said they understood my feelings but had to comply with the judge's orders. After a while, I did not mind going into the side room because one of my attorneys would have a can of snuff in his briefcase for me.

## DAY 1 - Tuesday, May 28, 1991....

Today was mainly for opening statements on the charges and the jury selection. The entire day I noticed the judge staring at me over the rim of her glasses, but I just stared right back because there was no way I was taking a plea.

My attorneys asked me, in the beginning and a couple of times during trial, if I was sure that I had not done anything with marijuana since my release from state prison and I assured them that I had not had anything to do with marijuana except to smoke it. He stated that the prosecutor said that they had something on me which contradicts my statement. All I said was, "We'll see later on, won't we?"

By the end of the day a jury of nine men and six women were chosen with two of the 15 being alternate jurors. Because of the time it took in choosing a jury of 13 with two alternates out 45 people, need-less to say, it was a brutal day.

## DAY 2 - Wednesday, May 29, 1991....

It was determined by the judge on day one that nothing was to be mentioned to the jurors or any witness about my prior conviction. So the jurors did not know that I had been arrested in 1985, plead guilty and served time. Nor did they know that I personally told everyone that I was finished with the marijuana business. This is something that, to this day, I don't understand. In fact, my entire trial was one-sided. There was very few times that she ruled in favor of us.

The judge started the day with instructions to everyone on how her courtroom was going to be run. She planned to have the trial Monday through Thursday beginning at 8:30 for her and the attorneys to go over any and all questions. Then the jury would be brought in at 9:30 for the trial to begin with plans to end at 4:00 with a one hour lunch break.

The jurors were sworn in and Mr. Furr began his opening arguments. Of course, everything he mentioned in his opening arguments was about my state case that I had already served time for. He mentioned that when I was arrested I admitted that everything in the trailer was mine. I did admit to that but back in 1985.

Once Mr. Furr was finished, my attorney, Mr. Ostrander started with his opening arguments. I feel that it was very tough for him to lay down the ground work for the opening arguments especially because he couldn't mention anything about my previous case. But I feel that he did a good job.

After opening statements by the government and the defense, the government called their first witness to the stand, David Livingston.

David was one of the lead investigators. He was sworn in as an expert witness on the cultivation of marijuana. He was asked how he became an expert witness and his reply was that he had three to four weeks of classes. But, later, when the government attorney asked, "Can you tell the jury why marijuana plants are hung upside down?"

He replied, "I'm not positively sure. I think they dry faster upside down."

They had a large map of Manatee County set up in court on an easel with 60 different colored dots marking the different marijuana fields that were eradicated over a ten year period with only 30 of the dots being a part of the conspiracy. My attorney objected to this stating that this was only to enflame the jury but the judge denied the objection.

David went over the 30 dots stating whose fields were whose, how much marijuana and the details about the fields such as going into the swamps with gators, snakes, spiders and fire ants. The other 30 fields he stated he didn't know whose they were or who they belonged to. Not once did he state to the jury that any of the fields belonged to me.

All afternoon the government grilled Livingston on the stuff that the officers confiscated from the ranch. They even showed pictures of the barn where I had the grow room. The government had David go into detail about the ledger book that was kept in regards to the marijuana growing in the swamps in drums that was taken into evidence from the ranch. They also produced a photo album of pictures that the sheriff's department compiled that was passed around for the jurors to see.

He also presented bags of marijuana with seeds and one of Bruce Hendry's PVC pipes that he had several bags of pot inside. They presented buckets, floaters and "pungee" plates (a metal plate that has spikes welded on one side to put in a trail or in water) for people to step on who don't belong in the area.

Of course, this was all evidence and information that was gathered from my arrest in 1985. But not once did Livingston or the government attorney mention a time frame therefore not allowing the jurors to know that it was in 1985. My attorney's tried to object to a lot of the questioning but was overruled.

## DAY 3 – Thursday, May 30, 1991

The morning started with the judge going over a few things with the attorneys then the jurors were brought in at 9:30. Livingston was still on the stand and the government began asking him to go over the photo album. They seemed to dwell on the pictures of the seed operation and the grow room. They also went over the map of the fields that Hendry and Gary Huffman had shown the Sheriff's Department. The government finished their questioning in the afternoon and my attorney, Smoking Gun, started his cross examination.

There were a lot of objections from the government's attorneys and most of the time the judge ruled in their favor. Most of the objections were due to the way the questions were being asked. Smoking Gun tried to tip toe around and wanted to get Livingston to bring up the 1985 arrest but never did.

The jury was sent home a 4:00 to be back at 9:30 on Monday. But our day was not quite over. The judge had a major sidebar after the jurors were out of the courtroom. She instructed the attorneys to be careful in their question/statement structures.

She said, "I'm not trying to interfere with counsel because that's not my role, but I'm going to tell you right now if somebody's trying to set up ineffective counsel and a get a 2255 in this case, before I let that happen I'm going to impose sanctions."

She even spoke of the court imposing jail time for the attorneys as possible sanctions but stated imposing fines to the attorneys seemed to be more effective.

## DAY 4 – Monday, June 3, 1991

The morning started as normal with the judge and the attorneys discussing a few issues in the beginning and then the jury was brought in. Livingston was back on the stand with my attorney finishing up his cross examination.

Smoking Gun touched on the map with all of the dots. He asked, " Can you tell the jury if any of these fields belonged to Donald Clark?"

Livingston said, "No."

Then he started asking about the evidence that had been pre-sented so far.

Smoking Gun asked, "You cannot say that the ledger books that are in evidence belonged to Donald Clark, is that correct?"

Livingston said, "Yes, that is correct. I cannot say they are his."

Smoking Gun then asked, "You cannot say any of that stuff be-longed to Mr. Clark, can you?"

Livingston replied, "I don't believe so."

Smoking Gun finally asked, "You cannot say any of this evi-dence presented so far to this jury belonged to Mr. Clark, can you?"

And Livingston replied, "I don't have any personal knowledge of it, no sir."

Smoking Gun finished his cross and the government briefly

re-crossed examined Livingston. He was relieved but put on stand-by in case they wanted to call him back. A recess was taken.

Bruce Hendry was sworn in and took the stand as the second witness for the government. He is the one that became the government's main witness in this entire case.

Bruce told everything and then some but not in the courtroom. I had his and Gary Huffman's debriefing in front of me and was reading their statements while Bruce was on the stand testifying against me. One of the statements that Bruce made that stood out was about the Schoolhouse Bay marijuana field.

Bruce and Brian Coker had an argument over grow lights, so Bruce drew a map leading to the Schoolhouse Bay marijuana field, wrapped it around a rock and then threw the rock into Deputy Don Rowland's yard.

Timmy and Brian Coker thought that the Sheriff's Office found their field by flying over it, but I read about it in the debriefing and told Timmy about it. It was a real big crop and only a few days from harvesting when it was found.

Bruce testified that he worked for Clark Seed Company on the Myakka ranch for a short time. He admitted to stealing two of my marijuana plants in the late '70s and that he bought pot from me in 1981. He told about the marijuana plants that Philip Coker screwed up that were the plants that I gave Philip to grow on halves. But after I saw how sorry the plants were I told Philip that I didn't want any part of them anymore, so Philip gave them to Bruce to grow on halves. Again all of this was prior to 1985.

Hendry even testified how he paid Tony Lee $15,000 to grow pot on his property. Tony Lee was arrested, but later did a set-up for the Sheriff's Department and got off without serving prison time.

The government finished their questioning but my attorneys wanted the rest of the day to read over Hendry's plea agreement. The jury and court was relieved at 3:15 for the day.

## DAY 5 – Tuesday, June 4, 1991

One of the jurors was sick so a delay was made this morning to determine what to do. Most of the morning was spent trying to find out what was wrong with her. The jury took their lunch break and then was released shortly afterwards for the day.

In the meantime, the courtroom deputy clerk heard from the juror's husband that the juror had an inner ear infection and would not be able to return until Friday. So the judge decided to recess for the day with the understanding that more information was needed to be obtained from the juror's doctor to see just when she could return. Everyone was to return to court the next morning for further direction.

## DAY 6 – Wednesday, June 5, 1991

Everyone was back in court this morning as usual. The judge spoke with the juror's doctor late the previous afternoon. He assured the judge that the juror would be available on Monday without any further problems. So the judge excused the jurors for the rest of the week. She went over several things with the attorneys before excusing the rest of us for the weekend.

## DAY 7 – Monday, June 10, 1991

Court was back in session with all jurors present. After going over things with the attorneys, the jury was brought in. Bruce Hendry was still testifying with my attorneys cross examination.

Smoking Gun really drilled him about why he seemed to always refer to me in his answers to the government's questions. Smoking Gun said, "Was it simply hearsay when you said 'Coker told you he got buckets, fertilizer and plants from Donnie?'"

His reply was, "Yes."

Smoking Gun said, "So you really don't know if Donnie Clark supplied them or not, do you?"

Hendry said, "No."

After going over a few other things, Smoking Gun finished his questioning and Hendry was relieved, but put on stand-by.

The government then called Philip Coker as their third witness. The government actually paid to fly him back into town because he lived in Mississippi at the time.

Both the government and my attorney questioned him. Coker stated that he knew absolutely nothing about growing marijuana until I showed him everything. He told about his involvement with me and our drug business together. He stated that I supplied all of the materials that were needed for growing and all of the knowledge to know how to grow it.

He agreed with Bruce's earlier testimony about me not wanting anything to do with the failed crop. He told about the marijuana that he sold for me in the '81 crop that I grew and about the grow room with the pot in it. He told about his ex-wife living with me and about having a shotgun to shoot me with. But as usual, the government was still using all of the information from my 1985 arrest as evidence.

His testimony wasn't that long and before the end of the day Timmy Young was sworn in as the fourth witness for the government. The government questioned him for about an hour or so and then the judge ended the day with instructions for everyone to return tomorrow.

### DAY 8 – June 11, 1991

Once again court started as usual and the jury entered the courtroom at 9:30. Timmy was back on the stand with the government questioning him for about a half of an hour.

My attorney cross examined him for about the same length of time. Neither of the attorneys got a lot out of Timmy in my opinion. He really just confirmed some of the dots on the map and testified that he and Bruce went into the grow room with one of my sons but that he did not have any drug business dealings with me. He actually stated that he had more to do with my boys than he did me because he felt like I didn't really like him.

The fifth witness for the government was Gary Huffman, who also testified that he had not had any drug dealings with me. He only stated that he had been to the ranch to go hunting with my sons and to get vegetables from the garden. But Gary was quite a babbler. He often gave more information than what was asked for. The government finished their questioning and lunch was taken with my attorney starting the cross examination afterwards.

It was mentioned during Hendry's questioning and quite a bit more during Gary's questioning how Buddy Parks was paid by some of the growers to be informed ahead of time as to when the Sheriff's Department would be doing a fly over on the Kibler Ranch. Buddy Parks was the ranch foreman but also very good friends with Johnny Potts. So Buddy always knew, through Johnny, when the Sheriff's

Department's helicopter would be flying.

And Buddy allowed some of the growers to use parts of Kibler Ranch to grow on, of course, with some type of payment from them. He kept the ranch hands and everyone else away from certain areas that he knew they were growing on. So he not only was acting as a friend to Johnny and the other officers involved in the investigation, but was also covering for the growers as much as possible. He was paid generously several times by several growers.

Gary's cross examination was completed shortly after lunch and a break was taken. Then the government called their sixth witness, Raymond King, after the break. He was only on the stand for about 30 minutes total including both sides questioning him. He testified that he was at the work release at the same time I was there which put everyone on alert because that had to do with my state time. He also testified that he had not had any drug business dealings with me. I'm not sure why the time was wasted on him because the only thing he really said was that he got some marijuana one time from Duane in trade for some four wheelers and he had been inside the grow room.

Rob Whaley was called to the stand as their seventh witness. He testified that he worked at the ranch for me off and on in the '80s at which time he saw a huge amount of marijuana on a big table. He also stated that Cande was present at the time when asked who was at the ranch.

He said that he had smoked marijuana with me but that he first smoked marijuana in his early teens. But the government made a big deal about this on closing arguments to the fact that I got this young boy smoking marijuana at an early age when Rob clearly stated in his testimony that he smoked pot long before he knew me.

When Smoking Gun cross examined him he couldn't say why or who told him to be at the courthouse that day. You could tell he wasn't sure why he was there and that he had been coached. The day ended with Rob and the jurors were sent home.

### DAY 9 – Wednesday, June 12, 1991

The morning was slightly delayed due to Smoking Gun getting to court late. The judge went off! She instructed everyone that court was due to start every morning at 8:30 and not a minute later. Smoking Gun apologized to the court and explained that the hotel where he was staying did not give him a wake-up call but that just infuriated her even more. She instructed him to go to the drugstore across the street at lunch and get an alarm clock because she was not going to tolerate tardiness in her court.

Once she cooled down and finished going over things, the jury was brought in. Brian Coker was sworn in as the government's eighth witness. During the government's questioning, they asked if he knew Buddy Parks. He answered, "Yes, he was my brother in-law."

The government asked, "Did he assist you in the marijuana business?"

Coker said, "Yes, he gave me information regarding when the officers might be out and around the Kibler Ranch where I had marijuana growing."

Then the government asked, "Did you compensate him?"

He answered, "Yes, I paid him $500.00 maybe $1000 quite a few times."

Furr also asked, "Do you know who spray painted the Myakka Post Office?"

Coker answered, "Yes, everyone knows who painted it."

Gary had painted "Anyone that rats is a dead rat, depositions included."

The government finished their questioning and then Smoking Gun cross examined him. Smoking Gun went over all of the indicted people with him. But Coker stated he never had any dealings with me whatsoever. He was released but put on stand-by.

Grady Wilgus, my former brother-in-law, was sworn in as the ninth witness for the government. He was questioned extensively by the government about my involvement with marijuana. But Furr kept referring to me growing in that late '80s which Grady denied.

Then Smoking Gun questioned him if the Myakka community knew about marijuana being grown there and Grady said yes. He asked Grady, "Did you know that Donald Clark was growing marijuana in the '80's?"

Grady said, "Yes, in the early '80s."

The defense rested but the government cross examined him again because Furr felt that Smoking Gun had opened up the door about my 1985 arrest and conviction. So he questioned Grady on the ledger book and the vegetables that were grown at the ranch. He asked Grady if vegetables could be sold in grams instead of pounds which of course Grady answered no.

During the redirect, Smoking Gun made several objections. Some were overruled but a couple of them made the judge so mad that she called a sidebar. At sidebar, after several minutes of discussion, everything got worked out but Smoking Gun was still not happy and he asked for a mistrial. She denied it of course. So Furr went back to his questioning again.

Once Furr was finished, Smoking Gun asked for a redirect on his cross which she granted. And it was during the second redirect that it all came out in the courtroom. Grady spilled the beans when asked, "Was there an occurrence that caused everybody in Myakka to talk about Donald Clark?"

"Yes...it was when he was arrested for growing marijuana."

Smoking Gun then asked, "Are you aware that after his 1985 arrest, that Donnie Clark would have nothing to do with marijuana?"

Grady answered, "Yes, he said he wanted no more to do with it because he got into enough trouble and did not want to go back to prison."

Grady was finally released but kept on recall status.

So it was finally out! The jury now knew that I had been arrested prior to this trial for manufacturing and cultivation of marijuana. They seemed surprised that it took nine witnesses and eight days of testimony to bring this out. Now, my question was, are they going to find out that all of the evidence that had been presented thus far was from my 1985 arrest?

None of the pictures that were shown had me in them. No one who had taken the stand stated that they had any drug dealings with me except for Bruce Hendry and Philip Coker but that was prior to my arrest.

Nancy Bryant was the tenth witness to be sworn in. The government started questioning her until she started saying that I didn't live at the ranch much after my arrest in 1985. They seemed like they didn't want to talk much about me not being at the ranch because they still wanted the jury to believe I was still very much a part of the marijuana growing after that.

Smoking Gun questioned her briefly then she was excused. Johnny Potts was sworn in as the eleventh witness. You should have seen my sister's face when he took the stand. Remember, he swore to God in front of her that he would not testify against me in court. That statement didn't go far and it really hurt me because I thought Johnny was an honest and truthful person. What a fool I was!

He was sworn in as an expert witness on marijuana identification and marijuana paraphernalia identification with approximately 400 hours of basic law enforcement training, intermediate training, advanced narcotics identification, and basic DEA training with narcotics investigation.

When Johnny was questioned about Buddy Parks he said that he and Buddy became good friends in late 1987 but their friendship ceased in April of 1991 after Potts realized Buddy was double dipping by receiving money from pot growers in exchange for information on the Sheriff's Office air surveillance over the grower's pot fields. Their friendship must have blossomed again, because not long after my trial Buddy Parks was working for the Sheriff's Department.

At the end of the day, the government wanted to show a video tape to the jury. Smoking Gun objected, because he stated he didn't know anything of a tape and thought the tapes were simply tapes of search warrants of some of the other indicted co-conspirators. But this particular tape was a tape of a BBQ picnic that was seized at Bruce Hendry's house.

The judge came down hard on the attorneys by telling them that they have had several months to look over all of the evidence. She adjourned for the day, but not until she told the attorneys, "All of you can look at all of the evidence to your heart's content but tomorrow morning this court is rolling."

## DAY 10 – Thursday, June 13, 1991

The morning started with the tape being shown. The tape was actually confiscated during the search of Hendry's house and was of a BBQ held at Crane Park in Myakka City. Potts pointed out several of the co-conspirators, as well as several of the "unindicted" co-conspirators. A lot of people were named during the showing of the tape, but I was not in the tape.

244

Mr. Page asked Potts, "In your opinion, can you give us an estimate of the plants that were grown from the beginning of the charged conspiracy until its termination?"

Potts answered, "I would have to say between 900,000 to a million plants."

Johnny was not just talking about me when he answered; he was also speaking of the entire group. But the others took a plea so why was all of this being brought into my trial?

A lot of times his answer to questions would be "I don't recall."

Another tape was shown of the marijuana fields in Schoolhouse Bay that was confiscated in 1987. A third tape was shown of a field labeled as the "McClure field" located on Buckeye Road and Carter Road in Manatee County that was eradicated in 1988. A fourth video was shown of a field which showed floaters that was used for growing.

Testimony continued with Potts stating how he went, on May 24, 1985, to the Myakka ranch that was being leased by me with a search warrant. So finally the jury was hearing all of the evidence of what was found during the search way back in 1985. They heard that marijuana was found along with some paraphernalia. They also heard that I pled guilty to the 1985 arrest and was convicted. But why were they not allowed to know this in the beginning? I felt like this was some type of conspiracy on their part by not allowing the jury to know from the beginning.

A video was shown to the jury of the search done at the ranch in 1985. Then the government attorney had Potts tell the jury of my violation of probation in 1987 due to the firearm that Gary left on the pool table at the ranch along with a small baggie of marijuana that I had.

Smoking Gun began his cross examination requesting a sidebar. He wanted Sandra put under the rule as a possible witness. To be "put under the rule" means to allow a witness to testify, but normally they are sequestered during the trial. Of course, the other attorneys objected because she was not sequestered and was in the courtroom every day of the trial. Smoking Gun wanted her to testify about the conversation that she had with Potts.

The judge really got perturbed with Smoking Gun on several occasions due to the way he questioned Potts. He asked Potts if he and the Delta Task force ever planted marijuana on someone in order to get information on other people. Then he got into the friendship with Potts and Buddy Parks.

Smoking Gun asked, "Why wasn't Buddy Parks arrested as a co-conspirator or co-defendant like the 27 others?"

Potts answered, "We had no more room...we had to stop somewhere."

Boy did Smoking Gun have a hay-day with that answer! Even some of the jurors seemed a little shocked at his answer. An afternoon break was taken and when we got back to the courtroom, the judge had to instruct the attorneys to not talk to the press until after the jury had reached a verdict. Apparently Smoking Gun had been talking to the press. Smoking Gun completed his cross examination with Potts and that completed the trial for the week.

### DAY 11 – Monday, June 17, 1991

The morning started with the twelfth and last witness for the government, Jeff Brunner. He was the DEA agent who worked with the other law enforcement agencies during the investigation. All of his testimony was about his credentials as a DEA agent. When asked why the DEA was involved he answered, "Because the investigation got too large. When a drug case becomes too large, agencies normally pool together, which is why in this case the DEA, the IRS, FDLE pooled together with the local Sheriff's office."

Furr finished his questioning with Brunner rather quickly and the judge asked if my attorneys wanted to cross exam and they answered no. So the government rested their case.

The judge then asked my attorneys if they had witnesses for the defense. Smoking Gun stood to say that he had two quick witnesses and then asked for the rest of the day to confer with me to see if I was going to take the stand. The judge had a fit! She said, "You both have had all weekend to confer with Mr. Clark and now you're asking for a half of a day or more delay. What did you do for three days?"

Then Furr had a fit when he found out who Smoking Gun was going to call as witnesses. He was going to call Gene Matthews, but because he was under a lawsuit with the Manatee County Sheriff's Office he wasn't allowed to testify.

Then my sister, Sandra, was going to be the second witness, but because she was in the courtroom throughout the trial, Furr argued she couldn't testify. So it boiled down to, prior to lunch, there wouldn't be those two witnesses testifying.

My attorneys then started requesting a mistrial due to the fact that Livingston testified that none of the fields that were brought into court as evidence had anything to do with me. So, therefore, I could not be tied into the conspiracy. Also it was clearly stated once Grady Wilgus opened the door to my arrest, conviction and time served, that I no longer was involved with the production or cultivation of marijuana.

The judge let the jury have an hour and a half for lunch due to all of the issues that she had to deal with. After lunch, prior to having the jury return to the courtroom, the judge denied my attorney's request for Gene Matthews to testify, as well as the request for Sandra to testify. She asked both of my attorneys if I was going to take the stand. They said no even though I wanted to.

Then she asked them if they were certain the defense rested their case and Smoking Gun stated, "Yes, the defense rests."

So closing arguments was the next step and both sides requested two and a half hours to prepare which she agreed to two hours for each side. She went over the evidence with the attorneys as to what the jury would be allowed to review in the deliberation room. Both sides agreed to allow them the photos only.

She then called the jury back in after lunch. She let the jury know that both sides had rested their case so they would be released for the rest of the afternoon to return in the morning for closing arguments to begin.

### DAY 12 – Tuesday, June 18, 1991

The morning started as usual and then the jury was brought in. Mr. Page started with his closing arguments. He went on about how I was conspiring with everyone in Myakka throughout the early '80s until the major arrest of the "Myakka Gold" team.

He painted the picture like I took this young kid, Rob Whaley, introduced him to marijuana and because of me he started smoking pot at a very young age. But as you recall when Rob testified he stated that he was smoking pot long before he even met me.

The indictment charged conspiracy and if the jury found that I conspired with other persons, both known and unknown, I was responsible for what happened later on even though I wasn't around.

Page said to the jury, "We know he pled guilty or no contest to the charges back in May of 1985 was convicted and served time. The basis of this conspiracy was formed because Donald Clark was out there with the growing operation where plants were in the fields (almost 900 of them), grow light operation in the top of the barn, secret stairway to the top of the barn, marijuana in the clothes dryer, marijuana in the house, scales and a ledger book of the sales."

All of this was from my 1985 arrest. When I was arrested in 1990, I turned myself in. All of the so-called plants, scales, grow light operation, and marijuana in the house or in the dryer were NOT any part of my 1990 arrest. They brought up all of the prior conviction information to prosecute me in my federal trial.

So all of the government's closing argument statements or information that was given to the jury, in my eyes, was double jeopardy which was why I was fighting so hard to beat the charges. I really did not think they could re-try me on charges from my prior conviction especially because I had quit. I did not have anything to do with marijuana after I got out of prison except to smoke it from time to time. But the final statement that the government gave to the jury was, "In a conspiracy, quitting doesn't count!"

A brief break was taken and Smoking Gun started with his closing arguments. He started by telling the jury that the government had not proven me any part of the conspiracy. He reminded the jury about the witnesses that testified on the information given to the court was the information from my 1985 conviction.

He stated, "None of the witnesses, not Gary Huffman, not Bruce Hendry, not even Officer Livingston testified about Donald Clark having anything to do with the several hundred locations of marijuana fields or plants that were seized. In fact, Officer Livingston stated, after direct questioning, 'Were any of these fields Donald Clark's fields?' 'Not that I'm aware of.'"

Smoking Gun reminded the jury that Potts testified that he did, in fact, arrest Mr. Clark in 1985, admitted no other conspirators were arrested or investigated at that time. He reminded them that Potts admitted that there was never a conspiracy back then. But he also reminded the jury that now, after five or six years, the government is now asking the jury to use all of the 1985 evidence to convict me of conspiracy.

Smoking Gun explained to the jury that it was his decision and his decision alone to not have me take the stand. He stated, "Although, Mr. Clark did, in fact, want to take the stand because he stated to me and Mr. Ostrander that he had nothing to hide."

It was a long and grueling morning with lunch taken at one. After lunch, Mr. Furr started with his final closing arguments. He was very pissed when he got started. He told the jury how the defense attorneys had berated the government; how the defense said that I shouldn't be in prison because I wasn't guilty.

Then he made the comment about why I didn't take the stand. He said, "If he had, we would have beat the ever living hell out of him!"

Of course, my attorneys objected to this comment but the judge overruled. Then Furr stated how the defense attorneys tried to get the jury to believe that every government witness was a liar. He said, "If Mr. Clark would have taken the stand, there would have been blood all over this courtroom in Tampa, FL because Mr. Page and I would have been fighting to get to him."

Furr finalized his final summation with some pretty subtle comments that I'm sure helped the jury in their deliberations. He stated, as he went over the case within the last several days with the jury that he couldn't help but feel sorry for the Clark family because they have basically destroyed themselves. Seeing the destruction of the family with two sons and a daughter-in-law pleading guilty and being sent to prison is sad.

He wrapped up his closing with stating to the jury, "Guilt is written everywhere. In the barn, on his farm and with all of the people who were arrested that pled guilty."

The judge then started with the jury instructions. After going through several minutes, maybe a half hour, the judge started on defining conspiracy. She stated that a person may become a member of a conspiracy without full knowledge of all of the details of the unlawful scheme. In other words, if a defendant has an understanding of the unlawful nature of a plan and knowingly and willfully joins in that plan on one occasion, that's sufficient to convict them on conspiracy even though they had not participated before and even though they played a minor role.

So at the end of the day the jury was sent home with instructions that they would return in the morning and be in deliberation. My only regret about the trial was that I didn't take the witness stand because I did not have anything to hide. I would have answered all questions truthfully but I think my attorneys were afraid that they might have had some tricky questions and so my answers could have been harmful. I do know that I put my foot in my mouth at times.

## DAY 13 – Wednesday, June 19, 1991

Shortly after the jury came in they began their deliberations. They only had two questions for the court throughout the day. One was, "Can someone sell marijuana to a buyer and that be considered a conspiracy?"

The other one was, "Can a person engage a 'cleaner' of marijuana and that be considered a conspiracy?"

The judge answered by telling them that either the court could read the instructions from start to finish all over again or the jury could read the instructions themselves. So she wasn't about to assist them in anyway. The jury went home after court was adjourned at four o'clock.

## DAY 14 – Thursday, June 20, 1991

The jury was back in deliberations and after returning from lunch a note was sent back to the court by the jury foreman that the jury was at a stalemate. The judge called the attorneys back and shortly after two everyone, including the jurors, was back in the courtroom.

The judge, at that time, read "The Allen Charge". Basically, it instructs the jury to go back to deliberations and to carefully reconsider their thoughts on guilt or innocence beyond a reasonable doubt.

So they went back to deliberations. At four, they came back to the courtroom requesting testimony from Brian Coker, Grady Wilgus, Rob Whaley and Bruce Hendry. The judge denied their request due to the court transcripts not being available. She told them that they had to rely solely on their individual recollections of the evidence and the testimony.

At the end of the day, the judge told the court that she had a commitment in Orlando that she couldn't get out of tomorrow, but that Magistrate Jenkins would be filling in for her though she would be available by phone with any questions.

## DAY 15 – Friday, June 21, 1991

The day started as usual and right after lunch the jury came back stating they had reached a verdict. After the jury was seated the jury foreman stood with their sealed verdict. Magistrate Jenkins asked the clerk to read the verdict.

We the jury finds the defendant, Donald Clark, **GUILTY!** All jurors were individually polled on their answers of innocence or guilt with each of their answers being guilty.

They also had to deliberate as to whether the Myakka Farm was to be forfeited to the Government. Their answers were yes to forfeit all land, buildings, machinery etc.

I was transferred to a Federal cell in the Sarasota County jail the first of the week where the other seven co-defendants were. We had one hour of rec each day on the roof of the jail that was enclosed with a heavy wire mesh fence that had a volleyball court net in the center.

I was only there one or two nights when Smoking Gun showed up for a visit. He asked for $30,000 to cover his additional attorney fees. I looked at him and said, "Look, do you remember when Duane, Gary and I had our first visit with you in Springhill jail and you told us that you could walk me with no problem?"

He said, "You know I didn't mean that."

I said, "I mean this...you ain't getting any more money from me. I'm probably going to get life without parole and you want me to pay you more money? I know I'm a little dumb but I'm not stupid!"

I spent four months there waiting to be sentenced and this was the beginning of my book reading when my Momma sent me four books to read. The books were a series by John Jake.

## November 4, 1991, my sentence

On November 4, 1991, my sentence came down as "LIFE WITHOUT PAROLE".

One thing Johnny Potts didn't lie about was the new drug laws.

But my mind was still reeling because I didn't commit murder but yet some of the criminals who do commit murder don't get this type of sentence.

On November 9, 1991, I was sent to Springhill County Jail in Brooksville so that I could visit my family before being sent to Federal Prison. A few days after being held there, I was taken to Orlando Airport where I boarded a Con-Air jet. Most all Con-Air jets are off to themselves at the airports away from the main terminals and inmates are transferred by buses or vans to the jets.

When I arrived at the jet that day, I was surprised to see the Marshalls surrounding the plane decked out with automatic weapons. The normal routine is when a convicted felon gets off the bus or van, his handcuffs and shackles are removed, he's searched and the Con-Air handcuffs and shackles are replaced.

The one thing that I remember the most about the Con-Air trek was trying to eat lunch. The Marshalls handed all of us a bag lunch, but I didn't know how I was going to eat my sandwich because when they cuffed me, they attached a chain around my waist and attached the chain to my handcuffs. So pulling my hands to my mouth was quite tricky. I asked the Marshall how I was supposed to eat my sandwich and his reply was "you'll figure it out".

Which I did, I pulled the chain that was around my waist up almost to my chest so that my hands would reach my mouth.

From Orlando I was flown to El Reno, OK, where everyone was unloaded, searched and loaded onto buses and once again, the routine of replacing the cuffs and the shackles. During that time, El Reno was the hub where all Federal medium and high level inmates were sent first before being sent to their assigned prison. So this was simply a two or three day stop for processing.

It was windy with light snow falling when the bus arrived and I only had prison clothes on, which was a t-shirt and pants with slip-on slippers. The guards had big laundry carts on rollers right outside of the bus with large military jackets in them so as we exited the bus, a guard would throw a jacket around our shoulders. We were all put in a large holding cell, and then taken out one at a time to another area where we had to change into our prison uniforms. Since it was late at night and the chow hall was closed, we were given another bag lunch.

We were then taken to a large room that had about 200 cots for us to sleep on; each had a towel, washcloth, soap, toothbrush and toothpaste to use. There were toilets, sinks and showers in this room, so after we ate our bag lunch, we showered and went to sleep.

At noon the next day we were assigned a cell and there was a desk located in the center with a guard stationed. On the wall was a chalkboard with the inmate's name and ID number listed as well as which prison the inmate was going to next. I located my name and saw the abbreviation of where I was being sent which was "THI". I thought, "Hot damn I'm going to Tallahassee".

The guard asked for my name and ID and told me I was being sent to Terre Haute. I said "Where in the hell is Terre Haute"?

He said, "Indiana."

Of course, I was disappointed because I thought I would be with my two sons who were in Tallahassee.

A few days later I was on another Con- Air jet heading for Terre Haute, Indiana.

## TERRE HAUTE, INDIANA—FEDERAL PENITENTIARY

I arrived at Terre Haute Federal Penitentiary a couple of weeks before Thanksgiving in 1991. It was a rough prison. Nearly everyone there was not getting out of prison anytime soon, if ever, and most of them didn't care if they ever did. The Federal guidelines at the time of my sentence were that all inmates with a life sentence had to be put in a Federal penitentiary and Terre Haute was the closest Federal penitentiary to Florida.

There were men from all walks of life – rich and poor, educated and not, city and country folk. And we had the time to learn more about each other than we ever could on the outside.

When I arrived at the Federal penitentiary, it was a big letdown because it was made of old looking brick. Terre Haute was built in 1940 which was the same year I was born. There were two 20 foot tall wire fences about 20 feet apart with razor wire on both the bottom and the top. There were gun towers located all around the parameters. It looked awful for me because I knew I was not that bad of a person.

After going through receive and departure (R & D), I was taken to the dorm area, a huge room, with about 40 bunks with each bunk having two lockers. The lockers were between each bunk at the head of the bed so you couldn't really see the guy next to you. At the back of the dorm was another room with showers and toilets along with washers and dryers.

The difference between a dorm and a cell is a cell normally housed anywhere from one to eight inmates but a dorm is a big open room that housed up to forty. The dorms were a lot more dangerous than cells because there were so many inmates in one big room with no privacy at all.

Each inmate had to purchase a fan because the dorms and cells were not air conditioned. The chow hall, medical area, library, commissary and main offices were the only areas that were air conditioned. There were two TVs mounted on the wall, on each side, above the entrance door. What a joke that was trying to hear them!

There were sliding bar gates that we had to walk through to help lock down an area if trouble started. There was trouble daily with fights every day and six or seven stabbings weekly. There was a lot of tension in the air at this prison.

The daily routine was like all Federal prisons. The cell doors were opened at five in the morning with the chow hall opening at six. At seven, work duty was announced over the PA system for all inmates who worked somewhere to report to their post. Every hour a ten minute move was announced to allow inmates to go from one place to another and we had only ten minutes to get there. All inmates had to have approved passes to go to wherever they were going and the passes had to be signed off on when they returned to their housing units. This didn't apply for work duty.

Lunch started at 11 with the unicorp workers eating first, then the morning workers eating next with the rest of the inmates eating last. All inmates ate with their housing units. The times varied for the housing units depending on their housing inspections which happened once a week. The guards inspected the housing units and each unit was given a grade on cleanliness, neatness and organization. With this grading system, one unit could eat first one week, but end up eating last the next week if their inspection was bad.

At one the hourly move begins again until 3:30 which is when recall is announced over the PA. When the guards called for recall we had ten minutes to get to our cells or dorms. All doors were locked and at four every day, there was an announcement for all inmates for a stand up count. All inmates had to be in their housing units and two guards would come by each cell door looking in the cell door window to count the standing inmates. By 4:30 the count was over and the all doors were unlocked and mail call was called.

Supper started at six and chow hall was usually closed by eight with the rec yard and library closing at nine with all inmates in their housing units by nine as well. At 11 all inmates were locked into their cells. The guards would shine their flashlights into the cell windows at all times during the night to make sure everything was okay.

The inmates were different at Terre Haute than the county jail or state inmates. The laughter or joking around wasn't there with these guys. Most of them had long sentences or were in for life due to violent crimes. I would estimate that over half of the 1200 or so inmates were very bad men who carried weapons of some kind at all times.

In the United States Penitentiary (USP), we had an evaluation every six months with my first being shortly after I arrived at Terre Haute. At that meeting, I asked why I was in a USP and was told that I would always be in a USP due to my life sentence. They did tell me that Atlanta, GA, was soon going to be a USP and that I could possibly get transferred there so I would be closer to my family.

There was man in his 70s who took me under his wing, maybe because I was from Bradenton and he was from Tampa. He didn't stay long because his time was up in December. I found out that his family owned the Produce Exchange, a vegetable shed at the Farmers Market in Tampa and I had actually taken some of my produce to them to sell before I was arrested.

Just before Thanksgiving in 1991, I was assigned a job in the chow hall, cleaning tables, sweeping and mopping. When I work, I work hard so it didn't take long before I got a good paying job (as good as it can get in prison) working as a goat man. The job was called that because the machine that ground up uneaten food was called a "goat".

It was located in the back of the kitchen and it didn't take me long to get my job completed. Once I finished my job, I would go around helping the other inmates. I didn't have to do that but I'm not one to stand around doing nothing. I only worked half days in the afternoon.

In the mornings I would work out with weights or walk around the track and other times I played putt-putt golf.

I have never seen the likes of mice as there were in the kitchen at Terre Haute. I bet I killed at least ten mice per day by using the hot water hose in the goat room. The one thing that I can say about Terre Haute was that they definitely had hot water; I mean scalding hot water. While I was washing the garbage carts out with the hot water hose, I would spray the shit out of the mice as they came running by.

Tom Pritchard, who was from the Keys, had a job in safety trapping mice. The next day he came into the goat room showing me three mice that he had caught and beaming with pride of his catch. I just laughed at him and told him that I kill triple that in one day with the hot water hose. I told him to come with me so I could show him where to put the traps. There were two old rotisserie ovens that did our baking, and we put the traps behind them. The next morning, Tom had over 60 mice trapped.

While eating in the chow hall, you could see the mice running around. When I first started working in the goat room, I would often go into the cooler for some cake. The bakers put the cakes there to cool so that they could put icing on them shortly after baking them. One time when I opened the door, the mice ran off the cakes and into a hole. That stopped me from eating any more cake!

Late one night, before lockdown, I was playing poker with some of the other inmates at a table in the back of the dorm, when all of the sudden there was a big commotion at the front of the dorm by the TVs. A young Negro came running towards us with five or six others running after him. That's when most of the other inmates started running in all different directions getting their shanks.

I thought "Holy shit, there's going to be some real trouble here."

There were two sets of Negroes, one at each end of the dorm, each of them threatening the other group with the rest of the inmates in the middle off to the sides. Anytime a fight would break out someone would always be watching the door in order to know when the guards were coming. The guards normally made their rounds every hour to check the dorms.

The guards came, making their last round, and everyone got back in their bunks as if they were already asleep. It was around midnight and they were still haggling back and for. I got so aggravated I just said, "The hell with this shit; they'll just have to kill me in my sleep 'cause I'm going to bed."

I was told the next morning by Doug, an inmate who I worked out with from Ohio that the incident went on until two. Nothing really happened; it was just haggling back and forth among the inmates.

That morning, while Doug and I were working out, some of the guards came in asking other inmates what happened the night before. After Doug and I worked out, he went to get his shower first and when he returned he told me that he was going to have to leave the dorm. I asked him why and he told me, while he was showering, that some of the Negroes told him he had to leave because they thought he was the one who ratted them out to the guards.

I said, "BULLSHIT! This is not right!"

I asked him to sit down on my bunk so that we could talk this out. I asked Doug who the Negroes were telling him to leave and about that time, a young, short but stocky bi-racial inmate from the DC area, who was causing all of the trouble the night before, came walking by the bunk coming from the showers. He didn't get along with anyone; even the other black inmates didn't care for him because he was always causing trouble.

Doug said, "That's him right there; that's the main one who told me to leave."

About that time, the inmate turned around to head back towards the showers. I was just glaring at him when he stopped and asked me, "What are you looking at me for?"

I told him, "I'll look at you any way that I want to."

As he headed toward the showers, he said, "We'll see about that!"

As I continued talking to Doug, all of a sudden the inmate jumped onto the bunk next to mine, and then leaped over the lockers right on top of me, pinning me to my bunk, straddling me and hitting me with his fists. Somehow I got my feet up under him and was able to kick him off me. I jumped off my bunk sliding towards him because I still had my socks on and the floor was slippery.

He started running towards the showers with me after him, but I was having trouble keeping my feet under me because of my socks. He stopped, turned around, and punched me a couple more times, which put me off balance. He took off again and I started after him. When I caught up with him, he punched me, knocking me onto the closest bunk. Then he jumped on top of me and proceeded to pound the shit out of me until some other inmates pulled him off me.

A couple of the guys helped me up and took me to the shower room where I sat down on one of the toilets. One of them brought me some ice in a towel to hold on my face to help keep the swelling down. I looked in the mirror and my face looked like a bag full of hickory nuts. It was bruised and bloody with small cuts.

When I went to chow, the guards saw me and took me to the Lieutenant's office, where they made me take off all my clothes and took pictures of me. The Lieutenant asked me what happened and I told him that I slipped in the shower. He told the guards to put me in the "hole" (solitary confinement) to let me think about what really happened.

The hole was a two man cell. You couldn't see the other inmates but could hear them hollering back and forth to each other. You could only see the walkway through the bars outside of the door. I mostly read books and played cards while in the hole.

That was the only time that I have been in a fight that I never laid a hand on anyone. I haven't won all of my fights, and there haven't been that many, but at least I knew I had been there.

While I was in the hole, I had a celly named "French Fry" because of the bad scars on his face and arms. He was burned in a plane crash and most of his nose was gone except for his nostril holes as was his ears. His arms and hands looked really bad as well. He really was a nice guy but just looked awful.

The next day the inmate who beat me up was also put in the hole and a few days later a guard came to take me back to the Lieutenant's office. He told me that he had found out what had happened and that I could go back to my dorm. I asked if I could be moved from my dorm to a cell block because the showers in that dorm were real slippery. He laughed and said that it would take about a week in order to get an empty cell, but said that I could go back to the dorm until then or I could to stay in the hole. I chose to stay in the hole because even a week was okay with me.

After a week, I was moved to "B" block, which had eight men in one cell, and was much nicer than the dorm set-up because I had more privacy. There were four bunks with two men per bunk. The bunks were along the walls with lockers in the middle. The cells were wide open without any privacy which put everyone right in the middle of everything that was going on, good or bad.

The cells didn't have doors on them and the bathrooms were at the end of the hallway of each cell block. There were doors that automatically shut in the main hallway in case of a lockdown.

One day, while in the bathroom, I looked out of the window and I could just see a little part of the "camp farm" with the tractors working the fields. There were times that I would stand there for hours watching them work the fields, wishing I could be there working, too.

The farm grew the vegetables for the prison. The watermelons and the onion scallions were the best with the tomatoes and cauliflower being the worst. The tomatoes were split with black spots and the cauliflower was black. The reason the cauliflower was black was because they didn't tie the leaves around the cauliflower head. The farm looked to be a good set up, but they obviously didn't know much about farming.

Terre Haute must have had about 40 or so inmates who were Indians. Any Indian who commits a crime on a reservation gets sentenced to Federal Prison. They all looked to be full blooded Indians unlike the ones at the other prisons where I couldn't tell if they were Indian or not. Each prison has a "sweat lodge" for them and on Sunday's they would spend the day in or around the sweat lodge.

Another interesting group was about the big-time mafia inmates. There were four of them in Terre Haute that I knew of. Each of the mafia group inmates had their protectors or "Lieutenant's". The Lieutenants were paid by the mafia inmates. The four of them would sit on a bench and talk with their Lieutenants standing close by. I never saw any of them in the chow hall because they made their meals in their cells. They had money to buy whatever they needed out of the kitchen from the kitchen workers. They also had what is called a "stinger" which is an electric rod to boil the water. This was how they would boil their pasta. If any inmate was ever caught with a stinger, it would mean a long stretch in the hole.

There was an inmate in the cell with us who was a total neat freak and he spent so much time folding his clothes in neat little stacks that he even took a ruler to measure the distance between the stacks. He spent hours getting his clothes just right.

My life sentence didn't change my ways because I still played jokes on the other inmates as much as possible. I remember when I came into the cell one day when no one else was there, and I went to neat freak's locker and shook it really hard. When he came back later, boy was he mad and cussing up a storm when he opened his locker. It took him two hours to get his locker perfect again. I was only able to do that a couple of times because normally there was someone always in the cell. He never did find out who messed with his locker.

It isn't often an inmate gets called to the main office but anytime an inmate gets a certified letter, that's one time when they're called. And I got a call from the main office one day. When I arrived there, they handed me a registered letter from the IRS. I kind of chuckled but opened it up and found the letter to read that I owed the IRS $7000.00 in taxes from 1990. This must have been my taxes owed from the watermelon crop that I grew before I was arrested.

I kindly wrote them back telling them "Good luck getting paid because I am serving a life sentence."

A few weeks later, I was called to the main office again but this time a Deputy Sheriff was there to serve me a subpoena. I thought to myself, what else could there be, I've got life in prison and the government got everything that they possibly could take, what else could there be other than killing me?

He handed me the subpoena and said that it was for child support. I said, "Child support?"

That can't be possible; all of my children are grown. I asked who the woman was and when he told me I had to think for a minute, and so I took the subpoena. I answered her back requesting a blood test.

I later found out that she had twins, a boy and a girl. I did have sex with her several times, so I'm not sure if they are mine or not but she never did the blood test. I think she was just saying that they were mine so that she could get the government to pay her. I never heard from her again until five or six years later when she wrote me a letter telling me that it was about time for me to start paying for the children. I wrote her back and told her that we needed to talk and to fill out a visiting form so she could visit me. That was the last time that I heard from her.

Jim Wardell was my appeals attorney and he filed my appeal after I got to Terre Haute. He told me that the prosecutor called and told him that I could get my sentence reduced if I would talk to Johnny Potts and David Livingston, who were the lead investigators from the Manatee County Sheriff's Department. He said that I didn't have to tell them anything in particular, but Jim advised me to talk to them. I told Jim that I would talk to anyone else, but I wouldn't talk to either one of them even if they brought a handful of pardons with them. They lied at trial and I would not have anything to do with them.

Before my trial, I liked Johnny Potts. He seemed like an all right kind of guy, we were just on the opposite sides of the law. I always thought that officers of the law were honest people, but boy this shows just how dumb and naïve I was.

Johnny swore to God and to my sister Sandra that he wouldn't take the stand and testify against me. And when he served the subpoena to me and my two sons, Gary and Duane, to go before the Grand Jury, he actually told me that he knew that I hadn't been growing marijuana anymore since my time served in 1987 but that they wanted me to tell them what I did know about everyone else. He made this statement in front of both of my sons.

When I was arrested in 1985, Johnny wrote out my arrest report and I signed it without reading over it apparently due to my trust in the law. He stated in the report that I said that I made a lot of money growing pot and that I paid my land payments with the drug money. I never said anything like this to him or anyone else because it wasn't true.

It wasn't long, maybe a couple of weeks, after talking with Jim about Johnny and David that I heard my name being called over the loud speaker that I had a visitor and for me to return to my cell. I was working out at the gym area and thought, "Who the hell would come to Indiana to visit with me 1100 miles from home."

I returned to my cell and asked the guard if he would call to find out who my visitor was. The guard came back and told me that there were two Manatee County Sheriff Deputies here. I told the guard that I wasn't going to see them. But he told me that I would have to go. I told him he could put me in the hole if he needed to but that I wasn't going to see them. I was later told that Johnny Potts was really mad about me not seeing them and said that I could rot in prison as far as he was concerned.

I became friends with a guy from Vernon, Texas, named Randy Adams who was about ten years younger than I was and had a 20 year sentence for loan sharking. We worked out together and both of us worked in the kitchen but his job was in the butcher room.

He never used or sold any drugs, he just loaned money to people with a high interest return, ran a junk yard and had some rental property. He loaned a guy $10,000 to buy drugs and was supposed to get a $20,000 return in two weeks. The drug dealer gave Randy the title to his truck as collateral. In two weeks, the drug dealer only had $10,000 but was supposed to have the balance paid the following week. But the drug dealer got arrested and ratted on Randy and that's where Randy's 20 year sentence came from. The drug dealer only received five years.

Most Federal prisons have events happening around the holidays. The events consisted of cards, dominos, pool, horseshoes, botchy ball, volleyball, basketball, softball, soccer, hand and racquetball. They also would have a 5K run, hundred yard dashes, relay races with different bands playing.

All of the Federal prisons that I have been in had good bands. I believe it was because all the musicians were in prison for drugs. Nearly every holiday, you could expect to hear the bands playing at the rec yard. There was almost every genre of music from many different countries.

Randy entered in most of the events but never participated in any of them. When no one else showed up for the event but Randy, he would be the one winning the prize. He entered me in the over 50 Easter egg hunt and the over 50 bench press contest. I was the only one that entered the bench press contest which was to press your weight as many times as you could. I pressed 205 pounds eight times and won a sweat suit.

I went to the rec area later in the day for the Easter egg hunt and there must have been around 30 inmates in that event. The guards had three dozen plastic eggs with some having a piece of paper inside of them with prizes. The guards hid the eggs in a small area around the rec yard, on the ball fields and around the bleachers. When the guards opened the gate to let us in, everyone took off. I was laughing so hard looking at all of us old farts running like a bunch of little kids hunting Easter eggs. They were running everywhere. I walked out onto the ball field and stood there laughing and watching them getting the eggs. Then I turned and walked a little farther into the field and kicked something in the grass. I looked down and saw a green egg, and inside was a paper with $30.00 commissary on it. I guess I didn't do too bad standing there laughing at the old kids running around hunting Easter eggs.

Randy's cell was a little ways from mine but Randy never went to mail call. The first time that I brought Randy's mail to him, he just put it in a box with all of his other mail. None of it was opened. I asked him why he wasn't opening his mail and he said that his family wouldn't have anything to do with him because of his arrest. So he wasn't going to read their mail. I really felt bad for him because with no family support while in prison, it really makes the time that much harder.

I always looked forward to my letters from family and friends but I remember one of the first letters that I received at Terre Haute. It was from Ellsworth Helm and I always enjoyed his letters because they made my life in prison seem so much better than his on the outside. All of his letters made me laugh because Ellsworth's life seemed to be one disaster after another. But it didn't seem to get to him; if it did, he didn't show it in his letters. If he wasn't being sued by one of his six ex-wives, sued by the IRS, his house being flooded, his car being repossessed, etc., I don't know how he kept track of everything going on.

The one letter that was the most memorable was when he wrote to me and said, "Donnie, you know that I've been playing and singing music for the past 25 years, but damn if you didn't get a record before me!"

I allowed an inmate in our cell block to talk me into playing softball once. As you know I played a little in high school, and I wasn't that great of a player then, but damn was I rusty. They had me play right field in the beginning, and the first fly ball came right to me. I started running forward when I should have run backward and of course, missed the fly ball. After a couple more errors, they moved me to first base. With me being left handed, I actually did better there, but not much. I don't remember a softball hurting my hand so much as it did then and my batting was awful. So this was my one and only experience playing softball in prison. That inmate didn't ask me to play again either. I wonder why?

Phil Sims was the only inmate in Terre Haute who I knew from Bradenton. I really didn't know him; I just knew of him and I had heard that he was a real bad ass. Phil and Paul Richardson ran around together back in their day and Phil worked in the kitchen at Terre Haute as well.

We would walk the track sometimes and there were a few times when I would come up behind him, slap him on the back or shoulders. I would jump back real fast because he would come back real quick, ready to throw a punch. I would laugh at him and he would say, "Donnie, one of these days, you're going to be sorry."

One morning Phil didn't show up for work and I asked an inmate about him who was in the same cell block. He said that he was in the hole because Phil was in the TV room when a big young black guy came in, and changed the channel, so Phil got up and changed it back. The black guy left the room for a few minutes, but when he returned he picked up a chair and hit Phil over the head with it. A few other inmates were in the TV room with Phil and told me that Phil beat the shit out of that black inmate.

This kind of stuff went on daily because there were some real mean inmates in this prison. I saw a few inmates who I thought were dead, but in a few weeks or so they would be back out on the compound. And then there were the weirdo's like this inmate in his mid-20s who was always destroying the property. He got fired from the Unicorp for throwing a big wrench into an expensive piece of machinery that cost the government over $20,000 to repair. He would, at times, come into my goat room area and turn on the water and leave it running. I don't know why the Bureau of Prisons (B.O.P.) didn't keep him locked down in solitary confinement because he would destroy something every day. He believed that by destroying property would break the government's account and eventually get him out of prison sooner.

The one thing that I did do in prison that I never did on the outside was read. Up until I was sent to prison, I probably only read three books in my entire lifetime. But with only time on my hands, I learned a lot by reading.

Someone sent me a book named the Emperor Wears No Clothes written by Jack Herr. Being the southern farmer and Florida Cracker that I was, I always thought that sunflowers and soybeans were the best plants on earth because so many things are made from their seed. But after reading this book, I know now that "hemp" is the best plant on earth. That made me really mad then because I am sitting in prison with a life sentence because of such a great plant. There are so many things made from hemp that it makes sunflowers and soybeans seem like nothing.

I was cussing and raising hell when a Spanish inmate asked me what was wrong. We were the only inmates in the cell at the time. I told him what I had just read and he said, "That's nothing compared to what I'm writing about and besides you don't get the big picture about what's really going on in this world."

So I asked what he was writing about and he told me he was translating books from English to Spanish. The titles were the New World Order, Council of Foreign Relations (CFR), The Trilateral Committee, the Bildeburg's and some on the Rothschilds family. He started telling me a little bit about the books, which I remembered a little about the CFR from school. He got me interested so I asked if I could read one of them and he gave me one to read. The first one I read was so interesting that I ended up reading all of them.

There were times while reading them that I got really mad so I would stop and go onto reading something else for a few days. I soon got accustomed to reading the involvement of the New World Order without getting so mad about something that I had no control over. If you want to read something that's really an eye opener, read the "Timeline of the Rothschilds family".

There were two tests that I had to take while at Terre Haute. The first test was a piss test, which was my very first. There were about 30 to 35 inmates taking the test, and as my name was called, I went into the room which had a toilet and sink in it. A guard was sitting in a chair beside the toilet with a tray of bottles, some filled and some were not. He told me to start urinating in the toilet and right after I got started that he would give me the bottle to piss in. I thought yeah right; this is going to be interesting. So I stood there but couldn't start a stream for the life of me, especially with him sitting there, holding the bottle and looking at my "lil pete".

He turned on the water in the sink, but that didn't work either. He finally told me to go drink some more water, so I drank and I drank until I thought I had drank enough. There was a Spanish inmate at the water fountain also. He was having the same issue. We started talking and he bet me that he would fill his bottle before me.

I went back in to try it again but still no luck! He was laughing at me when I came back out. He went in again and came back out with the same results. I was getting frustrated, but I kept drinking and I would walk around, go back and drink some more. Finally the guard told us that we had two hours to do the job and if we didn't have what he needed in two hours that he had a shot that he could give us that would damn sure make us go.

Within 30 minutes all of the other inmates that came in with us had completed their job and gone, so the Spanish dude and I were the only two left. My bladder got to where it felt like it was about to explode but I continued to drink more water just in case. I went back into the room with the guard still sitting there waiting. I stood there and still couldn't go, so I shut my eyes and concentrated on the water running in the sink. Finally...I started to piss and boy did I snatch that bottle from that guard. I handed it back to him but stood there for quite a while before getting my bladder empty. I walked out and waved to the guy laughing as I left. I saw him a few days later and he told me that he finally filled his bottle about ten minutes after me.

Another test that I had to take was a blood test, and this time there were about 35 to 40 inmates waiting to get blood taken. They called names in alphabetical order so I knew that I would be taken early. The man drawing the blood had a hard time finding my vein. He started on one arm and failed, so he went to the other arm, but failed on that one as well. Now with bandages on both arms, I asked him about the vein that was up on my wrist because you have to make a fist when they're drawing blood and that vein popped up real good. He attempted there and finally without any problems, he was able to get what he needed.

As I was leaving I could see the other inmates still waiting. As I went through the door, I folded my arms in front of me across my stomach and leaned over a little moaning. I walked toward the inmates, looking at them, unfolded my arms and said, "Look what that son of a bitch did to me; he ain't worth a shit for hitting a vein."

About eight or ten of the inmates jumped up wide-eyed with a look of fear on their faces and left the room. They didn't want any part of that.

I only had a few visitors while I was in Terre Haute and they were from family except for Paul Wilburn. Paul was a staff writer from the Tampa Tribune newspaper. He really did a good job on reporting my case in the paper. He had a front page write up on me for three days from June 7th 1992 through June 9th 1992. The headlines read "A Prisoner of Drug War".

In May of 1993, I went for an evaluation and they looked over my records and saw that I was a good inmate except for being put in the hole that one time, but I didn't get any points against me for that. I asked them when I would be going to Atlanta because I had heard that Atlanta was now a penitentiary. After going over my records, they told me that I was scheduled to go to Jesup, GA, which was a medium-high security prison. I mentioned that I was told that I would always be put in a USP due to my life sentence but they informed me that B.O.P. had changed the rules. I would be sent to Federal Correction Institutes (FCI) due to the rule change.

Did that make me a happy man! First I was getting closer to home and family and out of this hell hole. There were only two inmates who I met at Terre Haute who were also in Jesup with me. They were John Bonner and Tom Pritchard.

## JESUP FEDERAL CORRECTIONS INSTITUTE

I left Terre Haute without a tear in my eyes but with a lot more knowledge about prison. I realized what "time" was all about. I had all the time in the world to recall my life up to that point. And for the most part, there's not much that I would have changed.

I was getting closer to my family, that's what I focused on. If not for my family, I am sure my first several years in prison would have been rougher than what they were.

I didn't have many visits while I was in Terre Haute but I knew I would definitely have more family visits once I got to Jesup. Other than the two deputies and the reporter from the newspaper coming to Terre Haute, I only had three other visits. Uncle Harold and Aunt Margaret Smetzer visited once. Cande and Margarita visited once. And Duane, Sandra, Kelli and Bobbi Lee stopped for a visit while on vacation.

I left for Jesup on Con-Air early one morning, I think in August. There were several buses loaded with inmates leaving Terre Haute. We were not in the air long before we landed again. I don't remember where we were at any given time because we made about six or seven stops throughout the day, with every stop lasting about an hour or so. The Marshalls had to do the usual unload and reload procedure each time which took a while.

Our last stop that night before we landed in El Reno was somewhere in Michigan or Minnesota. I had been sleeping off and on throughout the day while the loading and unloading took place, and woke up when the plane was taking off. I was sitting in the aisle seat but looking out the window.

I started looking around the plane at the "new" inmates on the plane and noticed this little man sitting across the aisle from me. I knew that I had seen him before but couldn't place his name. I kept looking at him but still couldn't remember his name.

I finally asked, "I have seen you somewhere before, but I can't place the name."

He said, "Jim Baker is my name."

Then it dawned on me who he was. I then started laughing and said, "I know who you are now; I used to wake my kids up with you on the TV early every morning when your show was on."

I would turn the TV on at the ranch in the early morning when Jim and Tammy Faye were on their TV show. When Jim or Tammy were talking or singing, I would turn the volume up really loud. Boy, the kids would start screaming, "Turn it off; turn it off; we're getting up!" It worked; it got them out of bed.

I don't think he liked that very much because he wasn't laughing. I think the reason I didn't recognize him was because he is so much smaller in person than he looked on TV, and only weighed about 115 or 120 pounds. We didn't talk again after that because the other inmates were talking to him, mostly asking questions.

It was dark when we landed in El Reno and it took another hour or so before we actually got to the prison. The weather wasn't like it was before; it was actually hot without the snow and wind. Of course, the procedure was the same as before, changing our prison uniforms and going through the search. This time I had some Copenhagen in a plastic bag tied to my boxer shorts through the fly hole and over the waist band. The bag hung a little higher than my crouch. I was able to get the snuff through all of the searches by the Marshalls that day.

I hung back towards the back of the line so that when I laid my boxers in the laundry cart they would be on the top. This way upon my return after the strip search I could grab my plastic bag and put it in my pocket, which I did. We still received the bag lunch throughout the day and it was really late again when we finally got to the cell where the cots and the personal hygiene stuff were.

That evening I waited in line to call my sister, Sandra, to tell her where I was. I also told her about seeing Jim. She said, "Maybe God's trying to tell you something."

I said, "Yeah, right; a preacher in for embezzlement!"

On the third morning I boarded the plane with the other inmates to Atlanta. When we arrived onto the prison compound in Atlanta, I noticed the wall surrounding it. Boy, I had never seen a wall that high around a prison! It looked to be around 20 to 25 foot tall.

I was taken to a huge lockdown cell block that was three story's high. There were huge fans blowing down the walkway in front of the cells due to the heat. I never asked nor found out if the regular cell blocks were air-conditioned; but the "holding" cell block that I was put in was not air-conditioned. All along the corridors, outside of the cells, the inmates had pieces of cardboard sticking out from the bars trying to get as much of the air reflected into the cells. This helped some but damn was it hot in there. All of the inmates were stripped down to their boxers, but we still sweated.

I was in a cell with a black man about the same age as I was. The guards handcuffed us while still in our cell, and then we were led to the shower where the handcuffs were removed to allow us to shower. We were able to get a short shower every day. And boy, I never had a shower that felt so good.

I asked a guard why I was in lockdown and he said that there was someone on the compound that I couldn't be around. I later found out that it was Brian Coker, who testified against me, but I didn't have any real issues with him. But the B.O.P. kept inmates away from any snitches that had anything to do with their case.

After four or five days in Atlanta in lockdown, I was finally bused to Jesup, going through the same procedures. I knew when I left Terre Haute that I was going to Jesup but I never knew how long it would take to get there. I always felt like a bull going to market; I went from truck to truck, pen to pen; not knowing if I was going to be butchered or turned out to pasture with some cows. That's the prison way of life.

Our bus arrived at Jesup in the middle of the afternoon, so I was put in a holding cell in the R&D area with four other inmates. At R&D, I was told what unit and cell number that I was assigned to which ended up being a mop room. At all prisons, which are overcrowded, the mop rooms are converted to cells. But Jesup was the first prison that I had been to that converted their mop room into a cell that housed eight men in it.

While going across the compound from R&D to my cell, I was shocked. I thought I was close to heaven because it was so beautiful. The grass was neatly mowed, manicured and real green. There were roses and cabbage palms planted all over; it just didn't look like a prison. I couldn't believe my eyes, especially after being in Terre Haute, El Reno, and Atlanta.

After visiting some other inmates in the regular cells, I realized the cells here had wider beds with actual spring mattresses, a desk for writing, a sink, a toilet and a mirror. After seeing the other prisons, this was the Hyatt of the prisons so far.

When first arriving at any prison that I was going to be at for some time, I went through what they call the "merry-go-round" for three days. You go all over the prison at various times to various places such as the medical area, the library, the laundry, chow hall, rec yard and the schooling areas. This is so that I knew where everything was located.

On the first day, I met Jerry Godwin. He wanted me to work in the kitchen with him as a butcher. Jerry was from the Tampa area and knew all about me and my case. One of my co-defendants, Danny Godwin (no relation to Jerry), was at Jesup until a few weeks before I got there.

After my three days of the merry-go-round, I was able to get a job as a butcher. There were three of us, another inmate named Mike, Jerry and myself. Most of our job consisted of slicing whatever meat we were having, sawing the pork loins, ribs or getting the meat prepared to bake. We also made bag lunches for the "traveling" inmates.

We prepared the meat for the entire prison which consisted of about 1200 inmates in the medium high compound and another 500 or so for the camp. The one part that all of us hated the most was deboning the chicken when "chicken ala king" was on the menu. This was the most time consuming and boring part of the job.

Once we finished our job for the day, a guard would take us to the freezer and we would get the meat out for the next day. We would put the meat in our work room, which was pretty small, but air-conditioned, so that it would thaw. Whenever we were in the work area, we were locked in so that none of the inmates could get in to steal any of the meat. Stealing out of the kitchen was rampant in all prisons. If I had to guess I would probably have to say a small 8X14 box truck would be stolen out of every prison every day. I often wondered why the B.O.P. never tried to put a stop to that. I know that if I were in charge, a camera would be placed in every corner of the kitchen and chow hall. This may not stop it; but it definitely would cut it down.

They had about four or five guards overseeing the 25 to 30 inmates who worked in the kitchen. But there was always a market for anything coming out of the kitchen. Every time a guard's back was turned, food would disappear. From the kitchen area, inmates would hide food somewhere on their bodies. That inmate would then take the food to another inmate working in the chow hall area. This inmate was called the "mule" because he was the one who carried the food to the housing units. He was also the one who got caught by the guards most of the time. The mules had what they called blockers and sometimes they had two or three blockers. The blockers would watch the guards from inside the chow hall searching the inmates as they left chow. There were two guards at each door checking the inmates.

All of the inmates who worked in the kitchen and the chow hall wore coats to and from their cells. You were allowed to take only one fruit out of the chow hall. So the mules would stuff their jackets with fruit or food of some kind and normally leave in bunches of five to six at a time. The blockers would always have a fruit in their hand so that they normally were the ones that got searched leaving the mules to get past the guards. The guards would normally only search two out of the bunch which left the door open for the mules to slip right by with all of the food they had. The guards felt like they were doing their job because they did catch some of the inmates with extra fruit or vegetables. They had a plastic garbage can beside the door that they threw the extra stuff into, but they rarely sent the inmates to the hole. If inmates were caught stealing quite a bit of food, they were sent to the hole for two to three weeks unless it was cooked meat. They would spend about two to three months for cooked and raw meat was about six months.

If we ever wanted or needed anything out of the work cooler, we had to push a buzzer and wait for a guard to come. The kitchen guards stayed pretty busy, watching the workers and getting things for the workers. The bakers and produce workers were locked in their work area as well. The ones who were locked into their areas all had knives to work with. We had regular knives in the butcher shop. But they had knives that were attached to a three foot long cable and locked to the work table. The knives were all very dull so we didn't use them very often. They didn't have a stone to sharpen them with only a steel rod, so we normally used the gallon can lids as knives.

We would take the lid, lay it on the table with a ¼ of the lid hanging over the ledge, and take a towel or cloth and bend that about ¼ ways down at a 90 degree angle. Then bend it over again to the larger portion of the lid. This made a semi-circle sharp knife with a handle that wouldn't cut my hand. They were sharp but they would dull and we would just use another lid.

The first year that I worked in the kitchen, we worked from 5AM to noon but then they started another shift that worked from 2AM to 7AM so we switched and worked that shift. There were about 20 good working inmates on that shift but there were not any chow hall workers just a small kitchen crew. We got more done on this shift but still had the rest of the day to ourselves. The guards were more relaxed on this shift as well; they let us cook our own breakfasts.

The food would have been better if we had all of the ingredients to make it with. Take the baker for example, when the guard takes a baker to the storage room with a rolling cart, he loads everything onto the cart that he needs to bake with. He's then taken back to the bakery area and locked in. But because of the stealing, the baker's missing eggs, sugar, yeast etc, but he cannot say anything out of fear that he'll get beat up by the inmates. So he has to make whatever he's making with what he has. However, what comes out is what is eaten which sometimes doesn't taste that good. I got accustomed to the food after a while. It is much better than the county jail's food, that's for sure. So when we were able to make our own breakfasts, they were good because no one stole our stuff.

When I worked in the kitchen at Terre Haute, the inmates would always try to get me to steal food for them, but I told them that I didn't steal. They would say it wasn't stealing because the food belongs to us.

I said, "No it doesn't belong to me and I'm not stealing it."

That would tick me off because I knew that I probably paid more taxes when I was in business than any of them.

Jerry tried to get me to help him bring mostly raw chicken out of the kitchen one time. I told him the same thing. He never pressured me about it but he made about $30 to $50 a week, which was a lot in prison.

One day Jerry had a big order of raw chicken. All morning Jerry was on me about helping him carry out some of the chicken. He always deboned it so he could get more in the bag and not have to worry about it showing in his crotch area. We wore rubber boots and an apron which helped hide things better. The guards knew that we were hard workers and sometimes they would make us turn around with our hands out. We normally had some fruit or a few slices of bread in a plastic bag but they didn't really pay us much attention. They let us slide because of our attitude and work ethic; unless it was a new, young guard, then it was a different story. All inmates tried to stay away from the new ones, but after a year or so, they were just like the rest of the guards.

So I went along with Jerry on stealing the chicken this time to help him out. After that I stole every so often throughout my stay at Jesup, but I never stole again after leaving Jesup. That was the beginning and the end of my stealing career because if a kitchen worker got caught stealing from the kitchen, their kitchen job career was over and I would have been sent to the hole. Going to the hole didn't bother me as much as not being able to work in the kitchen. I really enjoyed that and would have missed it.

Something of interest to me was my realization of humans and how they are like some animals. Every chow hall has two chow lines on each side leading into the chow hall. The whites would be in one line which was always on the left side and the blacks would be in the other line on the right as we entered the chow hall. And believe it or not, the seating was the same…the whites on one side of the cafeteria area (left) and the blacks on the other (right). There would be some mix of blacks with whites but not much. Every prison that I was in, the lines and the seating were the same but not by any rules just by human nature.

My realization about this was the fact that cattle do the same thing. When you have a large herd of mixed cattle laying down chewing their cud, the mix breeds will do the same thing. The blacks mostly with the blacks, the whites with the whites, browns with the browns but with a few mixed in.

Jerry and I had another inmate working with us in the butcher shop for a while. His name was Eather and he was a big guy who was a good worker but he couldn't stand the cold in the butcher shop. After he was in the cold room for about an hour, his nose would start running and dripping. When we deboned the chicken, we would debone twenty 50 pound boxes of chicken at a time. We had to take off the skin and then pull the meat off the bones. We only got the dark meat of the chicken and there were times that small bone fragments or knuckles would get by us.

We would talk to each other most of the time while working. I remember one time Eather was deboning the chicken and I looked over at him and his nose was dripping into the chicken.

I said, "Eather, wipe your nose; it's dripping into the chicken."

Jerry spoke up and said, "Oh shit that pan is full too."

No we didn't throw away that pan of chicken because we would have had to get two more cases out of the freezer, cook it and debone that batch which would have been an additional three hour process.

After that Jerry got Eather a beard guard to wear over his nose to catch the dripping snot. I don't think Eather liked it because he quit within two weeks.

Brian Alday came to Jesup a couple weeks after I got there and my son, Duane, arrived about a month later. So a few of the Myakka crew were together again and we made the best of the time that we had together.

Duane was at Jesup about two weeks before he was able to be my celly. When new inmates first arrive at a prison, they normally are automatically put in the hole for a few days because of space. I actually never had to go to the hole when I first arrived at a prison because there seemed to always be an available cell. After a few days, the inmates are put into cell blocks where there was room. Since we were father and son, they approved his request.

On holidays, as mentioned before, there were all kinds of events going on. Duane entered the 5K run and Brian and I entered the horseshoe contest together as partners. When Duane started his run, we stopped to watch him.

There were about 15 inmates entered in the 5K race and when they first started there was a Negro that took off real fast and was about 100 yards ahead of the rest. There were some other blacks playing basketball by the horseshoe pit and one of them said, "That's my cousin; look at him go."

He stayed ahead of the pack for about a lap and a half and then fell out on the track from exhaustion. Duane won the race and passed the guy who came in second by a lap and a half.

Some of the inmates said, "Pops, that son of yours sure can run."

I said that he should be able to because he doesn't have watermelons under his arms. I remember Duane running alongside of the truck throwing melons up for someone to catch while loading melons from the fields.

Everyone in prison has a nickname and of course mine was Pops, Duane's was Skeeter, and Brian's was Hillbilly. There was an inmate who was called Tractor Tom, who was nicknamed that because he was as dumb as a tractor. He was good friends with Duane. His cell was in the same unit as Duane and I and he worked in the butcher shop with Jerry and me.

As usual we were always pulling jokes on one another from time to time. Our cell was next to the showers and Duane was making some peanut butter and jelly sandwiches for us when Tractor Tom came by. He tossed some bread at Duane asking him to make him a sandwich while he took his shower.

I was lying in the bunk reading when Duane said, "Look Dad at the sandwich that I'm making for Tom."

Duane took each slice of bread and wiped his ass with it and then put peanut butter on one slice and jelly on the other. He then pulled pubic hairs and put them in the peanut butter that was on the bread. We were eating our sandwiches when Tom came by to get his sandwich after his shower. Tom was half way finished with his sandwich when I asked him how good it was. He answered, "Real good!"

I told him it was probably because Duane wiped his ass with both pieces of the bread and topped it off with some pubic hairs. I don't think he believed me because he kept eating his sandwich and said that he didn't care because it was real good.

There was another inmate that we called Wobble Eyes because his eyes would wobble everywhere when he looked at you. He would often come to our cell because our unit was normally first for chow and his cell unit was normally last or next to last. Our unit had real good orderly's and kept on top of everything so our unit was normally the cleanest and neatest, therefore always scored the highest.

Duane told Wobble Eyes if he didn't quit coming in our cell in order to get to chow quicker, that he was going to butt rub him. Wobble Eyes told Duane that he couldn't do that to him, so Duane and Tractor Tom both jumped on him and threw him on the floor. Tractor Tom had his feet and Duane had his arms but Duane couldn't get a good butt rub. Wobble Eyes was hollering real loud so they let him up.

Wobble Eyes said to Duane, "I told you that you wouldn't be able to do that to me."

That did it, they jumped on him again but this time Wobble Eyes was ready. When they finally got him on the floor, he went wild, kicking and throwing punches with one of his kicks ending up kicking me in the bunk. That did it for me as well. I got out of bed, grabbed his arms and pinned him to the floor. Duane had his shorts off and was sitting on Wobble Eyes' face rubbing his ass back and forth. By this time Wobble Eyes was screaming but the door was shut so the guards couldn't hear him. If we would have got caught doing that, we would have all been in the hole for quite some time.

When we let Wobble Eyes up, he ran out of the cell and into the mop room. He came out with a mop ringer in his hands and we were all standing there laughing at him. Tractor Tom asked him, "What are you going to do with that?"

Boy was his eyes all wobbly and his face was red, he was so mad. He stopped and turned around throwing the mop ringer back into the mop room as he stormed by. That was the last time ole' Wobble Eyes came to our cell.

Wobble Eyes got fired and went to the hole for stealing in the kitchen. When we got a new food service manager, Wobble Eyes was begging for his job back. He would follow the manager around telling him how good of a worker he was and was saying just ask anyone, they'll tell you. Jerry and I had to have the manager let us into the freezer for the next day's meat and Wobble Eyes was standing there begging for his job when he said, "Hey Pops tell him what a good worker I am."

I looked at Wobble Eyes and said, "You aren't worth a shit."

That got Jerry and the manager laughing, but Wobble Eyes got mad and left. Later on in chow, Wobble Eyes asked me why I said that and I told him, "Because it's true; you don't do any work; all you do is steal."

Tractor Tom worked the early morning shift with me and Jerry. His cell was four cells down from Duane and I and both of us would take a nap until around ten or so after our shift. I would go wake him up just before we had to go for lunch. Tom always slept with his mouth open, which left me with a lot of tricks to pull on him. One time I dropped a pinch of Copenhagen in his mouth and another time I dropped some tabasco sauce in. Then Tom was onto me so he put a deodorant can on the door knob so that when it was turned the can would fall onto the floor which would wake him up.

I practiced opening our cell door with a deodorant can on it so that I could snatch the door open and at the same time catch the can before waking Tom up. So the next time I got ready to open Tom's door, I did just that. I snatched open the door and caught the can but Tom wasn't in bed. He was standing at his sink, which was right beside the door, jacking off with one hand and holding a Playboy magazine in the other. It startled me so I shut the door back real quick. As soon as I shut the door, I realized what he was doing. I was going to snatch it open again and holler at the other inmates to look but Tom had a hold of the door knob holding the door closed, so I turned and went back to my cell laughing.

On our way to chow, Tom said, "A man can't do anything around you, can they?"

Once we got to chow, I saw Tom's celly, Andy. I said to Andy, "Hey, you know the toothpaste specks that get on your mirror?"

Andy shook his head yes and I said, "Well, it isn't toothpaste."

After I told him about Tom, he told Tom not to do that shit anymore.

One day Brian and I were playing horseshoes against Pop Vargas and another inmate. Pop Vargas was real good at horseshoes even being 72 years old. He always had a pipe hanging out the side of his mouth. Brian normally only wore a cap with a pair of gym shorts without boxers shorts under them and no shoes or shirt. Brian and Pop's partner had just finished throwing their shoes when Pop and I went into the horseshoe box to pick up the shoes. All of a sudden we heard a big commotion at the other end. We both turned around at the same time and saw Brian jumping up off the ground naked and starting to run away.

Duane and Tom had apparently come up behind Brian with Tom pushing Brian over and Duane yanked his shorts down. As Brian was falling, his feet got tangled in his shorts which made him fall down. Once Brian fell on the ground, Duane yanked his shorts completely off and took off running. Brian got up to run after Duane for his shorts.

At first all Pop and I saw was Brian's ass and his balls hanging down between his legs as he was getting up. His balls are so big that when he started running his sack of balls would go from side to side hitting each leg, kind of like a bull's when they are running. He does have some big balls because I've actually seen him on the toilet before with his balls across his leg in order to keep them out of the toilet water.

The first thing Pop said was, "Golly, look at the balls on that boy!"

That was the funniest part of the whole thing, everyone around was laughing. Duane didn't go very far before he gave Brian back his shorts because if the guards would have seen that commotion they both would have been sent to the hole.

Brian smuggled marijuana into Jesup several times. The first time was by using a plastic cigar container, similar to a toothbrush holder, which was about five to six inches long and packed real hard with high grade marijuana. The price for drugs inside was two to three times more than it was on the outside. The cheap marijuana would go for $25 for a chap-stik lid and not even packed. I'm not sure how much Brian got for his but I know it had to be a lot.

He didn't really go into details on how he smuggled in, but he did tell me one time that he cut a real small hole in his pants and pushed the cigar container up his ass in the visiting room. I don't know how he managed to do it because there are cameras and guards in the visiting rooms all of the time. And when we leave, we have to push a buzzer to alert the guard that we're ready to leave. Once we are let out of the visiting room, we enter another room where we have to take everything off and be searched. As we are undressing a guard is searching your clothing. We have to stand in front of him and he tells us what to do. Raise your arms, shake your head, open your mouth real wide and lift up your balls. Then we have to turn around, bend over spreading your cheeks and cough real hard. Brian passed all of the tests but I don't know how because that cigar container should have come out at least a little ways when he coughed, but it didn't.

Another time, one of Brian's buddies couldn't come, so he sent another friend in his place. This buddy brought a cigar container but a little longer maybe two inches longer and Brian couldn't get it in enough. I saw Brian at the rec yard later and he was madder than hell because he couldn't get that container in. So he decided that the containers were out and balloons were in and from that point on he would get the marijuana in small balloons packed as small as your finger tip and tied in a knot which ended up about the size of a grape. While in the visiting room he would drink a soda and eat popcorn at the same time while swallowing the balloons. But then he would have to dig the balloons out of his stool which worked but the marijuana smelled like crap as well.

My first and last time smoking marijuana in prison was when Duane, Brian and I were sitting on a bench by the horseshoe pit talking and Brian brought out a joint. Marijuana joints in prison are the smallest joints that I've ever seen. The rolling paper came from the wrapper of a roll of toilet paper and was rolled as small as a pencil lead. Brian lit the joint and took a hit and handed it to me but I shook my head no. I passed it on over to Duane who took a hit and he gave it back to Brian.

Brian, once again, tried to get me to take a hit saying "Come on Pop, just a little, you haven't had a hit since we've been in prison."

So I took a hit and started coughing. It was almost gone but I didn't want any more anyway. It didn't take long before I had a hell of a buzz on. It had been over four years since I had smoked any pot and with the buzz that I got immediately, I also got paranoid as well.

I told them that I was going back to my cell on the next move. I kept my head down the entire time I was walking back to my cell. I knew my eyes were blood shot because my eyes always looked like a Georgia roadmap whenever I smoked. I finally arrived in my cell where I laid in my bunk and slept it off. So that's why I say that I smoked pot twice in prison, my first time and my last time.

Ronnie Fripp was from Stuart, FL, and quite the jokester like Duane and I. He liked to put lit cigarettes butts in other inmates' pockets. Duane paid him back several times. One of the best times was when Duane spotted Ronnie in the chow line and told us that he was going to pull his shorts down as Ronnie was walking to a table with his tray in his hand. We passed the word around the tables around us about what Duane was going to do. Shortly after that, Ronnie left the salad bar, and started to walk toward a table when Duane came up behind him and jerked his shorts down to his ankles.

There amongst everyone Ronnie stood naked as a jaybird looking from one side to the other with his tray in his hands trying to figure out what to do. Everyone was laughing at him and finally he set his tray on the floor and pulled his shorts back up. He picked up his tray and headed for our table. He was madder than hell by the look on his face, and everyone was still laughing at him. He came over to Duane, who was having a laughing fit, and told him that he was going to get him back big time.

Another time that Duane jerked Ronnie's shorts down was the funniest though. Ronnie was standing, slightly bent over, talking to another inmate who was eating his meal at one of the tables. He had his tray in his hand when Duane walked by and jerked his shorts down. Ronnie's reaction automatically was to stand straight up and the inmate who was sitting down was looking at Ronnie's privates about one inch from his face. That inmate jumped back and actually turned over in his chair like it was a snake that popped out of his shorts.

The British Broadcast Corporation (BBC) came to Jesup to interview Duane and me because they were doing a documentary in the U.S. about crime and punishment. They also interviewed Cande and attended the Families Against Mandatory Minimums (FAMM) meeting in St. Petersburg. The video was aired all over the world but never in the United States, because it told the truth about our system and the U.S. wouldn't allow it to be aired.

Mr. Wheeler, who was the commentator from BBC, asked me what I thought about the new drug laws and I replied, "My understanding of the new drug laws were, mostly, to put away the "drug kingpins" for long prison terms as well as take away their assets. But I've been in prison now for five years and haven't seen a "kingpin" yet."

A kingpin has anywhere from 50 to 100 people or more under him and when he starts telling on the ones under him, he will only get a five year or less sentence and be sent to a camp. The drug dealers at the end of the line are the ones that get the 20 to 25 year prison term. The last person in line gets the big time because he doesn't have anyone left to tell on. I told Mr. Wheeler, "Of all of the time that I have been in prison I never saw or heard of a marijuana grower having a life sentence."

I kind of laughed and said, "I guess that's why they call it 'justice' because it's 'just us' here in prison not the kingpins."

There was a couple, Eunice and David Pike, from England, who got my name and address from Mr. Wheeler. They wrote lots of letters to me and they thought it was awful that I received such harsh punishment knowing that nowhere else in the world would there be such a harsh sentence. She also sent photos of England and of themselves, as well as money.

The first year or so I couldn't read her letters because she wrote so small. The print was the smallest that I had ever seen and the phrases over there are so different than ours; it was hard to understand her English slang. There were a couple of inmates who would read the letters to me and she wrote long letters, normally four to five pages long. I called her when I was released and she cried and was still crying when I hung up the phone. I still try to stay in contact with them and hope to get to actually meet them one day.

It was April 2, 1996, when we left Jesup and got moved to Coleman, FL. There were probably about 300 Florida boys and men that couldn't wait for the prison to be built and ready for inmates. All of us signed up for the transfer and there ended up being about ten busloads of inmates.

One bus per week left for Coleman and Brian and Big Joe were on the first bus but it was about a month and a half before Duane and I left Jesup. Duane and Tractor Tom gave me a Mohawk before we left. My hair was almost to my shoulders and I wanted to shave it all off, but they talked me into a Mohawk to wear for a while. Some of the inmates from Florida didn't really care to leave Jesup because Jesup was such a nice prison and they thought Coleman wouldn't be as nice.

We left Jesup around 7:30 AM and arrived at Coleman around noon. It was really nice getting the few bus rides that I got because the scenery was different. And a change of scenery was good for a while after spending years in one place.

## Coleman Federal Corrections Institute

After arriving at Coleman and going through the regular routine of R&D, we went to our assigned housing unit. Duane and I were in B4 on the second floor. At this time, there were over 800 inmates in Coleman and of course, we had three days of the merry-go-round.

On the merry-go-round, I had to visit the psychiatrist one day. He was from Sarasota and looked to be in his late 20s. He saw in my file that I was from Manatee County. He said the files showed that I was a good inmate and a good worker for someone with a life sentence. He asked if I was having any problems handling my life sentence and if so, how was I dealing with it. I told him that I didn't have any problems at all; that life in prison was great! He just sat there and looked at me like I was crazy.

He probably was thinking I was some kind of serial killer sitting there with the Mohawk haircut and with that attitude to boot. I know he was thinking, "How can anyone who looks like that enjoy being in prison?"

Then he said, "Are you sure you're okay with everything?"

I said, "Life couldn't be better!"

He just shook his head and said, "You're excused! But if you ever have any problems come see me."

I said that I would but this would be the last time he would see me.

Soon after arriving at the prison, most inmates provide the prison with their phone and visitor lists. When using the phone, an inmate has to fill out a phone list form which consists of the relationship to that person with the phone number. There are two ways to make phone calls, collect or pay calls that are deducted from your phone account. An inmate can only have 20 people at a time on his phone list. The list can be altered by adding people but removing that same amount of people. Only the phone numbers on the list can be called with only 15 minute calls at one time. Calls could be made as many times as you wanted from 5 AM until lockdown at 11 PM.

The visitor's list limit was 15 people. When I was in the B4 housing unit, I had a good counselor, Mr. Rodersheimer, who would delete and add to my list as needed. The B.O.P. rule stated that we could only make changes to our visitors list twice a year. Since I had so many people visiting me, he made an exception.

On my first day, I went to food service to see about getting a job as a butcher. I didn't like the food service manager at all because he was arrogant and a smart ass. He asked about my last job and I told him I was one of the butchers in Jesup. He said, "We don't have butchers in this prison; butchers are the hottest men on the compound" (which meant that they were the biggest stealers).

So I asked, "Who does the butchering work?"

He said that he had 12 cooks that did that.

I replied, "Instead of having three thieves, you have 12", and I turned and walked away.

Our first meal there was supper and we ate with Brian Alday and Big Joe, who was also in Jesup with me and worked in the produce section. I have to say that was the best meal I had in prison.

Brian and Big Joe had already been at Coleman for about six weeks and knew the ropes. They wanted Duane and me to work with them at the rec yard, so we did. Coleman wasn't as nice as Jesup even though it was brand new. They didn't have pretty green grass, or roses or palm trees. Most of all, they didn't have weights, just exercise machines. The cells or the bunks weren't as good either. The cells had one locker for each inmate and the mattresses were not as thick.

The only two things that made it nicer than Jesup was the food and we were only two hours away from home which meant we were able to get more visits. Duane and I normally got visits from someone every week and sometimes twice a week.

When a new prison opens, there isn't a budget to worry about in the first year. The rec yard manager, Geo (pronounced "Gee-o") Rodriquez, who was Puerto Rican, took advantage of it. He spent money like crazy to have the rec yard completed like he wanted it before the first year was over, knowing that the following years would be budgeted.

So it was a busy year for the most of the inmates. The rec yard was basically an open field of about six or seven acres. Geo had about 50 or 60 inmates working on the rec yard when Duane and I started with about 15 of the inmates on our crew.

First we installed a six foot wide, ¼ mile shell track around the perimeter of the yard. Then two softball fields with bleachers, one soccer field, one football field, two basketball courts, two horseshoe pits, three handball courts, three racquetball courts, two volleyball courts and two botchie ball courts.

We also built a large lean-to coming off the rec yard building where six TVs were mounted on the building really high. We put together about 40 metal "picnic style" table benches that would seat about eight inmates at each table; the cost of these benches was $400 each. The tables were put under the lean-to so that inmates could play cards, checkers, dominos, etc. and also watch TV. We dug trenches to install water lines for watering the grass, installed spigots and two outside showers.

Our crew was in charge of the outside work so we put the games that we liked to play in one area by the one big oak tree on the entire compound. We put the horseshoe pits there along with five table benches under the tree.

It was set up nice after it was finished. We could walk the track and pretty much see all of the games going on along the track, as well as the TV under the open lean to. Later on we put exercise stations about every 100 feet or so along the track as well. These stations would be exercises like pull ups, sit-ups, dips etc. This way you could stop at a station, perform that exercise then go walk a little ways, and stop again to do the next exercise. The only thing missing were the weights. Nancy Reagan took care of that for us. Sometime in the early 1980s, she visited the prisons and made the B.O.P. get rid of the weights, as well as the tennis courts.

They were also having a problem with getting the grass to grow because after the Oklahoma City bombing all fertilizer was removed from prisons by the B.O.P. Everything looked good and worked out well except for the soccer field, which did not have grass. The Columbian inmates were taking care of it but were not having much luck. Brian told Geo that I could grow grass, so Geo asked me what it would take to get the grass to grow on the fields. I already measured the area and told him it would take $2500.00 a year for the four acres. The Columbians said they could do it for $300.00, so he let the Columbians do it.

There were about 12 to15 Columbians working on the field and they seeded it with $300 worth of Bahia seed. Every morning you could see them out there raking the ground where they had just spread the seed. By raking it, this never allowed the seed to germinate and I told them to stop raking the field but their reply was that they knew what they were doing.

Six months later, the inmates were bitching because there was still no grass and the area was just full of dust and dirt. Geo came to me again asking if I thought I could get the fields in good shape. I told him that I could if I had what I needed.

It was June and I knew that Bahia grass would take longer to grow in order to get the fields ready for the ball games so I decided to go with Bermuda grass. There was Bermuda growing all around the rec yard but nowhere near the ball fields.

So I had Duane, Brian and Big Joe help me by pulling up the Bermuda sprigs to plant. I also had Jerry Godwin cut the sprigs into six inch pieces. We took two broom handles and drove a nail into each one side ways about three inches from the end. We used the end to poke holes in the ground up to the nail every three inches apart. The sprigs were planted in the holes and then covered slightly with dirt. This process took us about two weeks to complete the two acre fields.

The other two acres had Bahia on them but it wasn't doing good either because of the lack of fertilizer. I put 400 pounds per acre of 15-15-15 fertilizer that had all of the minor elements in it and kept it watered good daily. The sprigs started growing two to three inches overnight. The way I was able to tell was by Duane, Brian and I taking some small sticks and pushing them into the ground at the end of each sprig to the same height of the sprig just beside several of them. The next morning we would check them and the sprigs would grow that much due to the hot days and nights along with the water and fertilizer.

So within six weeks I had all four acres solid with green, healthy grass. The soccer field was the roughest because Geo couldn't get a vibrator roller to smooth out the rough spots, but all of the inmates were satisfied.

Geo didn't know anything about growing grass except that it needed water, so when spring came he didn't have the money to keep the grass growing. I told him that I was quitting my job and he said I couldn't quit. I told him, "Watch me, all you can do is put me in the hole."

The next day Geo came to me again and said, "I will pay you $50 a month to supervise the grass and you won't have to do any work."

I said, "Supervise what? You can't grow grass without money. The work I can do, but the money I can't do."

So for $50 a month I supervised three inmates doing what I did, but the only thing they could do was water, so I just told them when, where and how.

What ticked me off was, Geo was paying me $80 a month when I started and I worked my ass off to get the grass to grow, which it turned out very nice. But now I was getting $50 a month for doing nothing. I liked the work especially when I got what I needed to get the job done. The fertilizer was the hardest thing to come by. Geo had to bring it in on a cart early in the morning and I had to put it out on the grass before some of the big shots saw me. Geo probably would have been fired or transferred to another prison over that.

In my life, I have planted, grown, and harvested thousands of acres of grass, but never had the problems that I encountered growing the four acres in prison. I went to prison for growing grass and was paid while in prison to grow grass!

For some reason, Coleman had a lot of thick fog and the fogs would sometimes not lift until ten or so in the mornings. At the first sound of thunder or sight of fog, everyone had to be in some kind of shelter. The early morning fogs were the worst and that's when all of the guards, office staff and other prison workers surrounded the housing units standing far enough apart to see each other making sure no one was trying to escape. I'm not real sure what the big deal was because we were all locked down in the housing units with a guard inside each unit.

Everyone has heard of the inmates who cannot be broken or the ones that will not follow orders. I would like to introduce you to diesel therapy. Diesel therapy is a type of therapy used on inmates who don't want to cooperate with the B.O.P. system. This is used on an inmate when putting him in the hole doesn't work either. So they put the inmate on a B.O.P bus for a month or so traveling around the United States.

The inmate never gets a hot meal except on Sundays or holidays and his ID card will not work at any other prisons for commissary. He cannot make any calls or write letters and he has nothing but the clothes on his back. After about a month of this therapy and he gets back to the prison where he started, he's a broken inmate who will do what he's told to do. I never had this experience, but have heard about it and I'm quite sure it's no picnic.

We got a new Captain around 1997 but he only lasted a little over a year. He apparently got into some trouble with a civilian on the outside doing what he does to inmates on the inside. The B.O.P. doesn't fire any one; they just transfer them to another prison, so he was transferred.

None of the inmates liked him because he would try to intimidate everyone and he reminded me of Johnny Potts. He would walk the chow lines real slow staring at everyone in the face but not saying a word and he kept the hole full most of the time. I've never saw anyone doing that to the inmates in the entire time that I was incarcerated. When possible, an inmate would go the other direction when they would see him coming.

One afternoon he came into our cell block and was standing at the guard desk. I just finished reading and was standing along the railing looking down on what was happening below. I saw Jerry Godwin standing at the Spanish TV room watching TV while the microwave was cooking his food. I knew I had to get Jerry's attention because the Captain was in our unit. I yelled Jerry's name, but not too loud to get anyone's attention.

Jerry looked up at me and I pointed down to the guard's desk and he immediately saw the Captain. He rushed over to get his bowl out and put it in the mop room beside the microwave. He came out of the mop room with a broom and started sweeping the floor. The Captain must have saw what was happening because he walked right over to the mop room, went inside, came out and said to Jerry, "That meat looks about done."

Jerry just kept sweeping as the Captain walked by but all Jerry could say was, "Yes sir!"

Jerry then looked up at me as the Captain walked out the door with Jerry swiping his forehead as if he was wiping away sweat. I was just laughing my butt off at Jerry! Why the Captain didn't put him in the hole I don't know. Being caught cooking meat meant big time in the hole, so Jerry was extremely lucky.

The Captain did one good thing at Coleman that I know of. In the winter time, the seagulls would be all over the compound especially around mealtime. As the inmates left chow hall, they would throw bread crumbs up to them. The gulls would be flying and dipping down for the crumbs, as they shit all over us and all along the sidewalks.

The first day the Captain saw this he decided to make a change so he would hand the inmate a mop and bucket or a towel if they were caught throwing the crumbs or bread. The inmates with the towels would have to use the towel to scare the seagulls away, but the inmates with the buckets and mop would have to scrub the sidewalks. They all had to work like this until the chow hall was closed.

One of Duane's volleyball buddies, Piss Willey, had to scrub the sidewalk one time. I came out of chow hall and saw him scrubbing the sidewalk and started laughing at him.

He said, "At least I don't look as stupid as the other inmates with the towels."

I said, "No, you don't…you're just the shit man that's all!"

The seagulls were a mess and most of the inmates told the others not to feed them but they wouldn't listen until the Captain put them to work cleaning up the mess. I think everyone got shit on at least one time or another but I think most all of the inmates felt that this was the best thing that we all knew of that the Captain corrected.

Duane and I are as close to being "two peas in a pod". Both of us like joking around, pulling jokes on people and always having the last laugh. Being in prison didn't change us much. Being sent to Coleman together only kept us playing the jokes and stunts, though sometimes the last laugh wasn't so funny.

Most mornings, Jerry Godwin and I would play gin under the oak tree, usually after I finished raking the horseshoe pit which took about ten minutes. This particular morning we were playing gin when I saw Duane running from the softball fields towards us. I could tell he was holding something with both hands and as he got closer I could tell it was a seagulls.

The bird was trying to bite Duane's hands but he managed to make a motion to me to be quiet as he got closer. Jerry had his mind on the card game and didn't have a clue what was about to happen. Duane snuck up behind Jerry with the seagull's head going from side to side. Duane was trying to get the seagull to bite Jerry on the ear but he bit down on Jerry's neck instead. All of a sudden Jerry hollered, threw his cards up in the air and jumped up grabbing his neck. Looking around he knew it was Duane. The seagull actually drew blood on Jerry's neck.

Another morning, Jerry and I were playing gin under the oak tree while Duane and Brian were sitting on the edge of the botchie ball court talking. Once again, Jerry had his back to them but I could see everything they were doing. There was a big fire ant bed not far from them, so Brian took a shovel and stirred the bed a little but because it was cold, they hardly moved. Brian scooped up some of the ants with the dirt and dumped it carefully beside Jerry on the bench. Brian stood back and watched, but again they hardly moved. So Brian went to get a small piece of moss and laid it in the ant bed. It took a while but he finally got some ants on the moss. He then laid the moss, very lightly, on Jerry's back almost to his shoulders and since Jerry had a sweatshirt on he didn't feel anything. Brian went back to sit by Duane and we kept playing gin as if nothing happened.

It took a while before Jerry felt anything but he started with a slap on his neck and then he slapped again but this time was rubbing it as well.

He did this a couple of times before he turned around asking me, "You see anything on my back?"

Of course I said, "No, I don't see anything," but there were ants all over his back. About that time another one bit him and he jumped up to start pulling his sweatshirt over his head. Then we were all laughing at him and Jerry was saying, "You sorry suckers you!"

Buster Strahan was my horseshoe partner, but I knew him from Jesup. We didn't become friends until we were both at Coleman, though. He was a very particular type of guy from Riverview and got busted transporting marijuana through Mexico in a car transport. He walked the track a lot smoking cigars and inmates always came to him to light their cigarettes from his cigar.

One morning, after an all-night rain, the fields were flooded. Duane caught a real big bullfrog on the softball field. Buster and I were talking with other inmates along the track area when I saw Duane running across the field through the water towards us with this huge bullfrog in his hands. This was the biggest bullfrog I have ever seen weighing probably five pounds and was a foot and half in length. Buster had his back to Duane and, of course I didn't let on that anything was about to happen.

When Duane got to Buster, he grabbed Buster's pants at the waist, pulling them out at the same time, shoving the frog down his pants. It happened so fast that Buster didn't know how to react. Buster started shaking his leg in order to try to get the frog to slide down his pant leg. The frog did, but it stopped at the top of his boots, because Buster always wore his pant legs tucked inside his boots. Buster was jumping around trying to get his pants out of his boots in a hurry. Buster told us later that he thought it was a snake because it was so cold and slimy going down his pants, but was relieved when he saw that it was a frog.

The area where we hung out and played different games was more secluded from the guards than anywhere else around the rec yard. This was mostly because of the 20 foot wall from the hand-ball and racquetball court. There were times that the guards would walk into the area and give inmates breathalyzer tests. The guards that we had to watch the most were the two guards who patrolled in the trucks. The seclusion in that area is why we had the opportunity to do a lot of mischief to each other.

For example, on an inmate's birthday or when an inmate was due to leave the prison, a group of inmates would take that person down in the sand in the volleyball court area. Their clothes, shorts and shirt, would be removed and they would be held down by the other inmates. An inmate would use a magic marker to draw a bull's eye around the cheeks of their ass, paint their balls and then pack their ass with sand.

One time that was funny was when they took Duane down on his birthday to give him the treatment. When they were finished, Brian told the other inmates to let him up because he had a hold of Duane. As Brian started standing up, he had a hold on Duane's pecker and started leading him around the volleyball court as Duane was walking on his tip-toes. Brian was pulling it up pretty high so Duane couldn't get away. The entire time Duane was tip-toeing he was saying, "Oh, Oh, Oh!" After everyone had a good laugh, Brian let him go.

Every day, no matter what, the B.O.P. has a four o'clock stand-up recall count so at 3:30, the announcement would be made for all inmates to return to their cells for recall count. I would read or take a nap most afternoons, but Brian and Duane would play volleyball or handball. When the announcement was made, I would go to the TV room to look out the window to see the rec yard. They would play until the guards came out and made them leave; always being the last inmates coming in. Duane would just make it to our cell before the guards were locking the cell doors. He would always be covered in sand from head to toe. Most of the time it would be a 30 to 45 minute wait before the count was clear so with Duane covered in sand, there were times that he would stand in our toilet and wash the sand off him. The guards would come by the window to do the head count in our cell and sometimes the women guards would catch him standing there naked washing himself. They would yell, "Clark, get your clothes on!"

After the doors were unlocked, he would take a regular shower.

One thing that I remember about the black population is that they cannot stand someone to fart. That's how we were able to have an "all-white" TV room. There was a bunch of us "rednecks" in our unit so when a black inmate came into the TV room, which was only when there was a new inmate who didn't know any different, everyone would start farting. It didn't take them long before they would leave.

Speaking of farting, Duane could do what he called "jump farts". He would run around the track and when he came upon someone he knew, he would jump up in the air turning his butt toward their face and fart.

Most of them would chase after him but soon gave up because they knew they wouldn't catch him.

The only time Duane went to the hole that I know of was when they were playing kickball. Most of the time they played kickball after a big rain because they played on the softball field where the clay was all soupy which made them a mess. It ended up being a wild kickball game after someone tackled a runner. Everyone jumped on top of the others making a big pile of mess. Everyone shoved each other's heads in the clay mud, but no one got mad. It was just dirty fun.

This particular time one of the new women guards somehow got by our watchful eyes and saw the pile. She thought it was a fight and she hit the deuces. I'm not real sure why they call it deuces but every guard or employee of the prison wore one on their belt. It was a transmitter that would send a signal to the main office when set off. The office would be able to tell where the trouble was on the compound and then it was announced over the walkie-talkies and all of the guards and B.O.P. employees would start running to that location. When a guard hits the deuce, someone is going to the hole.

It was always fun to watch the fat guards trying to run to the locations. The younger, faster guards would be taking the handcuffed inmate to the hole by the time the other guards got to the area. Most of the time, inmates stood watching this go down and laughed at the heavier guards because they were the last ones to the locations and always out of breath.

Since Duane was on the bottom of the pile and was bleeding from an old scab, he was taken to the hole. Afterwards the new guard felt bad for what she did, not realizing it was all in fun. Duane was only in the hole for a few weeks.

Larry Whitaker from Palmetto was in a cell next to ours and he had a celly named Dino, a much younger guy. Duane and I were coming back from the rec yard when we saw Dino looking out of their cell door window. We knew that when you see an inmate looking out of their cell door window there's something going on in the cell.

So we went to their door and Dino let us in but stayed at the window on lookout for the guard. Once we got into the cell, Big Joe was sitting on Larry's bunk with Larry standing in front of him with his shorts down and Big Joe had a hold of Larry's pecker tattooing a smiley face on the head of it. Damn, did I cringe when I saw what he was doing because I knew that had to hurt.

Larry had his fists balled up, his mouth was shut tight and both of his cheeks were quivering in and out. Duane was the first to speak and said, "Damn Larry, you're acting like it hurts."

Larry couldn't answer until Big Joe stopped with the homemade tattoo gun. Larry piped up and said, "Have at it big boy, let's just see what you think!"

So Duane dropped his shorts, stood up in front of Big Joe, who grabbed Duane's pecker and started with the tattooing. Immediately, Duane yelled and jumped straight in the air grabbing his pecker and running around in a circle crying, "Oh hell, Oh hell!"

We almost got the guard's attention because we were laughing so hard at Duane. I don't know how Larry did it for the pain but he had a nice smiley face on the head of his pecker in red and yellow.

The shower orderlies would raise hell when they found shit in the floor of the showers. I don't know why but the Haitians would always shit in the shower instead of the toilet. After the 4:00 count, the guards would open the doors and everyone would race for the eight showers. All of them would be full except for one and I would go to that one knowing that a Haitian had shit in it. I would step into the shower, turn the water on and start smashing the turds into drain with my toes and then proceed to take my shower. I didn't have to wait to take a shower because I normally had an empty "shitty" shower.

What made the inmates the maddest regarding the Haitians, was when they would break one of the microwaves. Each cell block only had two microwaves. They would put cans in to warm something or a raw egg and blow the door off which made whatever was inside go everywhere. When one microwave was destroyed, it would take about two to three months before we received a replacement, which made it rough for 130 inmates to use one microwave. Whenever a new Haitian would arrive in the cell block, all of the inmates would warn them about the showers and the microwaves.

Buster had hemorrhoids that I found out by accident one day when we were playing horseshoes. I was always catching Buster off guard by some of the stunts that I would pull on him. One of them was when I poked him in the ass. Whenever I would poke him, he would really jump and jerk around which made me laugh.

I had just poked him in the ass right before we started playing horse-shoes. I threw the shoes down to Buster and he bent over to pick them up with his butt facing me and I noticed a big round spot on his ass. I said, "Damn Buster, you shit in your pants!"

I was laughing really hard as were the other inmates when Buster reached around to feel his pants. He dropped the horseshoes and left without a word. It was probably close to two weeks before he came back to the rec yard. The next morning at breakfast Buster told me that he had hemorrhoids and I obviously disrupted them when I poked him in the ass.

The biggest trick or joke that I pulled in prison was on Buster. We both had visitors one day, so we were in the visiting room. He had just finished his visit with his brother and I was still visiting with an older couple from Myakka City, Joyce and Norman Proveaux. Buster was standing at the door of the strip search room waiting to go in when he noticed me talking with my visitors. He thought it would be a good time to play a joke on me since I was always pulling jokes on him. He also knew that I didn't like queers so he walked up to where I was talking with Joyce and Norman and stood in front of me acting like a queer. With his voice changed and moving his hands real feminine like he asked me, "Hi, Poppie, are we going to play horseshoes this afternoon?"

After seeing Joyce and Norman's face and noticing them looking at each other with the ultimate question in their eyes, boy I was pissed! I am sure they were thinking that I had been in prison way too long and now I've gone queer. About that time the guard opened the door to the strip room and Buster walked away swaying his hips and wiggling his ass.

At supper that evening in chow hall, Buster and I were sitting across from one another with Hal Kirk or "Big Bird" and another inmate at the table. I had finished eating so I put a dip in my mouth and used a paper cup to spit in. When Buster finished his meal he looked straight at me smiling and said, "I finally got you today in the visiting room, didn't I, Poppie?"

I just glared at him not saying a word but thinking, "You bastard… I'm going to get you back big time!" He could see that I was really pissed, so he was egging me on more.

At that time he was wearing his glasses and had a neat, clean cut, grayish beard. He leaned forward towards me saying, "Don't be mad Poppie...let's kiss and make up."

Then he closed his eyes and puckered his lips out like a big kiss at me. That was the worst thing he could have done, like slapping me in the face.

I was just about to spit a good juicy Copenhagen spit in the cup when I just jumped up, pushing my chair back, leaned over the table towards Buster's face with his eyes still closed and lips puckered up and grabbed him by the back of the neck. As I grabbed the back of his head, I pulled his lips to mine forcing his lips apart and squirted the juice in his mouth as I took my tongue under my lip and pushed the Copenhagen along with all of the juice that I had in my mouth into his.

Buster never moved; he was so stunned. I sat back down as Big Bird and the other inmate said, "I'm out of here!"

They took off because they thought the guards saw what I did and knew that would be some big time in the hole. I'm not sure why a guard didn't see me do that because there was always about 15-20 guards in the chow hall.

I could hear other inmates saying, "Did you see that inmate kiss that other inmate?"

Buster still hadn't moved and his eyes were wide open with a shocked look on his face and the juice and snuff was running out of his mouth all over his beard onto the table. I grabbed some napkins to start wiping his mouth and chin but didn't start laughing until he came out of his stunned trance.

Once he started grabbing some more napkins and wiping himself off is when I started laughing. I said to him, "You always tease me about giving you a kiss...so how did you like that one?"

Buster never teased me again about kissing him or about queers from that day on.

One day Pete Dakin and his two sons, Farren and Cameron, came to visit Duane and me. About an hour into the visit, Pete asked Duane if we could get marijuana in prison. Duane said, "Sure if you have the money you can get it."

Then Pete said, "What about cocaine and heroin?"

Duane said, "Sure if you have the money you can get the drugs, but it's a lot more money for them in here than on the outside."

Pete thought for a minute and then said as he was smiling, "I bet you can't get any pussy in here, can you?"

Duane said, "Sure we can get pussy, but it's a little shitty."

We all got a good laugh about that but Mr. Dakin didn't ask any more questions after that.

Just before Duane left Coleman for the "halfway" house on November 18, 1998, the inmates asked me who was going to be my celly and I told them that it didn't really matter who it would be because I read all of the time. They said that I would probably get a Negro if I didn't ask to get someone in particular. They were right…my first celly was a Negro, but he only lasted about a week. Negroes could not stand for me to be sitting on the toilet first thing in the morning.

I would get up early, long before chow time, so I would sit on the toilet to read in order to pass time. There was a light over the sink area so I didn't have to have the big lights on over the bunks. But the Negroes thought that I was taking a crap even when I explained to them that I was simply reading. That still made them nervous. Most of them only lasted in my cell a week before they were requesting "cop-outs" or transfers to another cell.

I left the B2 housing unit and moved to the A2 housing unit where they were starting a unit for the 50 and over inmates. It housed 130 inmates and was almost full with the older inmates. When the younger inmates filed a complaint on age discrimination, they stopped putting inmates only 50 and over in there. It was a nice cell block that was a lot quieter and more peaceful. We called this unit "The Assisted Living" unit. This was the best cell block unit that I had been in because most everyone was of the same age and we didn't have all of the loud-mouthed jitterbugs making all of the noise like in the other cell blocks.

Once I transferred to A2 housing unit, the counselor gave me a fit. She refused to change my visiting list like the other counselor did. She really got mad at me when I went over her head to her boss because he made her take care of my changes. Her boss was the one who wanted me to move to the A2 unit to start with. I wasn't sure I wanted to move due to the great counselor that I had in B4. So he assured me that my visiting list would be taken care of if I moved. It only took five minutes of her time to make the changes to my list.

John Bonner and Tom Pritchard and I went through all three prisons together. John taught GED classes and wrote sports results in the prison paper. John is the only inmate that I met in prison that fiend on women. If his head was busted wide open nothing but women would come out. It didn't matter if a woman was pretty or ugly, fat or skinny, tall or short, he would stop whatever he was doing to fiend on that woman. So that's why I always called him "Fiener".

When Duane left prison, John asked him to send some nude photos back to him. Every time John knew that I was going to talk to Duane, he would tell me to remind Duane about the photos. A few months later, Duane sent John some pictures in some magazines. John and I were standing beside one another waiting for our mail. John got his magazines, went back to his cell to look through them and came to my cell saying, "There are no photos in these magazines."

I called Duane that night and asked about John's photos. Duane told me that they were in between two pages that were glued together. John went to scrambling through the magazines again and it wasn't long before he came back to my cell saying, "Don't ya'll have any women in Myakka City?" Then he handed me the photos that Duane had sent.

At that time, Duane was working for Farren at the dairy and the first photo showed a man artificially breeding a cow. He had one arm shoved up the cow's ass to his arm pit with the other arm holding the cow's tail out of the way and a long straw with the semen in it held between his teeth. He was looking at the camera with his eyes wide open, his teeth showing, holding the straw and a big grin on his face. It was a real look of enjoyment and quite the sight.

The other photo was of Duane, behind the cow spreading her twat open with both of his hands and with his tongue right that at it. I started laughing real hard at the sour, disgusted look on John's face. After I quit laughing, I knew what he meant by "not having women in Myakka City". I told him that these were the photos that he asked for but he said, "That's not the kind I meant!"

Duane later sent him some other photos that he wanted.

I was put into a cell with a Negro who had been in that cell for over a year, but he left within a week of my arrival. Then my next celly was Ron Whitaker who was from Sarasota and was there until he was transferred to go to a camp. John Peoples from Venus, FL, was my third celly and Brady Hilton from Bradenton was my last celly.

Ron knew the Bible very well and explained some of the Bible to me. He finally got mad at me for not believing in God and the Bible. Everyone in my family believes in God but me. I guess that's why I am the "black sheep of the family"!

The one thing that is in the Bible that I do believe in is the "Golden Rule". I could lie to myself and say that I believe in God, but that's not me. I wish I could believe but God hasn't gotten to me yet. From what I have learned about the Bible is that man has written what God has said, and man has always screwed up everything that he has done.

Maybe one of these days it will sink into this hard head of mine. If there is a God or something that has given me a chance to live my life on this earth and who has enjoyed life as much as I have and continue to, I would like to thank him. From all that I have read, all over this earth, man has believed in something or someone who has more power than man. There are two things that have gotten my attention and they are the Pyramids and the Maya Ruins. That is something you can see and feel and I wonder how they were built way back in those times.

As I've written this chapter about the other two prisons and about the different inmates in the prisons, Coleman was no different. Terre Haute was by far the roughest of the three Federal prisons. Jesup and Coleman were about the same as far as being fairly laid back.

So here I am still in prison having spent nine and a half years with inmates. I have been getting a lot more visits from family and friends which has helped. I stay busy working and reading but still pulling jokes on people even if they are inmates.

GARY CLARK

*Gary, visiting me & Duane at Coleman.*

*Me, watering the ball fields.*

# Recreation Worker of the Month

Every month the Recreation Department will select one inmate detail worker as that months Recreation Worker of the Month. Any staff may nominate any Recreation detail worker to Shawn Sharbaugh. This nomination must include name, number, detail shift, and a brief description why the inmate should be considered as the Worker of the Month. Mr. Sharbaugh will forward all nominations to Mr. Ramirez, Supervisor of Recreation, for his selection. Once selected, the Worker of the Month will receive a minimum of a $5 bonus at the end of the pay month.

For the month of May 1998, the Recreation Worker of the Month is **Donald Clark** from B-4. Inmate Clark works the Rec 1 AM shift Monday through Friday. His job assignment is the Chief Landscaper/Field Maintenance. Inmate Clark has been a

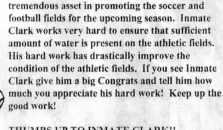

tremendous asset in promoting the soccer and football fields for the upcoming season. Inmate Clark works very hard to ensure that sufficient amount of water is present on the athletic fields. His hard work has drastically improve the condition of the athletic fields. If you see Inmate Clark give him a big Congrats and tell him how much you appreciate his hard work! Keep up the good work!

**THUMBS UP TO INMATE CLARK!!**

Gio Ramirez, Supervisor of Recreation 6/1/98

*How about my Mohawk.*

300

*Sandra & Mom visiting me.*

## CHAPTER 7
# 2000 – 2010

At the beginning of the ***New Millennium,*** though I was still in prison, the outside world was ever changing. A few of the most critical happenings was when the World Trade Center was blown up on September 11, 2001. Nearly 3000 people were killed when one airliner crashed into one of the twin towers and another airliner crashed into the other tower. Then a third plane crashed into the Pentagon while a fourth plowed into a field in Pennsylvania. This was the beginning of our country realizing the power of terrorists as well as our country becoming a nation under alert.

Then there was Hurricane Katrina that originally made landfall on August 25, 2005 on the east coast of Florida packing 125 mph winds and killing 14 people. On August 27th, it regained strength while churning in the Gulf and doubled in size to a category three. On August 29th, Katrina made another landfall in Louisiana as a category three with wind speeds of 140 mph. Over 1,800 people lost their lives in Louisiana and Mississippi.

In January of 2006, a University of Florida survey showed Florida land value increased by 50% to 88% during 2005. The demand for land by developers, investors and speculators pushed the value of land to record levels. A lot of people bought houses and would flip them for a quick gain. That's just how quick the prices were increasing. But by 2009, home prices dropped more than 50% in most areas.

By 2008, the market was taking a deep nose dive. The entire country, the state of Florida itself and especially Manatee County was in a critical downward spiral. People were losing their jobs and walking away from their homes.

The population census was 281,421,906 as of April 1, 2000. Manatee County grew by leaps and bounds during this era as well. The county's population increased from approximately 35,000 residents in

1950 to almost 265,000 in 2000. As of 2010, the United States Census Bureau estimated Manatee County's population to be 325,000.

The county ranked in the top 10 of Florida's 67 counties in agriculture sales. And at the end of the '90s and the beginning of the new decade, East Manatee, east of the Interstate, was absolutely booming. Lakewood Ranch had become its own town.

As for me, I was still at Coleman Federal Correctional Institution. At Coleman, we normally had steaks on New Year's Day, if you want to call them that. They were small and real tough. Some inmates couldn't eat them, so they threw them away or gave them to other inmates.

On New Year's Day, John and I were in chow line waiting to get our tray when two inmates came by pulling garbage cans back to the kitchen's goat room to be ground up. I had to step back away from the door so they could go through and as they went through I noticed this piece of steak in one of them so I grabbed it. As I started eating on it, it took all John had to keep from puking. I heard other inmates behind me saying, "Did you see that inmate eating out of the garbage can?"

The only time John and I were in the same cell block together was at Coleman in the Assisted Living unit, but John made sure his cell was as far away from mine as possible. He was on the bottom floor and I was on the second floor, but I could see John's cell from my cell door window.

The guards would open the bottom cell doors first and I would watch John as he went to take a shower. He would have his boxers on, a towel on his shoulder carrying his soap, shampoo, etc. By the time my cell door was open, John would be in the shower so I would sneak down to his shower stall and lean down to see which way his feet were facing in order to snag his towel and boxers off the shower door. It wouldn't take long before I could hear him hollering and cussing me.

I received hundreds of books while I was in prison from family and friends. The first thing that I would do was write my initials, with the book closed, on the top and bottom of the pages and my name on the side. This way I knew the book was mine because inmates were always borrowing books from me. I kept a list writing the inmates' name, the date they borrowed it and the title of the book. Once the book was returned I'd write down the return date. I donated the books to the library once I was finished with them. The other inmates would often tease me for having more books in the library with my name on them than the library had of their own.

Bill Priesmeyer was my book man. If there was a new book that I wanted, all I would have to do is call Bill and tell him about it. By the time we finished talking, the book was on its way to me because Bill was on the computer ordering it as we were having our conversation.

Another list that I kept was of the books that I read. I had my cousin Joe Clark put one list in alphabetical order by author and another list in alphabetical order by title. I read anything from Stephen King to the Wild West books to the historical fiction of South Africa. I read over 600 books while incarcerated.

Lewis and Janie Schofield sent me some real good books on health and nutrition in December of 2000. I wish I would have received these types of books earlier, because I would have read them all over several times. I definitely would be more versed when it comes to health and nutrition because when I read in prison, I was a lot more focused.

I have a lot more to learn about health and nutrition but I'm a firm believer if we take care of our own bodies instead of allowing the doctors to prescribe drugs, we would live a longer, healthier life. After cancer and heart disease, doctors are the leading cause of death in America and for the first time in history, our children are dying before their parents. I don't have much room to be talking about health and nutrition as I sit with a dip of Copenhagen in my mouth, but I do try to eat healthier than I did.

Every Christmas I would send Christmas letters to the list of addresses that I had. Each year I would have more addresses to send the letters to and more information in my letters which took more time to do my Christmas letters. I had to start doing my Christmas letters the first week of September.

I would write the addresses and return address on the envelopes first and then begin buying stamps every Monday and stamp all of the envelopes. I couldn't buy more than three books of stamps at a time and I couldn't have more than three books in my possession because stamps and photo tickets were like money in prison. So as soon as I purchased my three books I started stamping the envelopes until all 400 or so were finished.

Photo tickets were two dollars each and I had to have a ticket in order to have a photo taken. Whenever I would have a visit throughout the year I would have a photo taken with the people who came to visit me. While I was purchasing my stamps, I would arrange my letter with the pictures of my visits throughout the year. This process took until the latter part of October to complete.

Again, Bill and Kathy Priesmeyer helped with my Christmas letters and they wouldn't have been so good if it wasn't for them. By the first of November I would send them all that I had done, which was nothing compared to what they had to do. They arranged my pictures on the page with whatever I had written in the middle and then send a copy for my approval. Once approved, they would send me my original back along with the 400 copies. I would then put them all in envelopes to be ready to mail by the first of December.

We were not allowed to seal the envelopes. The guards had to read the mail first and then they would seal them. One year a guard called me to his desk and said for me not to send that many letters at one time anymore. It was the night guard's job to go through all of the inmate's mail and it took him all night to go through my mail.

My last Christmas in prison, I was called to the Lieutenant's office and she stuck a photo in my face pulling it away fast asking me if I recognized the picture. I told her, "No, but I couldn't see it real good because you did it so fast."

Then she handed it to me, but I still couldn't tell what it was. She said, "That's the bag of mail you sent out last night and I'm putting you in the hole!"

I asked her why and she said, "Because you had over 400 stamps on the envelopes."

I explained how I did it by only buying three books a week but putting them on the envelopes immediately. She said, "I don't believe you!"

I said, "Everyone in my cell block knows about it."

She then asked for some names and stopped me after I gave her 20 or so names. She sent me back to my cell and said that she would be seeing me later. But she never did.

A few days later, the new Captain, a middle-aged Spanish man, called me to his office. He asked me, "Do you know Lamar and Kathleen Parrish?"

I told him yes and he then asked how long I had known them, which I told him all of my life.

He then said, "Did you know that they sent you a check for $50 but wrote 'donation' on the check?"

I said, "You know I don't get to see the checks or money orders only the receipts that you all send me. But yes I knew they sent me $50."

He got real mad with me then and said, "You're scamming these people!"

I said, "No, I'm not. I've got over 400 addresses that I send Christmas letters to each year."

He then sent me back to my cell to get my list of addresses. When I returned with my list he looked at it and told me he would be getting back to me. It was almost two weeks before I was called back to his office. He handed me my list and said, "I know you do not know that many people; no inmate knows that many people!"

I answered, "Look, I have lived in Manatee County all of my life and actually know a lot more people than that. I just don't have all of their addresses."

It was very hard to keep up with the addresses every year. I would get 15 to 20 letters returned due to a change of address.

On Saturday, January 20, 2001 at 3:45PM I was released from prison. President Clinton signed my commuted sentence on his last day in office.

It was around two that afternoon, Brady and I were reading in our bunks and I was starting to fall asleep. I put my book down before going to sleep and I thought about Bucky Godwin, who was one of my co-defendants.

He was out of prison and was a part-time bouncer at a bar. After breaking up a fight at the bar, he almost killed a man and was going to court over the incident. So I got up out of the bunk and told Brady that I was going to call my daughter, Tammy, to see if she knew anything about what was going on with Bucky. After I got in touch with Tammy, the first thing she said to me was, "How does it feel to be getting out of prison?"

I said, "What are you talking about?"

Tammy said, "Haven't you heard?"

And I told her no.

Tammy told me that Cande told her that Julie Stewart, the President of Families Against Mandatory Minimums (FAMM), called to tell her that President Clinton had signed my commuted sentence at 10:30 AM.

I said, "Tammy, don't be joking with me!"

Tammy was shocked that I hadn't heard about it and I reassured her that I had not.

I saw my case manager, Mr. Ford, looking at me while I was on the phone, so I told Tammy that I would call her back in a few minutes. I was always joking and pulling jokes on inmates and there were several other inmates on the phones around me. As I hung up the phone, I yelled, "I'm out of here!"

They all turned to look at me with their phones to their ears and I said to them, "My daughter just told me that President Clinton signed my commuted sentence this morning!"

Most of them said, "Yeah, right" and kept talking on the phone.

I turned to walk over to Mr. Ford and I told him what Tammy had told me. I asked him if there was some way that I could find out if this was true. Mr. Ford was looking over my shoulder, so I turned to see what he was looking at. The inmates that were around were looking at me and Mr. Ford. He told me to come with him to his office to look on his computer. While we walked to his office, all of the inmates were watching us.

We entered his office and then through another door into a conference room that had a large table surrounded by chairs. I walked over to a small desk that had a computer on it. Mr. Ford walked over to a large filing cabinet and opened a drawer. He brought a large file jacket over to the table and sat down in a chair and started going through the papers in the big file.

I looked back at the computer wondering to myself, "What the hell was going on?"

I looked back at Mr. Ford who was reading a piece of paper and he looked up at me and asked, "You got a life sentence for growing marijuana?"

I replied, "Yes, sir."

He started reading the papers again and I was thinking, "What the hell is he doing; I thought he was going to get on the computer?"

He then said, "I see that you got your life sentence down to 27 years."

Again I replied, "Yes, sir."

Not long after I got to Coleman, a jailhouse lawyer, from St. Petersburg, named Pete Ireland was able to get my sentence reduced from life without parole to 27 years. I paid him $50.00. What a contrast from spending thousands of dollars on appeals and receiving nothing.

Mr. Ford then looked up at me and said, "Yes, it's true; Clinton has signed your release."

He looked up at me with wide open eyes and said, "Are you alright?"

I said, "Sure I'm all right."

I was still standing by the computer at this time and looked down to see both of my hands and legs were shaking. I looked up at him and said, "I'm okay!"

But I was really just trying to convince myself, I think. He then said, "Today is my day off, but I was called back to work because I'm your case manager. We don't know what to do with you right now because we have never had this happen at this prison before."

He then instructed me to go back to my cell until they find out exactly what the procedures were going to be. He also instructed me not to say anything to any of the other inmates about my release because it may cause trouble among some of the inmates.

As I left his office, I saw some inmates watching me. I noticed Duke Olson coming out of his cell. Duke was in his mid-60s and was working in the law library doing law work for other inmates. Duke knew the laws very well so I walked over to him and said, "Hey, Duke…I have a question for you. If a judge, a warden or someone with authority signs your release from prison, when will that inmate be released?"

Duke said, "The day the release is signed, the B.O.P. must have that inmate out of prison before the four o'clock stand up count."

He also stated that if the inmate was not out by the four o'clock count and should anything happen to that inmate, the B.O.P. would be responsible for the welfare of that inmate. I thanked Duke and started to walk away when he asked me, "Why, what's up?"

I just replied that I would tell him later.

I started to go to my cell but thought about calling Tammy back to tell her to come and get me. She asked if I was out and I told her no but that I would be out before she arrives.

She asked, "How do you know that?"

I explained what the jailhouse lawyer just told me and that I believe the jailhouse lawyers more than the lawyers on the outside. After hanging up the phone with Tammy, I headed back to my cell. My mind started racing for it was now 2:30 in the afternoon and I knew that I only had an hour and a half left before I had to be out. But I also knew I had a lot to do. Some inmates started questioning me, but I told them that I would tell them all about it later.

When I opened the cell door, I yelled to Brady, "I'm outta here!"

He dropped his book, removed his glasses and started getting out of his bunk. He said, "You're shitting me?"

I told him that it was true but that I didn't have time to talk about it. I had to make the three 'o clock move to go to the rec yard to get my legal papers and other stuff out of my locker and be back by the time the ten minute move was over.

Brady still didn't believe me because I was always joking around but when I opened my locker and handed him my radio, tennis shoes and other stuff, he started believing me. You don't start giving away stuff in prison unless you're leaving.

There were only a few things that I wanted to take with me and most of it was in my rec yard locker. I put what I wanted in a box and gave the rest to Brady and John Bonner. I was at the door when the three 'o clock move was called over the PA system and I went to the rec yard as fast as I could without running. No running was allowed on the compound.

When I reached the lockers, Jerry Mosby, was watching TV in the equipment room. His job was signing out the rec yard equipment to the inmates. Jerry was leaning against the lockers in a chair but in the same area of my locker. When Jerry saw me he asked, "Damn, Pop… what are you doing here at this time of day?"

He knew that I should have been taking my nap at that time. I said, "I'm going home."

Jerry answered like all of the other inmates, "Yeah, right!"

He asked me again what I was doing there and I told him again that I was going home and told him to get out of the way so that I could get to my locker. I explained that I had to be out of there before the move was over. Once I got the combination lock off my locker, I gave the lock to Jerry and told him the combination. Jerry always wanted his own locker at the rec yard and when I gave him the lock he said, "Damn…you really are going home. What happened?"

I told him that I couldn't explain it right then because I was in a hurry. I took my legal papers and told him that he could have everything else in the locker. I told him, "Goodbye and good luck" and out the door I went.

I just made it back to my dorm when the move was over. Now I only had 30 minutes before the four o'clock stand up count. Inmates have to stand up and be counted by two guards from cell to cell and if the count isn't right, they have to start all over. When the recall count is clear, the guards will unlock the doors and shortly after that they call mail-call.

When I got back to my cell, there were inmates around talking to Brady and they started asking me questions but my mind was on other things. My mind was spinning. I was trying to make sure I had everything that I wanted to take home with me.

Then I thought about my ID card so I started asking if anyone knew anything about inmates keeping their ID cards. Some of them said that it would be okay as long as there wasn't any money left on the card. So I told them to follow me to the vending machines so that I could run the money off my card. This ID card had a photo of me on it with a Mohawk haircut and my Federal ID number which was 11808-018. My hair was like that when I arrived at Coleman and I never had the picture retaken. I still have that ID card and I have had fun with it on the outside when asked for my ID.

Before we returned to my cell, a guard told me to get my belongings and wait by the cell door. I had two boxes to carry out with me so John Bonner helped me. I was shaking hands and hugging inmates saying goodbye. The guard came up just before the 3:30 recall and said for me to keep walking not stopping for anything or anybody.

When recall was called (recall, recall, all inmates report to your housing unit for the four o'clock stand up count), we started across the compound towards the R&D building. The compound is rectangular with a flag pole in the center of the yard.

Inmates were coming from all directions toward their housing units and the prison grapevine is something else. Within that hour and a half, everyone knew about my release. They did not know how it happened just that I was going home.

First, all of them were yelling at me, "Good luck and goodbye", then it started...the chanting "Donnie...Donnie...Donnie" and this went on until we reached R&D where the main gate was. It made my hair stand up on my neck.

A younger guard asked me if I wanted to punch him for anything, and that now was my chance. I told him, "No, I don't have anything against anyone."

That's when John spoke up and said, "Hey, Mr. Macho...son of a bitch, what about all of that macho shit that you have been telling me all of these years that you would never leave the prison system until the judge apologizes to you!"

I looked over at him laughing and I said, "So I lied, so what!"

That's when John said, "You lying son of a bitch!"

When we went inside R&D, John sat my box down and we shook hands and hugged each other. They searched through my boxes to make sure that nothing was leaving the prison that wasn't supposed to. They fitted me with a shirt, blue jeans, under shorts, belt, socks and shoes and gave me $500.00 cash from my account.

I was then taken to a room where visitors wait prior to being processed to be allowed into the prison for visitation. This room was considered outside of the prison and I was in that room about ten minutes before the four o'clock count was called. Duke Olsen the jailhouse lawyer was right. I was out of prison before the four o'clock count.

If it wasn't for FAMM (Families Against Mandatory Minimums), I would still be in prison until my scheduled release which was June 6, 2014. FAMM has been lobbying in Congress since 1990 and still is in order to do away with the unjust drug laws with the mandatory minimums. I would like to say thanks to Julie Stewart and her staff at FAMM, my family and also to Former President Bill Clinton for my early release.

Of all of the ten and a half years that I spent in the Federal Prison system, I only met or heard of one person who received a life sentence for growing marijuana. Mark Young wasn't a grower or a seller but was the middle man that hooked the two up. He was charged with their charges, went to trial and ended up with a life sentence.

But I am convinced that my life sentence was just a way to pay me back for all the tricks and stunts that I had pulled on so many people throughout my life. Marijuana was just the tool but all in all, my prison life didn't stop me from pulling jokes on people. And once I got out of prison and got back to my normal self, I was back to pulling tricks and stunts on people.

Around five o'clock, Tammy, Sandra and two of the grandkids, Kyle and Kayley, came to pick me up. I hugged them all and we put my two boxes of possessions in the SUV to start my new life of freedom. I was in the front seat with Tammy but turned around talking to Sandra when Tammy handed me her cell phone. She said, "Here, Momma wants to talk to you."

When I took the phone from her, which was the first time that I had ever had a cell phone in my hands, I said, "Where do you talk in or where do you hear from?"

They were all laughing at me as Tammy had to explain how to use a cell phone. After I finished talking to Cande, Tammy confirmed with her where we were all going to meet, and then she asked me what I wanted to eat. That was the easy part, I simply told her "tripe". Tripe is the first stomach in the cow's belly and the largest of four stomachs. Tripe is prepared several ways but I like it best fried in cornmeal or flour.

On the two hour trip home, Tammy kept getting calls from family members wanting to talk to me and then the TV stations were calling to set up interviews with me. I started getting very confused about all that was going on and that's when I started losing it.

Mostly everyone was asking all sorts of questions that I couldn't answer such as, "How does it feel to be out of prison?"

"Where are you going to live?"

"What are you going to do?"

"Where are you going to work?"

All of this was overwhelming.

The TV networks kept calling for interviews also. I finally told someone to call Jim Wardell, who was my appeal attorney, to set up a time and place for all of them to come for a one shot interview.

It didn't seem like it took two hours before we arrived at Duane and Sandra's house. She said that I could stay with them until I figure out what I was going to do. The family decided that we would all meet at the house in Elwood Park for the family get-together.

By the time Sandra, Duane and I arrived, my confusion was getting worse. Here I was confined for 10 ½ years, being told what to do, when to do it and how to do it, but all of a sudden I didn't have control of my mind for some reason.

Seeing most of my immediate family there at one time together was more than I could bear. I felt like a zombie, I was mostly in a daze. I think it was because I had not been around all of them at one time since I went to prison. I do know one thing for sure, I was screwed up!!

I think I only ate two pieces of the tripe and couldn't enjoy the taste. If I wasn't in the shape I was in, I could have eaten the entire plate by myself. I really don't remember much about that first night except that the bed sure did feel good.

I had never had that feeling before. It was the first time that I didn't feel like I could control my mind. Everything was like a blur and I was this way for about two weeks. It reminded me of an animal that had been locked up in a cage for 10 ½ years and one day someone opened the door. That animal will not go out of the cage right away; it will take some time before it will get too far away from the cage. That is exactly how I felt.

Normally, most all inmates know when their release time is. So a year before they're released they attend classes to prepare them for the outside world again. Also, most of them have a job waiting for them upon their release. This didn't happen with me and I wasn't prepared for the sudden change. You can ask anyone who saw me in the first two weeks and they will tell you that I was not the same Donnie Clark as before.

There is also quite a difference between commuted sentence and being pardoned. If an inmate is pardoned, they are free to the outside world and have all of their rights back. If an inmate receives commuted sentence like I did, they are still considered a convicted felon, usually receive probation and do not receive their rights back. I cannot vote and cannot be around firearms. I also received five years of probation that I had to fulfill.

The probation requirements were that I had to fill out paperwork monthly about my work history for the month, my salary, my bank account balance, my current address and phone number. I also had boundaries within the State of Florida that I could travel without having to get special paperwork filled out to have with me at all times. And I couldn't leave the state without this paperwork filled out.

I had a probation officer who visited me every month for the first six months that I was out of prison. He would do a piss test every time. I think once they found out that I was stable, after about six months, the officer would normally visit about three to four times a year. But every time I had to give them a piss test which was a problem at times like the problems I had at Terre Haute. It was a pain having to do the paperwork every month and have it sent to my probation officer on time, but it was better than being locked up.

Early the next morning, I asked my brother-in-law, Duane, if he could ride me around Manatee County. I wanted to see what changes had taken place while I was away and boy was I shocked.

I knew Schroeder-Manatee Ranch well, which is now where Lakewood Ranch is. I caught wild horses in 1959, worked cattle on the ranch, planted and harvested seed, cut sod, hunted wild hogs and caught gators through the years. But all of this was now a huge subdivision and seeing this sure did not help my mind any.

On Monday, Lee Sly and Floyd Smith drove me to the Myakka area. I was ready to see the ranch that I had before I went to prison but we didn't make it there. As we rode most of the roads, Lee and Floyd were explaining things to me.

We did not stop to talk to anyone, because I still wasn't comfortable with people and the outside world. Other than more people living in Myakka, the roads surprised me the most. I would have to say that 90% of the roads were now paved and as we drove by the County equipment yard, I realized they had more equipment since I had lived there.

As we went by, I said, "Look at the two new road graders they have; when I lived in Myakka, there was only one old grader with miles of roads to grade. And now they have two new ones with fewer roads to grade."

I was always asking, "What's that or when did that happen?"

After seeing two days of all of the changes in the few areas that I visited, I realized this wasn't the Manatee County that I knew. Knowing that my release date was supposed to be June 6, 2014, I felt as though I should have stayed in prison.

I believe it was Tuesday that Jim Wardell set up the interviews to take place at Sandra and Duane's house with all of the TV networks. I don't remember much about the interviews except all of the microphones and the questions.

I remember some of the things that took place shortly after my release, like when Duane took me to get my driver's license in Arcadia. After I got my license, my nephew, Wade, asked me to drive him to the doctor in Oneco. He had knee surgery and was on crutches so he couldn't drive. This was the first time that I had driven since I went to prison and he had a four-door extended cab dually Ford pickup truck which seemed huge to me.

I was dreading driving along I-75 because the traffic seemed to be going too fast even when I was riding with someone. But before we ever made it to the Interstate, I was turning off Fort Hamer Road onto Old Tampa Road and didn't turn sharp enough so we ended up in the ditch. Wade's eyes were big and he was grabbing for the dashboard. He asked, "Uncle Donnie, are you alright…can't you drive?"

I couldn't believe myself either because I was having such a hard time driving and shifting the gears at the same time. By the time we arrived at the doctor's office, I was getting better.

For those first two weeks, it seemed like I couldn't do anything. I had trouble riding horses, working cows, operating a back hoe as well as driving a vehicle. It was like I had never done any of it before even though I had grown up doing it all. I went once or twice to the Manatee County Fair with Duane in the latter part of January. I followed Duane around like a scared child, still not wanting to really talk to anyone.

The first Saturday of February, which was the second Saturday after my release, everyone threw a big party for me at Bill Manford's barn on Verna Bethany Road. It was the biggest party that I ever had, just for me. We had BBQ hog, swamp cabbage and all kinds of other foods with desserts with a band there as well. I talked to everyone and visited but didn't feel comfortable about any of it.

When the band started playing, Sandra came to me and said, "Let's dance, Brother."

Now dancing is something that I really love to do but I told Sandra that I couldn't do it. Everyone that knows me knows how much I like to dance and joke around. But for those first two weeks, not pulling jokes on anyone, not dancing at the party and not really enjoying myself, I was really screwed up!

Once I got over the shock of my release, I started settling in a little at a time. I had several job offers but didn't take any. One day, Wade asked me to help him do some silt fencing work. That was another thing that was new to me…there wasn't such a thing as silt fencing before I went to prison. But work was what helped me the most, because I was keeping busy and not having to answer questions which helped my mind a lot.

One of the first things that I bought after I got out of prison was a camera. When I was in prison I didn't have a lot of pictures to look at because I never took the time to take pictures. I was always too busy doing other things.

I bet I took over 2000 pictures the first year I was out. I wanted to make sure I had pictures to look at if I ever went back to prison. Not that I was planning on going back, but my fear was going back on a firearm violation. As a felon, I would be sent back to prison for life without any questions asked if I were in a vehicle that had a firearm in it.

The first year I was so skittish about this that I asked everybody before I got into their vehicle to go somewhere with them. Of course, most of them said yes, but I made them take them out before I would go anywhere.

By the way, the camera didn't last a year. I took it to a camera shop to get it repaired and the man asked, "What in the hell did you do to this camera?"

It was all beat up and scratched up and could not be repaired so I had to buy a new one. I think I have bought about four cameras since I've been out, but I've got lots of pictures.

I bought a used ¾ ton Ford truck with Sandra and Duane co-signing with me. We went through the Manatee River Community Bank where Allan Langford was the president. Allan was a different banker that I had ever dealt with before. All of the previous bankers that I dealt with would loan me $75,000 when I was asking for $100,000 and then I would have to give a pint of blood and my first born.

I stayed busy working with Wade and soon I was close to my normal self. When the jobs came up, I would start work at daylight and work until dark and sometimes after dark. But not having any personal possessions upon my release, I had a lot to buy so I got a part time job working for Farren Dakin at the dairy. Later, I worked for Jerry Dakin, at night, moving dirt with a pan for the site of his new dairy barn. I worked two jobs, day and night, until the dairy job was complete, which helped me with my finances.

A few months after my release from prison, FAMM had a party for the 37 people that President Clinton commuted their sentence like mine was. Cande went with me, but only about 10 or 12 other former inmates showed up though.

In May, Farren wanted me to go fishing with him, Cameron, Jerry, Allen Langford and Larry Thomas in the Sam Crosthwaite fishing tournament. Mostly, I just watched them fish, because I felt that I needed to be working, not playing because I needed the money.

Other than the part time work with the Dakins, I worked various jobs with Wade. We did silt fencing, hydro-seeding, seed and hay mulch, working cattle and wire grassing. Every November, Wade planted wire grass, palmetto berries, acorns and various other native vegetation of Florida. It was an environmental project that involved reclamation of phosphate mines and mitigation of wetlands. We would plant anywhere from 200 to 600 acres every year. I would have never thought that I would ever be planting wire grass and palmetto berries because in my early years, I was always killing them.

In October, Duane Rawls, Wade and I went to Moultrie, GA to the Farmer's Expo. I had always wanted to go to the Expo, but never went before. There was 600 acres of buildings and farmland and they had everything pertaining to agriculture. At the Farmer's Expo is where I got the idea of making shavings out of pine logs for the horse owners to put in there horse stalls.

When we were silt fencing on the big jobs, I would see piles of pine trees being burned or ground up into chips knowing that it was such a waste to see such good trees go to waste. At the Expo we saw a lot of different types of portable band saws but sawmills took a lot more labor. The log shaver looked more appealing to me as we watched it being demonstrated and I asked questions about it.

There was another man at the Expo who was interested in a shaver as well and I asked him what his need for the shaver was. He said he planned to use it to absorb the chicken manure in a long shed that he raised his pullets in. I asked him, "Why don't you use "sister" pulp?"

The man doing the demonstration on the shaver was getting aggravated with me because I was trying to talk this man out of buying a shaver. Then the chicken man asked me, "What's "sister pulp"?"

Duane and Wade immediately started laughing because I have always pronounced "citrus pulp" as "sister pulp". Wade explained to him what I meant and told him that it was dried orange peels that would be cheaper than shavings. Then I told him about a man from Florida that uses it in his chicken barn and then he feeds the citrus pulp and manure mixed with feed to his cows. Duane and Wade still tease me about my pronunciation of "sister pulp".

A few months after my release, Sandra brought home my granddaughter, Jamey, my oldest daughter, Sherie's youngest child. Jamey was getting into some trouble with the law, so Sandra was trying to get her back on the right track by letting her live there. So there we all were, Duane, Sandra, Jamey and myself with Momma there sometimes on the weekends. That's when Duane started saying that he and Sandra were running a halfway house for the Clark family.

While silt fencing with Wade, the machine he was using was wasting a lot of time. We came up with an idea to build a different type of machine. So in November, with the help from Steve Pope, he built a silt fencing machine that buried the silt fencing material eight to ten inches into the ground. After several modifications, we finally got it perfected and this allowed us to lay twice as much fence than we did the old way. I should have obtained a patent on the machine, but after a year if a machine is in use in the public eye, it is ineligible for a patent. To this day, Wade still uses that machine.

My son, Duane, was supposed to pick up his daughter, Heather, from school one day but couldn't make it, so he asked if I could. She was attending Haile Middle School at the time and he knew that I was leaving Lakewood Ranch heading back to Parrish to drop off the equipment that I had.

As I pulled into the school I saw Heather standing there talking to some of her friends. She wasn't looking for me to pick her up so I had to honk the horn and holler for her. You should have seen her face when she realized she was being picked up by me driving a big dully truck pulling a gooseneck trailer with a big tractor on it.

She got into the truck and said, "Popa, why did you come pick me up in this truck? I am so embarrassed."

I said, "Embarrassed? You should have to ride a horse or a Brahma bull or drive a tractor to school like I did and then you could say you would be embarrassed."

I really wasn't embarrassed by riding the horse or the bull or even the tractor. I actually enjoyed it and most of the kids today should have to do just that. Maybe they would have more appreciation of what they do have.

Late one afternoon, Bret, my oldest grandson and I were in one of Wade's trucks bringing back equipment to the barn after a silt fence job. As we pulled around the barn we saw the rest of the crew standing around Wade's truck drinking beer. So Bret and I unhooked and unloaded the equipment then we got into my truck to leave.

I turned the key to start the truck like always, but I got the biggest electric shock of my life. I felt the electricity throughout my entire body and immediately jerked my hand away. Bret, knowing something was wrong because I yelled and jumped in the seat, was looking at me with big eyes.

After sitting there a few seconds I felt my ass burning so I jumped out of the truck and started rubbing both cheeks of my ass. That's when I heard the rest of the crew laughing their asses off. Then Stevie Johns came over to the truck opening the hood and took the coiled wires that he had hooked up to the battery in order to give me my jolt.

I told Stevie that I was going to get him back big time for that trick. So far I haven't been able to get him back, though I have had several chances; none seemed to be good enough for what he did to me. I damn sure do not like any type of electric shock.

In January of 2002, Wendell and I were talking at the Manatee County Fair just before he started auctioneering the steer sale. Bob

Walton came up behind Wendell and jerked his cowboy hat off. He began beating Wendell's hat on his leg. Wendell said, "Man you really don't want to live long, do you?"

Bob handed Wendell his hat back when he realized he wasn't who he thought he was. He apologized saying he thought he was Lee Sly. Wendell said, "Now I know you don't want to live long!"

Wendell couldn't get real mad because I was laughing so hard about what happened. Lee and Wendell were about the same height; both had mustaches and did look similar from a distance.

I believe it was around February 2002, when Duane, Gary and I got into the shaving business part time. Duane and I were still working for Wade and Gary was working for Mike Alday cleaning windows. So we were only able to do the shaving business after hours and on weekends.

Farren Dakin co-signed a note for us and again Alan Langford loaned us enough money to buy the shaver along with a dump trailer for delivery of the shavings. Before they delivered the shaver, Gary found some logs at Mr. Whaley's sawmill on SR64 near the Hardee County. Mr. Whaley was very ill at the time and was no longer able to run his sawmill. His wife agreed to let us use the sawmill and have the logs under the condition that we clean up the mess. She also allowed us to use his Michigan loader, which we ended up buying from her later.

The three of us worked making shavings for the nearby horse barns in the evenings. The logs were old and hard on the shaver making the blades dull. The shaver was supposed to shave about 18 yards an hour but we could only do 11 to 12 an hour.

All of the logs had to be cut in eight foot lengths to fit into the log box. Then the box would go back and forth over the whirling blades underneath the moving box. The shavings were then blown into a pile where the loader would be able to dump the shavings into the dump trailer so Gary could deliver them.

After we shaved up all of the logs and burned the trimmings, Gary got Roger Musgrave to let us use a small piece of his property on Lena Road. We were able to get new logs and we used Wade's gooseneck trailer to haul the logs there.

We were only there a few months when Rodney Dakin made us an offer on his ten acres off SR675. The land had a building on it which was originally owned by Lewis and Brian Banks. The building was their vegetable packing house.

Rodney's offer was that we could use the building and land for one year free of charge. So we moved everything over there and put the shaver under the barn. We decided to buy six peanut wagons from North Carolina that was used to dry peanuts and we used them to dry the shavings. Everything worked well except the shaver was still not doing what it was supposed to do.

At the end of the year, we made Rodney an offer on the land and went back to Alan Langford for another loan with Cande co-signing for us. Around this same time, Gary found a used wood miser saw, so we bought it and set it up in the barn as well. Now we were in the saw mill and the shaving business.

Gary and his wife, Angel, quit their jobs and started sawing logs for lumber and made sod pallets from the smaller slats. Some of the grandkids started making the pallets after school and on the weekends. Duane and I would go get the logs in Wade's truck and trailer and bring them back to the barn.

We were doing okay with sawing the lumber and making pallets, but not so good with the shaver. So we sold the shaver and the peanut wagons for about half of what we paid for them.

The old saw was always breaking down so we ordered a new diesel wood miser which was a great machine. We also bought a used logging truck from North Carolina that had a grapple hook on it so that we could load our own logs onto the log truck. Up to this time we were having the loaders load them for us at the job sites.

Rick Chivers went with me to look at the log truck. It was real cold when we got there. The first thing Rick did was check out the headers which were in good shape. The worst thing about it was that it smoked really bad and burned a lot of oil.

So now with the log truck I could get the logs myself, cut them in the right lengths and bring them back to the saw mill. When I wasn't sawing logs, I was metal detecting them because most of the logs that we got from in town had nails in them.

Gary bought a John Deere loader that had a bucket and forks. It was a bigger loader and newer than the one that we had. With having all of the equipment, we were able to get more logs and produce more lumber or pallets. Once the word got out, we were starting to get busy with lumber orders and tree removals around residential houses.

We also started cutting oak lumber to replace on some local low-boy trailers which we also installed. We were getting the logs free but had a hard time getting workers to work at the saw mill for any length of time. It was real hard work but for some reason I liked it. Duane and I were still working for Wade and I was doing as much as I could with the saw mill. Wade didn't have jobs everyday so that's when I would work at the saw mill or pick up logs.

Angel was needed more for taking the orders and doing the office paperwork than running the saw, so we built an office in the front part of the barn. We hired more workers to help run the saw to relieve Angel. We added a small bedroom for me since I was still living at Sandra and Duane's.

Angel and Gary did most of the work and Angel hated working at the saw mill. Gary would load the logs on the saw while Angel did the sawing and then Gary would take off the sawed lumber or the cut slats.

The saw was on the south side of the building out in an open area. When the wind would blow from the east, it would blow all of the sawdust back in your face. Angel hated having to run the saw and especially on windy days. Even though she had protective goggles on, the sawdust would get all over her. It would be in her hair, up her nose, in her ears and down in her shirt and bra.

One afternoon when I came back from picking up logs, she was covered in sawdust and I started laughing at her. That's when she said, "I never had to work like this when I was growing up."

I was still laughing at her and said, "Angel, you know when you said I do,

when you and Gary got married. Well, you really said I did."

I then told her, "Ya'll just need to change your religion."

And she asked, "Why?"

I said, "Well if you and Gary were Mormons, Gary could marry two big German women and they would be able to do all of the hard work."

She liked that idea and told Gary about it later. But Gary said, "That would be fine but they would have to be young and not big."

Needless to say Angel wasn't liking my idea anymore.

322

On New Year's Eve of 2002, most of my family and I were going to meet at the Pewter Mug for a New Year's Eve party where Ellsworth Helm's band was playing. No one showed up but Cande, her boyfriend Donny Foley and I because it started absolutely pouring rain around seven. By eight it was a monsoon. The rest of the family lived in Myakka City and didn't want to make drive into town because of the bad weather.

Tammy called to tell me that she called her friend, Sonya, to come since she lived so close. I vaguely remembered Sonya but was glad that someone else was going to be there for me to dance with.

When she showed up, I did remember her after all. I didn't realize she could jitterbug as well as she could. Although I found out she did have a problem with leading. We stayed until after midnight and had a real good time. I asked for her number at the end of the night and we've been together ever since. At times I'm not sure how we have stayed together because Sonya reminds me a lot of breaking a horse. She still doesn't neck rein good and most of the time I have to pull each rein to turn her head in the direction I want her to go. Also she fights the bits most of the time.

And after all of these years, she still fights the bit and doesn't neck rein. One thing I have broken her of is leading me on the dance floor. So I guess I won't have to shoot her but I sure wish she would neck rein better.

Sonya and I dated for almost a year before I moved in with her. Her son, Brandon, had graduated high school and moved to Orlando to attend college, so I was spending more time at her house anyway. In the beginning, we went dancing every Friday and Saturday night. We would start around nine and go out to breakfast afterward not getting home until two or so in the morning. Boy did that get old, or should I say I realized that I was getting old. Trying to go out on Friday and stay out that late and then get up to go to work sawing logs. Damn that was tough!

I think it was around the first part of the summer of 2004 when Sonya started trying to get me to work half days on Sundays. I didn't like it a bit because I have always worked seven days a week most of my life and especially since I had been out of prison. After several Sunday's of knocking off around one, it actually was kind of nice. Half day Sunday's eventually turned into all day Sunday, so now I was only working six days a week, but it didn't kill me.

Around this same time Sonya and I took a weekend trip to St. Augustine. We had to get paperwork filled out and approved by my probation officer, George, before we could go since I was still on probation. I had to have the paperwork with me at all times in case we had a run in with the law.

I was still working for my nephew, Wade, at the time and at the saw mill. I remember the day that we left Wade called on the walkie-talkie about two hours into our road trip and said, "Uncle Donnie, we have a 911 job. When can you be here?"

You should have seen Sonya's face and heard what she had to say. There was no way in hell that she was turning around for me to go help them. After three years of not being able to get me away from work and finally getting me to get away, there was no 911 job going to make her turn around.

It was a short but nice little weekend getaway. We didn't do much, but she was happy to get me away from work for a couple of days.

My daughter, Tammy bought 280 acres off SR 70 just west of Arcadia in 2004. It was a pretty piece of property with lots of oaks and pine trees. She bought it to resale but had to keep it for a year because of tax purposes.

Just after she purchased it, Hurricane Charlie came through the southwest part of Florida on August 13. It came in through the Punta Gorda area and almost straight through her property blowing down hundreds of trees.

I took the log truck and some chain saws a few days later to start sawing the downed pine trees in 12 foot and 16 foot links. After sawing them, I loaded them on the log truck and took them back to the saw mill.

After getting the pine logs out, about nine truck loads, she rented a track hoe and a large loader with a root rack on it. Roy Smith and I went back out to start cleaning up the rest of the mess. Roy was operating the loader and I was using the track hoe and we made several big brush piles to be burned.

That property sure was a pretty piece of land, but had a lot of destruction after the hurricane. Tammy sold it in November of 2005 and made quite a bit of money on it.

Right before I quit working for Wade, we were working on a silt fence job at Lakewood Ranch at the site where Lake Club is now when we ran out of stakes. We only had less than a quarter of a mile to go, so I left the crew to go back to the trailers to get more stakes. Wade's crew consisted of me, my son Duane, Ryan, Pat, Scott and Bert, Sonya's dad. I drove the tractor and the rest of them did the hard work.

While I was getting more stakes, they were taking a break. As I was driving back up to where they were all standing, I noticed Bert was eating something. I shut off the tractor and as I was getting off Ryan asked, "Hey Donnie, do you want some brownies?"

I asked, "Who made them?"

He said, "Duane."

I said, "Hell no!"

That's when I noticed Bert immediately stop eating what he had in his hand and spit out what he had in his mouth. But it was too late...he had already eaten one and was on his second one. Everyone knows that Duane's brownies are laced with marijuana and will definitely screw you up. Just eating a half of one will get you high.

We all went back to work after I got a drink of water. We only had about an hour left to finish the job which we did. Bert and I were planning to go pick some tomatoes afterwards, so I asked him if he wanted to follow me to the field. He looked a little pale and said, "I don't believe I can drive my car."

That's when I said, "Come get into the truck and I'll bring you back to your car after we finish picking tomatoes. Hopefully by then the brownies will be worn off."

I headed north on Lorraine Road and turned east on SR70 when I noticed Bert was wiggling around in the seat. I told him to pull the lever up to lay the seat back more which he did. I was almost to SR675 when he said to me, "Man, I am fucked up. I think I'm going to puke."

I told him that I would take him to the saw mill where he could lie down in the bed to sleep it off. It was around one o'clock when we got there. Angel and Gary were working and I explained to them what happened. After I took Bert into the bedroom, I asked Gary if they could check on him because I was going to pick some tomatoes which they said they would.

I was back about two to three hours later and woke Bert up. He was much better, so I took him to his car. I don't believe you will have to worry about Bert eating any more of Duane's brownies.

One day I was telling Floyd how my life has changed over the years. Here I am living with a woman who is 20 plus years younger than me and having to put up with all of the crap from her that I've never put up with any other woman. She's got me going grocery shopping with her and I've even became a house bitch, as I call it, by sweeping and mopping the floors. She's even got me doing some cooking. And one thing that I've never done before is tell my family members that I love them.

But she does a lot of things for me though. The biggest is cooking what I like to eat. One of the funniest things she cooked was mountain oysters or bull balls. She had to wear rubber gloves when she cooked them because she couldn't stand the texture of them.

We are both hard headed as hell and I still find myself trying to neck rein her but she is an Aries and those rams are hard to neck rein. But after being together going on ten years we have really come to know how far to go with one another and have come to really love each other.

After telling Floyd about how my life has changed all he had to say is, "Poor Ole Donnie." And he's been saying it ever since.

Early one morning when I was in Parrish I decided to stop and see my Momma, who was living at Reba's Place. Reba's Place is an assisted living type place that Momma lived at until she died. Reba normally has about eight to nine residents that she takes care of.

Momma was sitting at the dining room table eating breakfast and drinking coffee when I got there. The other residents were sitting in the living room watching the morning news. I sat down across the table from her and we started talking about different things and she was taking her pills one at a time.

I remembered that Tammy's daughter, Jessica, had just had her baby a few days earlier so I thought about telling Momma about it. I said to Momma, "You know you're a great-great grandmother again, don't you?"

She said, "Who?"

I said, "Tammy's oldest daughter, Jessica."

Momma thought for a minute and said, "When did she get married?"

I said, "She's not married."

Momma kind of dropped her head with a disappointed look on her face and said, "Oh."

As she was reaching for another pill, I said, "But that's not the bad part. The baby's black."

She immediately dropped the pill and threw both of her hands in the air with a shocked look on her face and yelled, "Oh no!"

Now I haven't seen Momma get excited like that in a very long time. And with her yelling like she did it startled the other people in the other room causing them to look around to see what happened.

Of course, knowing me, I dropped my head on the table laughing my ass off. Momma just sat there looking at me in total disbelief. When I finally stopped laughing, I told Momma that I was just teasing with her and that the baby wasn't really black.

We started talking again and she finished taking her pills and she asked, "Is the baby really white?"

I said, "Yes, Momma the baby is really white. I just wanted to pull another one of my jokes on you."

As I left there, I thought about telling Sandra what I had just done knowing that she normally stops to see Momma about twice a week. After telling Sandra what I had done she said, "You shouldn't have done that. That will stick in her mind for a long time."

A week or so later I was talking to Sandra and thought about asking if Momma had said anything to her about my joke. Sandra said, "Yeah, Momma said that she could take it better than Donnie could."

So it seems as if another one of my jokes backfired on me.

In January 2006, I finally completed my five years of probation so Sonya applied for a passport for me. After receiving it several weeks later, she planned a surprise vacation for us to Cancun, Mexico.

Sonya had on her favorite pair of jean shorts that had a slight snag around the right pocket area. When we landed in Cancun, she stood up to get out of the seat and the snag got caught on the hook from the table rest on the seat in front of her. Not realizing her shorts were caught on the table hook, she continued to scoot out of the seat and ended up ripping her shorts from the middle part of her pocket all the way down to the bottom. Luckily she had a light weight jacket to wrap around her ass, because she couldn't have walked around with them ripped as bad as they were.

She arranged for us to stay in an all-inclusive hotel which I had never heard of before. The hotel had four or five different restaurants in it with a bar in the pool along with a tiki hut that served hotdogs and hamburgers out by the beach. It was a really nice hotel and the weather turned out to be nice as well.

Gary, Angel and I were still trying to run the saw mill but my age and the hard work was getting to me. The fall and winter times weren't too bad but the summer time was killing me.

There were several times that I had to stop using the chainsaw because of my hands and fingers cramping real bad. I think I went to the chiropractor two or three times due to lower back pain and had a massage therapist come to the house two or three times as well.

Sonya did not like it at all because she could see how it was affecting me. It sure was hard work but for some reason I liked doing it. We finally closed the sawmill down in 2006 and put the ten acres up for sale.

After I quit working full time at the saw mill, I started taking care of our yard that had pretty good St. Augustine grass. But I managed to kill the yard twice by putting too much chinch bug poison on it. I sure did kill the chinch bugs but it also killed the entire yard.

I got teased a lot about doing that. Especially from the people that knew me. They would say, "Man, you can grow thousands of acres of Bahia grass but you can't grow a small yard of St. Augustine."

Or some of them said, "Gosh, you grew how much of that potent marijuana but you can't grow the real grass."

After doing that twice, I now read the directions on the bags of fertilizers or poisons. We now have a very nice yard that we get a lot of compliments about.

A few months after we closed the saw mill, I started working with Buster Strahan, one of my prison buddies, selling metal buildings and metal roofing. The best part about selling the metal was getting to see a lot of people that I had not seen since my release from prison. I drove around trying to see people who I thought would be in need of metal roofs or metal buildings.

I liked the money but I didn't care for the job mainly because I couldn't talk the talk. I didn't know a damn thing about metal. After I received the orders for the metal, I would get asked questions that I didn't know anything about and had to call Buster. So that's why I always felt like I couldn't talk the talk. It took me some time to say metal roofing instead of tin roofs which always pissed Buster off.

In October of 2006, I got into the Mon A Vie business. I went to a meeting with George Hooper one day and signed up. It was a network marketing type of business where I got people to sign up under me and my business would grow from there. I have never been in a business that I enjoyed so much.

I worked at my own pace, pulled jokes on people and had lots of fun. The best part about Mon A Vie is it is the best health juice a person can put into their body that I know of so far. It's made from the acai berry that comes from the rain forest. Everyone knows that I went to prison due to the "Myakka Gold" case so when it came to creating a business name I came up with "Myakka Blend".

They had meetings all of the time and I really got into it. So much so that I was spending a lot of time going around to people and going to meetings. A few weeks into it Sonya got really mad and put a bottle of Mon A Vie on the table and said, "It's either going to be me or the Mon A Vie, not both."

I said, "Well, I love you but I'm getting into this business so I guess I'll be moving out."

She said, "Really!"

I said, "Yes, really because when I make my mind up to do something, I'm going to do it. And I've made up my mind this is what I'm going to do."

She ended up getting into the business with me. I ended up getting 167 people under me and the business was doing fairly good so I borrowed $25,000 against the saw mill. The Mon A Vie business went to hell when the economy went to hell. I lost a lot of the people because of it. People started cutting back on things that they didn't have to have and Mon A Vie was one of them.

Needless to say, I lost my ass and my $25,000, but mainly because I was giving away a lot of the bottles for people to try instead of having them buy them. I'm not in the business part of it anymore but I still drink it. I still believe it's the best thing you can put into your body.

After I started living with Sonya I didn't work as late as I did when I lived with Sandra and Duane. So I actually watched TV a little more. While watching TV I found that the Professional Bull Riding (PBR) was on one of the stations and from there I was hooked.

In February of 2006, Sonya bought us tickets to see the PBR in Tampa. I didn't really want to go because I thought it was better to watch it on TV than live. But when we went that changed my mind because it was so much better live than on TV.

The finals are always in Las Vegas at the end of the season which is normally around the end of October or first of November. Sonya arranged for me, her son Brandon and herself to go to the last two events in Las Vegas this same year. Brandon turned 21 so he was excited about going knowing he could gamble. I was excited as well knowing that we will be there live for the last two events. We all enjoyed the bull riding with Adriano Moraes winning the million dollars and crowned the champion bull rider of the year.

So far that is the only finals that I have been able to go to but wish that I could go to all of them. But living on my Social Security check, I'm not able to afford it. I've been teased a lot about digging up a PVC pipe that I supposedly have money buried everywhere in but that's a big joke. When the government and the attorney's got through with me, I was lucky to have any blood left.

After my Momma died in September of 2007 and then a little over two weeks later Wendell Cooper died, I got motivated to get to work on this book. With their deaths, I made a promise to myself that I was going to finish this book come hell or high water. I had been working on it here and there but really wanted to spend as much time as possible to get it done. You never know when your tomorrows will be over.

I'm not sure if Wendell would agree or disagree with anything that I wrote about here because he once told Sonya, "When Donnie gets finished telling his side of the stories, you come see me and I'll tell you the truth about us!"

Wendell passed away September 18, 2007, before she could get the truth. So it is what it is and I have tried to give you the truth as I remember it. I thought I could finish it in a year but at the end of the first year I was nowhere near finishing.

We finally sold the saw mill and the land at the end of 2007. We actually split the property in two five acre tracts. Gary had a couple from their church that we sold the back five to and we ended selling the front five, that had the saw mill building on it, to an Asian couple.

In 1991, when I was in prison, I mentioned I had received a certified letter from the IRS stating that I owed income tax money on the watermelon crop. Apparently they put a lien on my name in case I was to ever get out and have money that they could get back from me.

When we got ready to sell the sawmill property this lien popped up. The title company researched it and found that it had expired, so we were clear. It expired, because they didn't renew it. The title company said that a lien like mine is only good for ten years after that it has to be renewed.

You should have seen Floyd's face when I answered his question about the book. One morning while having breakfast at Big L's in Ellenton, Floyd asked me what all I was putting in the book. I said, "Everything that I have ever done in my life."

He asked with a shocked look on his face, "Everything?"

As I was laughing I said, "Don't worry about it because there's going to be two books but the last one can't be published until I'm dead."

Floyd said, "You son-of-a-bitch."

I have had a lot of fun telling people about the two books especially the people that don't want me to tell everything. But this is it...the one book is enough for me.

In June of 2008, my son, Duane, went to live in the woods. For the five years that Duane and I were in prison together, he would often talk to me about one of the things that he wanted to do before he got too old was to see how long he could survive living in the woods. He talked about going to Central or South America. But I told him he should just try Florida first because he already knew the dangers here such as the types of animals, plants and the weather.

I really didn't hear much more about it until his youngest son, Kole, finished high school. That's when Duane told Cande to do whatever she wanted with his house and the 20 acres of land because he was going to go to the woods and live off the land.

He had been saving money for this adventure so that he could buy supplies when he had to. My first thought was after about three to four months he would have his fill of living in the woods. But I was sure wrong about that. Three years later and he's still living in the woods.

At first he went down south in the Charlotte and Lee county area. Then he went north around the Gainesville and High Springs area. He normally stays in the woods for a few months at a time before coming back home. He is normally home for special occasions like Thanksgiving or Christmas.

In 2010 he trekked the Appalachian Trail which is a 2200 mile trek and did it in a little over three months averaging about 30 miles per day. He was also on the Continental Divide Trail when I was writing.

When I first started working on the book in 2007, I would get frustrated and wouldn't be able to finish what I was writing. When this would happen, which seemed like a lot in the beginning, I would go out to Myakka just to get away from the book. While I was in Myakka, I would get to talk to a lot of people and sometimes get more information to write about.

But in 2008, the price of gas went up and with living on my Social Security check every month, I had to stay home a lot more. When this happened my only solution to my frustrations was taking it out on the yard along with doing house bitch work and whatever else I can think of to help around the house.

Sonya had a three inch well that had been capped off when the county hooked the neighborhood up with county water and sewer. With the help of Terrell Green, we hooked up a pump and got the well going again in January of 2009.

Then I sprayed the entire backyard with round-up to kill the grass. I borrowed a rotavator from the neighbor, Ed Wilson, to rotavate the ground several times. Ed and his son Scott helped by fixing things for us a lot and Scott's ten year old son, Wesley, helped in the garden as well from time to time. Once I had the ground tilled up, I then took a soil sample for testing and got some Hi-Cal from the Keen Brothers to spread over the area.

With Duane living in the woods I was able to get his drip tape system and a few other things that he had to get the watering system going. I also got a few fittings and things from some of the area farmers here and there.

When spring came I planted the backyard in black-eyed peas,

crowder peas and bush beans. I had 18 rows that were 60 feet long, which produced quite a bit of vegetables for us along with our family members and friends.

This was the first time that I had used a drip system before and I actually used it to fertilize with as well using liquid fertilizer. Boy, what a difference in farming.

I really enjoy it and I call the yard work, working in the garden and the house bitch work my mind therapy. Somehow it helps work out my frustrations. I have to say of all the things that I've done in my life, writing this book is by far the hardest thing I've ever done. Putting the time frames together has been the hardest.

My first cousin Anita Kilcrease Henderson and her husband George were having their 50th wedding anniversary in Alva. George is a preacher at the First Baptist Church in Alva and their anniversary reception was held there in the fellowship hall.

Sonya and I rode over with Sandra and Duane to the reception. After we ate and visited with family and friends, they announced that it was time for Anita and George to renew their vows. So they went to the back of the fellowship hall to wait for everyone to get seated and quieted down.

Sonya was seated in between Duane and I and Sandra was across from Duane on the other side of the table. Just before the music started Sonya said we need to get the hell out of here before someone says that we need to get married. That's when Duane turned around to Sonya and said, "Don't you want to get married?"

She said, "Hell no!"

Duane grabbed her by the arm pulling on it and said, "Oh come on, everyone ought to be married to a Clark at least once."

That's when Sandra turned from the person she was talking to and said, "Shut up asshole."

We all started laughing. Anita and George's renewal of their vows was very nice and we had a good time.

Sonya and I went to my 50th year class reunion in 2009. We sat at the table with Richard and Nancy Strickland and his brother Tony along with his wife Jane Ellen. Jane Ellen was actually my high school sweetheart, until I had to marry Betty Lou. She did, however, go to the high school prom with me and was teased for going with a married man.

Mrs. Parrish, who was our English teacher, came over to the table to visit with us. She was 92 years old then but still looked good and her mind was still pretty sharp. I asked if she remembered me which she did and it was probably because I was one of her worst students, besides the fact, I am sure she couldn't forget about me coming to school smelling like a skunk.

What was really funny was when Nancy told Mrs. Parrish that I was writing a book. Sonya and I were standing there talking to her when Nancy said that and Mrs. Parrish said, "Oh my God."

Sonya started laughing and said, "I know what you mean because his spelling isn't any better now than it was then I'm sure."

Mrs. Parrish said, "He had the most red marks on any paper that I ever graded."

It was a pretty good turnout for being our 50th and we had a pretty good time. We didn't stay long after dinner because we went out dancing afterwards.

Sonya and I have been going dancing most every weekend since we met on New Year's Eve of 2002. She already knew the basic jitterbug dancing but over the years we have really gotten good at it. Most of the places that we go everyone tells us that they really enjoy watching us dance. When they ask how long we've been dancing and we tell them a little over eight years they are very surprised because they think we have been dancing together for twenty years or more.

Before I went to prison, there were about 50 vegetable farms in the county. Now we only have a handful which is mainly due to the strict government regulations. Some of the few that are left, I would like to say thanks for giving me their vegetables through the years like tomatoes, potatoes, watermelons, sweet corn, sweet onions, peas, beans and berries. My thanks go out to Ben King, Joe and Mark Cincotta, Paul, Robert and Greg Harloff, Darrell and Chris Parks, Jim and Robert Grainger and Brent, Chris, Gary, Doc and Lamar Shackelford.

Mentioning Ben King reminds me of the first time I saw one of the detectives who testified at my trial since I had been out of prison. Sonya's Dad, Bert and I were picking vegetables at Ben King's farm on Wauchula Road in Myakka one day. While we were pulling sweet corn, we noticed a flatbed dually pick-up going through the fields with two vegetable bins and two inmates wearing prison clothes riding on the flatbed.

As we were leaving the corn field and going to the black-eyed pea patch, the dually was coming towards us and stopped beside us. When the truck got beside us I realized it was David Livingston, who was one of the lead detectives that headed up the Myakka Gold drug bust back in the '90s. Once he saw it was me he started backing up.

I said to Bert, "I wonder what his problem is? He seems to be afraid of me or something."

While we were picking peas, David was driving all through the fields. As we were leaving, we ran into him again but this time I stopped him. As I pulled up beside him I said, "David, you need to get to work and stop driving through these fields."

He didn't have much to say so I just drove away. That was actually the first time that I had run into him face to face since I had gotten out of prison. I don't have any hard feelings about anything but he sure acted strange.

A few months later, while working on the book, I wanted a photo of the marijuana growing in the swamp in the floaters. Mark Massey and Duane had started using the floaters shortly after I got out of state prison. I never took any pictures of marijuana growing and thought a picture of the floaters with snakes and gators around it might be a good picture for the book cover.

Of all the people who grew pot in Myakka none of them had any pictures, so I thought that the Sheriff's Office would probably have some. After several calls to David, he finally called me back. I told him what I wanted and asked if he thought there might be some around. David said that there were a lot of pictures but he would have to get permission before he could show me any.

Several weeks went by and he called to say that he had some to show me so I met him at the substation in Ellenton. I looked at all of them but none of them were really good enough for the book cover.

After talking with him for several minutes, I asked him why he was avoiding me when he saw me at Ben King's. He told me that he was told that I was going to shoot him if I ever saw him. I started laughing and said to him, "I'm not mad at anyone or have hate towards anyone. There are a few people that I don't personally approve of but I don't have any hard feelings about anything."

Since then I have kept in contact with David. One of the fall gardens, I planted way too many collard greens. After several months of giving away collards to the neighbors, friends and family I could hardly give anymore away. So I called David to see if he would bring some of the inmates out to pick the collards which he did.

The first time they came out they filled eight vegetable bins with collards. He came back several weeks later and they filled another ten bins. The neighbors that saw them here didn't know what to think about inmates being in the backyard.

David stopped by one afternoon and brought me a shirt that he had embroidered with 'Clark Seed Company' above one pocket and 'Donnie' above the other. I have worn it several times around people that have known me for a long time and knew that I got out of the seed business back in the '70s so they asked where I got the shirt. When I tell them that David Livingston gave it to me they are shocked. Some of them say, "David Livingston? That SOB put you in prison. How can you even talk to him?"

After I finish laughing, I tell them, "He didn't put me in prison. I did that to myself."

David was just doing his job. But Johnnie Potts is a different story. I don't hate him and am not mad at him but just feel really hurt. For I thought he was a good honest man but that changed when he took the stand at my trial. He told several lies.

He put in the report that I was making my payment on the farm with the money I was making from selling marijuana which was a big lie. Then when he filled out the report when I was arrested for violation of probation in 1987 he wrote that I had a half a pound of marijuana in a baggy which was only maybe a joint worth. I found all of this out when I read my Pre-Sentencing Investigation (P.S.I.) report.

My personal feeling about Johnnie is on the outside he seems to be a good man but on the inside he's a much different person. As for David, I've never known where he lied about me.

Lee and Debbie moved into a house off Pope Road and a few weeks afterwards I stopped by to see their new place. After seeing the house and the barns, Lee took me on his golf cart to show me his pasture and cattle.

Lee asked me how I liked his Brahma heifers which there were about 20 or 30 of them. I told him that they looked good for Brahmas.

Then I asked him, "What are those four old cows doing in with the heifers?"

He said, "Well, I put them in with the heifers so that they would show the heifers about having calves."

I had to grab a hold of the roof of the golf cart to keep from falling out of it because I busted a gut from laughing so hard. As I was still laughing, I look at Lee and his face was red as fire and I said to him, "Now where the hell did you hear that?"

Lee said he read it in a book. I have never heard of such a thing but Lee is like that. He's always doing something that no one else has done before.

Now that I'm in the first stages of my "golden years", the only gold that I'm seeing so far is the gold piss stain on my boots. It looks like I'm going to have to do some more mind therapy. I have realized that I cannot do what I used to do. This old mind of mine thinks I can but this old body tells me differently. All I have to worry about now is staying healthy and trying to live life to the fullest.

Thank you for taking the time to read about my life. I have tried to keep this book as interesting as I could but telling the stories as I remember them. I have enjoyed most everything I have encountered and have few regrets. The best that I can describe my motto if I had one would be "Live, Laugh, Love and always have fun".

*Ellsworth Helm, Dicky Betts & Donnie Clark.*

*Five generations:*
*Back Row: Sorrell Vickers, Donnie & Joanna Vickers.*
*Middle Row: Jamie Vickers Nelson holding Kaylin Nelson.*
*Front Row: Edna Clark & my oldest daughter, Sherie Vickers.*

*Five Generations*
*Back Row: Tammy Clark Lowe and Donnie.*
*Front Row: Jessica Lowe holding Caden Catlett and Edna Clark.*

*2001 Crosthwaite Fishing Tournament.*
*L to R: Lawrence Thomas, Allen Langford, Donnie Clark, Farren,*
*Jerry and Cameron Dakin.*

*Me and Sonya in Key West.*  *Me and Sonya at Maggie Valley.*

*Me helping Charlie Brown*
*butcher his beef.*

*Me working cows at*
*Rutland Ranch.*

*Floyd Smith, Donnie Clark, Varnell Green & Lee Sly.*

CPSIA information can be obtained at www.ICGtesting.com
Printed in the USA
LVOW130554061112

306028LV00003B/2/P